George Sylvester Morris

Hegel's Philosophy of the State and of History

George Sylvester Morris

Hegel's Philosophy of the State and of History

ISBN/EAN: 9783742812001

Manufactured in Europe, USA, Canada, Australia, Japa

Cover: Foto ©Klaus-Uwe Gerhardt /pixelio.de

Manufactured and distributed by brebook publishing software (www.brebook.com)

George Sylvester Morris

Hegel's Philosophy of the State and of History

PHILOSOPHY OF THE STATE AND OF HISTORY.

AN EXPOSITION

By GEORGE S. MORRIS,
PROFESSOR OF PHILOSOPHY IN THE UNIVERSITY OF MICHIGAN.

CHICAGO:
S. C. GRIGGS AND COMPANY.
1887.

Copyright, 1887,
BY S. C. GRIGGS AND COMPANY.

𝔘𝔫𝔦𝔟𝔢𝔯𝔰𝔦𝔱𝔶 𝔓𝔯𝔢𝔰𝔰:
JOHN WILSON AND SON, CAMBRIDGE.

PREFACE.

THE attempt is made in this volume to present, in substance, the argument of two of the masterpieces of German philosophy contained in the works of Hegel. The limitations of space necessary to be observed have compelled the author to abstain mainly from comment or criticism, whether defensive or offensive, on the doctrines expounded.

Passages translated from Hegel will be generally recognized by the quotation-marks in which they are enclosed.

GEO. S. MORRIS.

SEPTEMBER, 1887.

CONTENTS.

Part First.

THE PHILOSOPHY OF THE STATE.

INTRODUCTION.

The "Encyclopædia of Philosophical Sciences"	1
The Argument of the Philosophical Sciences	2
Their Order	3
Man and Nature	4
Ethical Character of Political Philosophy	8
Method	9

CHAPTER I.
ABSTRACT RIGHT.

Abstract Will and Personality	12
Objectification of Will in Property	13
A. Property	14
(1) Possession	14
Inequality in Possession	16
(2) Use, or Consumption	17
(3) Relinquishment of Property	19

CONTENTS.

B. Contract 19
C. Injustice and Crime; or, Wrong 20
    (1) Unconscious Wrong 21
    (2) Fraud 22
    (3) Violence and Crime 22
Punishment 25

CHAPTER II.
MORALITY.

The Person a Moral Subject 30
  A. Purpose and Responsibility 31
  B. Intention and Welfare 33
  C. The Good, and Conscience 36
Happiness and Right 37
Abstract Duty 39
The Subjective Conscience 40

CHAPTER III.
THE ETHICAL WORLD.

The World of Organized Ethical Relations 43
  Sect. I. The Family 49
    A. Marriage 50
      Not a Contract Relation 51
      Why Monogamic 52
    B. The Fortune of the Family 53
    C. Rearing of Children and Dissolution of the Family 54
  Sect. II. The Civil Society 55
    A. The System of Wants 58

CONTENTS.

(*a*) Human Wants and their Satisfaction	58
(*b*) Labor	60
(*c*) Wealth	61
The Three Classes of Civil Society	62
B. The Administration of Justice	66
(*a*) Right in the Form of Law	67
(*b*) The Existence of the Law	68
(*c*) The Court of Justice	69
C. Police and Corporation	71
(*a*) Police	72
(*b*) The Corporation	77
Sect. III. The State	79
The State a Spiritual Value	79
Not to be confounded with Civil Society	80
A. Internal Polity	82
Reconciliation of Public and Private Will	82
The State and Religion	88
1. Internal Constitution	89
The Three Powers of the State	91
(*a*) The Power of the Prince	93
(*b*) The Governing or Executive Power	96
(*c*) The Legislative Power	97
Representation	99
Public Opinion	103
2. External Sovereignty	105
War as an Ethical Factor	106
B. External Polity	109

Part Second.

THE PHILOSOPHY OF HISTORY.

CHAPTER IV.

INTRODUCTORY IDEAS.

The Philosophy of History a Sequel to the Philosophy of the State	111
History an Ethical Development	114
God in History	116
Law of the Growth of Freedom	118
Geographical Conditions	126
Historical Characterization of Africa	132

CHAPTER V.

THE ORIENTAL WORLD.

Beginning of the Process of History	138
A. China	139
The Chinese Empire a Magnified Family	140
B. India	146
The Hindu Spirit a Dreaming One	147
C. Persia and the Persian Empire	153
I. The Zend People	156
II. The Assyrians, Babylonians, Medes and Persians	158

CONTENTS.   xi

III. The Persian Empire and its Component Parts   160
 (1) Persia   161
 (2) Syria and other Semitic Nations . .   162
 (3) Judæa   165
 (4) Egypt   169
 (5) Transition to the Grecian World . .   176

CHAPTER VI.

The Grecian World.

Greece presents the "joyous view of the youthful fresh-
 ness of spiritual life "   179
A. First Period: The Elements of the Grecian Spirit   180
 Geographical Environment   181
 Heterogeneous and Foreign Origin of the Elements
  of the Grecian People   181
 The Early Royal Houses and their Extinction . .   182
 Relation of the Grecian Spirit to Nature . . .   184
 The Grecian Spirit essentially Artistic   187
B. Second Period: The Creations of the Grecian
 Spirit   189
 I. The Subjective Creation: Mastering the Body   189
 II. The Objective Creation: the Religion and
  Mythology of the Greeks   190
 III. The Political Creation   193
  Grecian Democracy   194
   (a) The Wars with the Persians . . .   197
   (b) Athens   199
   (c) Sparta   201

(d) The Peloponnesian War 203
   The ruin of Greece proceeding from
   the development of Individualism . 207
(e) The Macedonian Empire 208
C. Third Period: The Destruction of the Grecian
   Spirit 210

CHAPTER VII.

The Roman World.

Grecian and Roman Civilization contrasted 212
A. Rome till the Second Punic War 214
  I. The Elements of the Roman Spirit 214
  II. History of Rome till the Second Punic War . 217
     The Early Kings 217
     Gradual Advancement of the Plebeians . 218
B. From the Second Punic War to the Empire . . 220
C. Later History of the Roman World 223
  I. The Empire 223
  II. Christianity 226
     Preparation for Christianity in the Roman
     World 228
     Christianity fully revealed Man to himself as
     a Spiritual Being 238
     Christian Truth as formulated in the Doctrine of the Trinity 239
     The Historic and the Spiritual Christ . . . 243
     The Christian Principle as first announced by
     Jesus 244
     Its Development 246
     The Organization of the Church 250
  III. The Byzantine Empire 251

CHAPTER VIII.

The Germanic World.

The Principle of the Germanic World, derived from Christianity, is Universal Freedom	255
A. The Elements of the Christian-Germanic World	255
I. The Barbarian Migrations	255
Original Character of the Germanic Nations	256
II. Mahometanism	260
III. The Empire of Charlemagne	263
B. The Middle Ages	264
I. The Feudal System and the Hierarchy	265
II. The Crusades	273
III. The Transition from Feudal Rule to Monarchy	277
C. Modern Times	281
I. The Reformation	282
Its Watchwords "Faith" and "the witness of the Spirit," or Christian Freedom	284
II. Influence of the Reformation on Political Development	289
III. "Illumination" and Revolution	291
The Revolution in France	300
Contre-coups of the Revolution in other Lands	304

HEGEL'S PHILOSOPHY

OF

THE STATE AND OF HISTORY.

Part First.

THE PHILOSOPHY OF THE STATE.[1]

INTRODUCTION.

IT is necessary to preface our exposition of Hegel's political and historical philosophy by a few words of explanation regarding the general character and method of his treatment of the whole subject.

In his "Encyclopædia of the Philosophical Sciences" our author distributes the whole matter of philosophy under three main heads, — (1) Logic; (2) Philosophy of Nature; (3) Philosophy of Spirit. The Philosophy of Spirit is primarily the Philosophy of Man, and is again subdivided into three parts, entitled, respectively, Subjective Spirit, Objective Spirit, and Absolute Spirit. The first of these sub-

---

[1] G. W. F. Hegel's *Grundlinien der Philosophie des Rechts, oder Naturrecht und Staatswissenschaft im Grundrisse*, Berlin, 1821; in Hegel's Complete Works, vol. viii., edited by Eduard Gans, with additions from Hegel's lectures.

divisions considers what may be termed the *natural* character of man as a spiritual being, and includes such tributary sciences as Anthropology and Psychology. The second is the philosophy of the State, or of man in his domestic, economic, and political relations. The third exhibits man in the perfection of his spiritual character and functions, and comprises the Philosophy of Art, the Philosophy of Religion, and Philosophy pure and simple, the supreme and perfect object of which is the Absolute Spirit, — the self-conscious and self-revealing God, through whom and for whom are all things. For man, it is found, approaches the character of absolute spirituality only so far as he recognizes and lives in conscious and voluntary dependence on the everlasting and truly Absolute Spirit, which is God.

Thus the "Encyclopædia of Philosophical Sciences" is not, as the name might at first suggest, a mere aggregate of separate and unconnected disciplines, brought together for convenience in a single compendium, like the words in a dictionary. These "Sciences" constitute a system, all the parts of which belong together, and stand in a definite and necessary relation to each other. The "Encyclopædia" exhibits them in their systematic order and their articulate relation the one to the other.

All the "Philosophical Sciences" are parts of one high argument, the conclusion of which is formally announced in the words of the title of the last subdivision of the Philosophy of Spirit, as mentioned above. It is to the fuller recognition and comprehension of Absolute Spirit that all knowledge progressively tends. Of all human experience, deeply, accurately, philosophically considered, God is the Alpha and the Omega; He is the beginning and the end of all absolute reality. This is the argument of the "Encyclopædia," — this is the argument of Philosophy as exhibited in all of Hegel's works.

The order of the Philosophical Sciences is from the abstract to the concrete. It is — otherwise and variously described — from the part to the whole, from the surface to the centre, from the conditioned effect to the conditioning cause, from that which needs explanation to that which explains itself and all things. Logic considers abstract notions. It is a scientific exposition of the fundamental and determining categories of all thinking experience. Beginning with the most abstract, elementary, and contentless of all thoughts, — the thought of pure being, — it ends with the "Idea" of an absolute self-conscious personality, as the thought in which all other thoughts are included, the one which they all imply, to which in their order they with increasing fulness point, and which they collectively and in their system demonstrate. But abstract thoughts, as such, are shadowy and void; they are ideal and subjective, and presuppose an objective realm in which they have reality, and, so to speak, actual validity. Nature is such a realm, and the second part of the "Encyclopædia" considers Nature accordingly as the scene of a progressive (though but partial) realization or objectification of what Logic contemplates only as abstract terms of thought. So it appears that the proximate ground or condition of thought is the objective reality called Nature. Its fuller or more concrete (though still not final) ground is found in that being — Man — in whom Nature culminates, and who constitutes the primary subject of the " Encyclopædia's " third part. Man, self-conscious, thinking, willing, acting, is subjective and objective, ideal and real, in one. What Nature is implicitly and imperfectly, Man is (or is to be) explicitly and more perfectly. Nature, we may say, is spiritual in a figure or in potency: in man the figure and potency are measurably converted into literal and accomplished fact. So the Philosophy of Man is in a conspicuous sense the Philosophy of Spirit. It extends the experimental demonstration, begun in Logic and carried forward in the Philosophy of Nature, that the common and eternal, self-explaining and all-explaining, ground, both of thought and of objective reality, is Absolute or Perfect Spirit. For every step forward in the argument is, as Hegel repeatedly reminds us, a step " backward " toward the eternal cause, or " inward " toward the eternal ground, of all development and all reality. God is not the result of development, but its eternal, omnipresent, and ever efficient pre-condition. The " potency" of Nature is not a power lodged in Nature to bring forth man independently of God. It is wholly relative to, and is but the sign or index of, a power and a nature eternally actualized in God, without whom neither thought nor Nature nor man were in any degree possible. All existence is, in varying degrees, an incarnation of living Reason, and reflects, as in an image, its spiritual source. In man, self-knowing and self-acting, the incarnation and reflection are most complete. Man, conspicuously, is "in the image of God." In him the finite, experimental revelation of Absolute Being becomes most perfect. In knowing his own thought, in knowing Nature, and in knowing himself, he is raised, as on a stepping-stone, to an elevation from which he knows God.

Such is the character of the great argument of philosophy, as Hegel understands and develops it. And now some things may be mentioned with reference to his special treatment of the topic which is immediately to engage our attention. First, it is impossible for Hegel, in considering man in his social and historical relations, to abstract him from the ties that bind him to Nature. Apart from these ties man is not intelligible. It is a necessary and demonstrable part of the character of man that he should have a side of unity and correlation with Nature and her laws. Nature is his matrix, and the umbilical cord that connects him with her is never in this life severed. Because man is a spiritual being he is not therefore merely supernatural, and cannot in a scientific treatment be so regarded. Nor is he thus regarded by Hegel, — a fact which becomes even more conspicuously evident in his handling of the Philosophy of History. It cannot justly be complained that the method of Hegel is inhospitable or indifferent to any application of the "physical method" in the treatment of man and his relations which is warranted by the facts. But while man is not merely supernatural, while he is subject to natural conditions and to the secondary influences of environment, he has yet a side of distinction above Nature; and this is the characteristic thing about him. To neglect or ignore this would be to miss the most essential thing in the science of man; it would be Hamlet minus the *rôle* of Hamlet. This is the error and defect illustrated in the works of those numerous and influential writers on political philosophy in modern times, to whom "there is no logic of spirit;" who, in other words, profess and practise agnosticism with reference to the spiritual nature of man (as also with reference to the really spiritual side of Nature herself), and apply exclusively an abstract "physical method," which would make of all human problems mere problems in mechanics. Against this narrowness the work of Hegel will be found to constitute a most energetic, practical protest. To him man, the State, history, are decidedly spiritual values. As such, however, they do not run counter to Nature; they enter into no rivalry with her. The rather, they find in her their connatural servant and instrument, and they honor her by fulfilling her prophecies.

Secondly, the work of Hegel has nothing in common with theories, ancient and modern, devoted to the speculative construction of a merely "ideal State." "This treatise," he says, in the preface to the *Philosophie des Rechts*, "must, as a philosophical work, be furthest of all removed from an attempt to construct an ideal State; as a work of possible instruc-

INTRODUCTION. 7

tion its end cannot be to show the State how it must be, but rather to show how it, the ethical universe, is to be comprehended." And our author immediately adds, "The task of philosophy is to comprehend that which is; for that which is, is Reason. The individual man is always a son of his times; so, too, philosophy is the time in which it exists, apprehended in thought. It is just as foolish to suppose that any philosophy is in advance of its present world as to suppose the like in regard to any individual. . . . If the theory of an individual does in fact transcend [and so exist out of direct relation to] the actual world of which he is a member, if in his

  world as it must
  c , that it exists,
 h s ney. — a plinth
  it ly may be rep-
  riendly criticism
  des Rechts, to
  to warrant the
  d only with the
  et work to date
  I political condi-
  the year of the
  Whatever of ap-
  charge, there is
  of its conspic-
  tribution to the
  te, and of social

contain no treatise bearing the express title of "Ethics," his *Philosophie des Rechts* is distinctly and profoundly ethical, and is a very substantial contribution to ethical science. Any different treatment of the subject would have been impossible for him, in view of his conception of the connection of all of man's social relations with man himself. This connection is viewed by him, not as accidental, but as essential. The language of a recent writer, who declares the State to be "simply the *res interna* of human nature changed to a *res publica* or *externa*," fully expresses, as far as it goes, the thought of Hegel. Only Hegel would go further, and say explicitly that the *res interna* is a mere unknown potentiality until it has become a *res externa*. To him, therefore, all the organic-social relations of man, as included in the State and in universal history, are simply, and in their measure, the objective manifestation or actualization of man. Without them man were not man; without them he were not the spiritual being that he is. The State, says Hegel, is the human spirit "as it stands in the world." The State exists in obedience to the command which man's spiritual nature lays upon him, — first, to know himself; and, secondly, to be himself. The science of the State cannot, therefore, but be ethical. It is, in its measure, the science of man coming to the knowledge of himself through the objective realization and organization of his existence in social relations, and at the same time, on the basis of the self-knowledge thus acquired, going on to perfect this his existence. It is the science of man at work in "the laboratory of moral experiment;" or, rather, it is the science of what man accomplishes in this "laboratory," and of how he accomplishes it.

Fourthly, it will appear in the progress of this work how, bearing the relation above described to the essential spiritual nature of man, the State is vitally connected with that final sphere of human consciousness and activity which is termed Religion.

Fifthly, with reference to the subject of method, it is the professed aim and claim of Hegel in all his works not to approach the subjects treated by him with a preconceived method to be arbitrarily applied to them, but simply to trace and exhibit the method followed by the things treated themselves in their own development. In the present instance the subject-matter is man himself, as a spiritual being, "standing in the world." Thus regarded, man is a being who, with the aid of a growing self-knowledge, progressively realizes himself, or approaches to the stature of the perfect man; in other words man, centrally considered, is "*thinking* will." Now, Will thus and truly considered is not merely a brute force, nor simply an original and full-fledged endowment; it is something to be acquired, or, more accurately, to be developed. The method of its development must determine the method to be followed in the present work. In the introduction to his *Philosophie des Rechts* Hegel treats at length of the laws of the development of Will from its purely formal beginnings to the stage of concrete and "substantial" fulness. It is enough to state that the order of development is not different from that illustrated in all cases of organic growth, — "first the blade, then the ear, and then the full corn in the ear;" or first the "abstract" and finally the "concrete;" first the partial and tentative, and then the complete, the state of finished achievement. A still more exact illustration would perhaps be, — first, the advancing foot; then the resisting earth; and then, as the "unity" of these two, actual locomotion (thesis, antithesis, synthesis). The terms mentioned in parenthesis indicate the relation to each other of the three chapters of the Philosophy of the State, the respective subjects of which might be expressed as (1) Will Objective; (2) Will Subjective; (3) Will both Objective and Subjective.

It must not be forgotten that this order is to Hegel primarily a logical one, or an order adapted to meet the necessities of a scientific treatment, rather than a temporal one. And, above all, it must be remembered that Will in its completed conception is not regarded by our author as an abstract faculty, but as the whole spiritual and intelligent nature of man in action. Accordingly, one of the intended results of Chapters I. and II. is to show that the attempt to conceive Will as merely objective, — that is, on the side of its visible manifestations alone, as is mainly done in abstract treatises on civil law, — and to found thereon the whole theory of man in his social existence, or to regard it with the like end in view as purely subjective, must fail. Objective (or objectified) Will presupposes subjective Will, and points to it as its immediate and necessary condition. Hence the necessity of the transition from the subject-matter of Chapter I. to that of Chapter II. In like manner subjective Will presupposes and points to, not simply the Will that is merely objective, but the Will in which, as also in all true intelligence, the subjective and objective exist in vital unity. This is the concrete and actual Will, which realizes itself in the social-organic relations of humanity. Objective and subjective Will, or Abstract Right and Morality, are therefore relative abstractions. The concrete from which they are abstracted is the Ethical World, or Man as he concretely exists and realizes himself in that world.

Finally, it must not be forgotten that, as just indicated, to Hegel the term *ethical* has a broader and more concrete meaning than *moral*. To overlook this circumstance would lead to fatal misunderstandings. The temptation to overlook it arises from the fact that in popular usage no such precise distinction is made between the two mentioned terms.

CHAPTER I.

ABSTRACT RIGHT.

OUR beginning is to be made with the abstract conception of Will, by which Hegel means the conception of Will as an "immediate," or undeveloped, potentiality. Thus viewed, Will is the attribute of the single individual, placed in the midst of a world having manifold particular relations to him. Into any or all of these relations he may, with his will, actively enter, and so practically identify them and the world with himself, or himself with the world. But into none of them has he, by hypothesis, yet entered. He simply possesses the abstract power of entering into, or "willing," any or all or none of them. This power, unexercised, is of course only formal. But the possession of it is the possession of formal freedom. The subject possessing such freedom is a Person.

Personality is the condition of legal competence. The conception of personality "constitutes the basis — itself abstract — of abstract and hence formal Right."[1] The whole sum and substance of Abstract

[1] The word "right," as here, in accordance with German usage, employed by Hegel (German *Recht*, as distinguished from *Gesetz*; compare the French *droit* and *loi*), carries with it the notion of organic law. It is law considered as organic to human will and purpose. It is, as Hegel remarks, on account of this organic relation between "right" and "freedom," that the former is usually termed "sacred."

ABSTRACT RIGHT.

Right, or law, is therefore contained in the command, "Be a person, and respect others as persons." This command in form is positive, but in substance and application negative. If the question is respecting particular things to be done, in order that one may "be a person and respect others as persons," Abstract Right is silent. At most it only extends to the authorizing of particular actions, on the negative condition that the action shall not tend to the violation of personality or of anything that depends thereon. Abstract Right contains therefore only prohibitions, and its apparently positive commands are ultimately founded on a prohibition. (Compare the Ten Commandments, which are mainly prohibitory.)

Let us now return to our "person," as abstractly considered and defined, with his formally universal but as yet undeveloped, or unexercised, freedom. As thus defined, he cannot and does not exist. The truth of the latter part of this statement — the empirical statement of fact — is obvious enough. The former part is true, because there is a formal contradiction contained in the notion of an inactive, undeveloped Will. Such a Will would be something purely "subjective," possessed by definition of the formal, or potential, attributes of *infinitude* and universality, and yet distinguished from and so *limited by* a whole universe of *objective* nature with which as yet it has no real connection. The very actuality of Will must consist in and result from an activity whereby this limitation is in some degree annulled, and a measure of objective reality is given to the

Will. In other words, the Will must first acquire for itself objective existence, and so actualize itself, by usurping as it were, or appropriating, the natural existence with which it is confronted. The sphere of Abstract Right will include whatever is immediately contained in or directly flows from this act. Under this head we have therefore to consider —

(*a*) *Possession*, or *Property*, in which the free personality of the individual gives itself objective manifestation;

(*b*) *Contract*, as concerned with the legal transmission of property from one person to another;

(*c*) *Injustice* and *Crime*, consisting in the involuntary failure or inability to conform to, or else in wilful transgression of, a standard of justice as yet unformulated, but which the development of the contract-relation itself obliges *persons* to recognize as a binding ideal of all voluntary activities, and as the implicit presupposition of all legal relations.

A. — PROPERTY.

(1) *Possession*. — That which man reduces, or elevates, to the rank of property is a natural object, which as such is self-less, impersonal, unfree. It is a mere *thing*, without rights of its own. Man's right to appropriate it is absolute. Having the appearance of independence, it is in reality dependent. It is not self-centred, having a " soul of its own." This lack, man, as far as the nature of the case permits, supplies, by making it *his* own, or through his will identifying it with himself.

For property is objectified Will.[1] It is an object into which I have introduced my will, which by my will I have made *mine*, — have made to become, as it were, an attribute or property of *me;* have, in short, so identified with myself that he who touches it therein touches me, and touches that Will which is my living substance.

In property, or possession, my will first acquires objective existence. The necessity of the existence of property, or of the appropriation by man of objects external to his formal will, is as great as the necessity that, if man is to be man and a person, his will shall not remain a mere subjective possibility, but by objectifying itself become actual. The circumstance that I find the occasion for making something mine in some special need, instinct, or fancy, and that property is a means of satisfying the same, is accidental. The essential point is that my free-will takes the first necessary step toward becoming objectively real in the possession of actual objects; and the essential *truth* is that just as the free-will cannot be conceived as a mere means to an end foreign to itself, but only as an end for and in itself, so property, being according to its true conception and definition simply the primary form in which the free-will renders itself objectively real, has something of the like character of an absolute end, and is proportionately sacred and inviolable.

[1] Legal science recognizes "things" only so far as they are capable of standing in relation to the human will. — T. E. HOLLAND, *Jurisprudence,* p. 78, 2d ed., Oxford, 1882.

From the conception of property now before us it only follows that the possession of external things as property is something essentially rational. But nothing follows as to just what or how much property any individual shall possess. This is something that, at least in the sphere of Abstract Right,[1] is quite accidental, being determined by the special needs of the individual, his arbitrary preference, his talents, external circumstances, and the like. From the natural abstract equality of all individuals, considered simply as so many persons, can be inferred neither a natural equality, nor a natural right to equality, in possessions. The assertion of this right on such a ground is "empty and superficial," since it is made in forgetfulness of the fact that abstract equality may and must co-exist with concrete or actual inequality. All persons are abstractly equal, since each in the census counts for one and no more; or they are, as we may say, *formally* equal; but *materially*, or considered with reference to the substance, character, and development of their personality, they are unequal; and if one must indulge in abstract argument, one might with better reason argue from the actual inequality of persons to the natural justice of an unequal distribution of property among them. But what is more important is that the assertion in question is made without due appreciation of the truth (to be developed in subsequent chapters) that the free-will, or practical

[1] "Abstract Right" is distinguished from "concrete" right, the nature and conditions of which are the real subject of the third chapter.

reason, of man fully realizes itself only in an "organism of reason" called the State, wherein are many members, having necessarily different and unequal positions and functions, though they constitute together one body. The State itself, in which alone property can be permanently held, presupposes and is conditioned on the perpetual maintenance of concrete differences and "inequalities" among its members.

An object is converted into property either by simply taking actual possession of it, or by the expenditure of "formative" labor upon it (*e. g.*, cultivation of the earth), or by putting upon it some token of my will.

(2) *Use, or Consumption.* — We have seen that property involves fundamentally the relation between an appropriating personal Will and an appropriated object. Now, it is plain that the terms between which this relation subsists are neither similars nor equals. The appropriating Will is active, internal, positive; it exists, and in its action manifests itself, as an end in and for itself, and so corresponds to the philosophic conception of a true *substance*. The appropriated object, on the other hand, is passive, external, negative; its nature, as an article of property, is to exist not for itself but for another, and in this sense it is properly to be termed, not substantial, but insubstantial. Now, property is not fully property unless it be treated by its possessor according to this its negative and insubstantial nature; that is, unless it be *used*, or, as the case may be, *consumed*. Moreover, true proprietorship

implies that both use, or consumption, and possession shall be more than merely partial or temporary. The complete liberty of using that the abstract title to which belongs to another, constitutes me no proprietor. "It belongs therefore to the essential nature of proprietorship that the latter be free and complete." Hegel adds that "something like a millennium and a half have passed since, under the influence of Christianity, the doctrine of *personal freedom* began to be accepted, so that among a restricted portion of the human race it has come to be acknowledged as a universal principle. But the principle of *freedom of proprietorship* has, we may say, only since yesterday, and then only here and there, been acknowledged."

The active and permanent manifestation of the personal appropriating Will, through the use or consumption of the appropriated object, is then essential to the perfection of the property relation, or to true proprietorship. So it is that merely through such constant manifestation I may acquire property, as it is said, by *prescription;* while through continued neglect or disuse of my possessions I cease to be their proprietor, and may forfeit my title to them.[1]

[1] Hegel adds, in a note, that "the principle of prescription has been introduced into the law, not merely in view of some extrinsic consideration in conflict with strict justice, such as the desirability of preventing the disputes and confusion affecting the security of property that would arise through the admission of old claims or the like. On the contrary, prescription has its intrinsic reason in that note of proprietorship which constitutes its very *reality;* namely, the actual manifestation of the will to possess."

The holder of an article of property being proprietor of its use, is proprietor of its *value*. For in the usefulness of an object — so far as this is capable of quantitative comparison and determination — consists its value.

(3) *Relinquishment of Property.* — Property in a purely external object may be relinquished just because it is and remains external. My free-will, which alone is inalienable, is objectified in it only *per accidens*. The connection established between it and me is therefore not essential, and may be broken up at will.

B. — CONTRACT.

Property does not really become property until it is at least constructively relinquished, and then reacquired by virtue of contract. If the human race consisted of only one individual, the property relation would never be developed. There is no " mine " except in relation to a correlative " thine ; " and there is no mine or thine except so far as both thou and I have consented to hold our possessions, not alone on the basis of our own individual wills respectively, but on the basis of a common will, in which we both agree. The property which is mine becomes thus the objectification, not simply of my own individual appropriating will, but also of the consenting will of my neighbor ; and the important point is, that my will is not really objectified in the object that I may *de facto* possess until it is recognized therein and allowed by another. Such recognition and allowance constitute the logical essence of Contract.

The general necessity of contracts is implied in the notion of property. But respecting all contracts in particular it is to be noted — (1) that they are subject to the arbitrary determination of the parties concerned; (2) that the "common will" expressed in them is "only common, and not intrinsically and essentially universal;"[1] and (3) that their subject-matter is "only particular external things, for such only can be relinquished at the arbitrary choice of the individual."

C. — INJUSTICE AND CRIME; OR, WRONG.

The *common* Will expressed by contract differs, as just mentioned, from the *universal* Will which flows from the essential nature of man as a rational being. The latter Will is, or in case of its realization would be, perfect practical reason, and its fruit absolute justice; in it nothing would be accidental or arbitrary, but everything would be necessarily and fully determined, or would have its complete and sufficient and all-reconciling reason. In contrast with

[1] The family and the State exist, not by contract, but by a necessity grounded in the nature of man. They are the objective expression, therefore, not of a merely accidental or "common" will, but of a "will essentially and intrinsically universal." The modern "subsumption of marriage under the conception of contract" is therefore stigmatized by Hegel, in passing, as "infamous;" while in the like error with regard to the State our author finds the origin of the greatest confusions in the theory of public law, and in many modern attempts at the actual constitution — or reconstitution — of political relations.

this ideal of universal and essential, perfectly rational and just, Will, the Will of Contract, which we have been considering, is particular and accidental. Further, what we are terming universal Will must be realized, if at all, in and through particular Will. But the particular Will of Contract, as we are now considering it, has come into existence without any express reference to the universal Will. It is a product which has been exposed, in its genesis, to the effects of accident and caprice. It is the result of the accidental intelligence and the capricious volition (the arbitrary liking, or good pleasure) of the contracting parties. It contains no guarantee of its own agreement with the universal Will or of its essential justice, and no assurance of that good faith on the part of the contracting parties on which it must depend for its own maintenance. Under these circumstances nothing but accident can protect it from being, or becoming, essential wrong. Having it in mind, we may well say, "It must needs be that offences come."

(1) *Unconscious Wrong.* — The wrong now in question may be unconscious or guileless (*unbefangen*). The making and recognition of contracts implies the establishment of particular rights, on the ground of which, in case of dispute, corresponding claims may be set up and defended. But the subject-matter of contracts being external things, incapable of immediate and visible identification with the persons and wills of any particular owners, it is obvious that different parties, both acting in perfect good faith, may conceivably acquire at one

and the same time what they suppose to be perfectly valid claims to the possession of the same objects. In the assertion of his claim, each contestant necessarily supposes his opponent to be in the wrong. Such contentions involve the recognition of right as the universal and decisive factor, "so that the thing is to belong to him who has the *right* to it."

(2) *Fraud.* — Fraud is conscious wrong. It respects the form of right, which form it employs for the concealment of its own disregard of the substance of right.

(3) *Constraint, or Violence, and Crime.* — My will, projected into an external object or article of property, becomes obviously so far exposed to attack. Through my property the hand of violence may be laid upon my will, or through such violence I may be coerced into making some sacrifice or performing some action, as the condition of my retaining any possession.

Such use of violence or constraint contradicts itself; it attacks the foundation of right, and is therefore wrong (*unrechtlich*). It attacks the foundation of right; for this foundation is the free-will, and the use of violence or constraint is an attack upon free-will as practically objectified in an external object or relation. And it contradicts itself; for the act of constraining violence proceeds, presumably, from the free-will of the aggressor: in it we are therefore to see an attack of freedom upon freedom, — freedom turned against itself. The case would indeed be relieved of contradiction, if we

ABSTRACT RIGHT. 23

could regard the freedom of the aggressor and the freedom of him who is violently attacked as two separate things, whose relation to each other is indifferent. But this we cannot do. Freedom is something which in its nature is incapable of being merely an article of private individual use and possession, like a member of the physical organism or a material instrument; besides being a particular and private possession, it is of necessity also a universal and, as it were, public attribute. In this sense the freedom of one is the freedom of all; and he who first employs aggressive violence against another's freedom wars, not only against his neighbor, but against himself. His act is thus inherently, or "in conception," self-contradictory and self-destructive; it is in accordance with its own nature that it should defeat itself and come to naught.[1] When, therefore, by the hand of resisting violence it is in fact defeated and brought to naught, it but meets the fate the seeds of which are sown in its own nature. Hence, while we may justly say that the use of violence or constraint is "abstractly considered" wrong, we must also admit that where it is employed to resist and defeat the results of a first act of aggression, it is not only conditionally right, but ideally necessary.[2]

[1] In the English language, the negative, ideally empty character of an act such as that considered in the text, and at the same time its ethical turpitude, are expressed by the term *naughty*.

[2] Hegel mentions, in a note, that any infringement, whether positive or negative, of a contract, is to be considered as an act of aggressive violence. The use of measures of constraint by the pedagogue against a natural tendency of the will of his pupil toward rudeness and unculture, may at first appear to be purely aggressive and

From the point of view now reached, we may say that abstract right is right of compulsion. For that wrong which may be defined as an infringement of abstract right consists in attacks on my freedom as it exists in, or in relation to, an external object; and the defence of my freedom against such attack must consequently be itself an external action and a use of force. But it is obvious that the foregoing description could not be regarded as a strict definition. To *define* abstract right as right of coercion would be to define it in relation to a consequence which comes in at the door of wrong, — the negation of right, — rather than in relation to its positive principle.[1]

hence abstractly wrong; but it is not so in fact. "The purely natural will is *per se* violence against the essential idea of freedom, which it is at once the business of the pedagogue to protect against the violence of such uncultured will, and to bring to realization in the latter." Hence, also, the justification of the State in the employment of coercive measures for the like ends, — or, antecedently to the existence of States, of "the heroes who founded States and introduced marriage and agriculture;" whose actions, though not authorized — as they could not be — by existing and recognized or formulated law, and so appearing arbitrary, were yet essentially lawful and right, being justified by the higher law and right of the idea of man and of his freedom, as against the insurrectionary and usurping pretensions of the "state of nature," — that is, the state of universal and unregulated violence.

It may be added that the "dialectic" of the general situation under consideration is expressed by one of Shakspeare's characters: —

"But such is the infection of the times,
That, for the very health and physic of our right,
We cannot deal but with the very hand
Of stern injustice and confused wrong." — K. JOHN, v. 2.

[1] Samples of such definition (taken from Bentham and Kant) are given by Professor Holland (*Jurisprudence*, p. 58).

ABSTRACT RIGHT.

The act of aggressive wrong, considered on its external side, consists in a damage done to the property or fortune of an individual. The cancelling of the wrong is termed, under established social conditions, civil satisfaction, and takes the form of restitution or compensation.

But the act of wrong, viewed on its internal side as a manifestation of free-will, is an offence against freedom in its universal sense. It is an attack on the foundation of right as right, and thus regarded is a crime.

Where, now, does the crime have its "positive existence"? Where can we find it so as to undo it, and by undoing it to maintain and manifest the inviolability of right? Damage we can easily find; it exists in an external object, where it can be measured and repaired. Crime has no such existence. Right, of which crime is the violation, is not an external existence, and is in this sense inviolable. We are compelled to say that crime has no positive existence except in the particular will of the criminal. Here, then, it must be attacked; here its denial of right must be contradicted and defeated. Such treatment of crime is Punishment.

Punishment is *per se* just; and its justification follows, first of all and essentially, from the circumstance that notwithstanding the flat contradiction in which it at first appears to stand to the will of the criminal, it is in reality but the completion, or actual and full development, of his own act considered as an act of *will*. For a real act of will can proceed only from a rational being; and the peculiarity of such an act proceeding from such a source is, that, besides its *particular* side or character, it has a *universal* one, or that by it there is virtually set up a universal law of action for all men, — a law which the agent thereby implicitly recognizes, and in accordance with which he in effect demands to be judged and treated. The law thus implied in a free act of aggressive wrong is indeed a law of violence, or of abstract wrong. But when the law recoils, in the form of punishment, on the head of the offender, he is treated in accordance with *his* right; his act is developed to its logical consequence, and the offender in receiving punishment is really being treated simply with the honor due to a presumptively rational being.[1] Further, we are not to forget that the act of wrong-doing is an inherently negative one; it is a negation of right as right. We are to beware, therefore, of thinking of it as something original and positive. What is original and positive is right as such, which is eternal, absolute, and inviolable; and if punishment is itself negation, it is the negation not of something purely affirmative and positive. Punishment is a mode of making visible the negative (or *naughty*) character of crime, and is at the same time simply the negation of negation, and thereby the declaration, manifestation, and restoration of the positive character of right.

In view of the foregoing results, derived from

[1] The true attitude of the criminal as a *rational* being is that of Socrates, who desired that if injustice were found in him he might be punished.

analysis of the nature of crime as proceeding from that free-will of man which is the proximate source of right, our author finds himself compelled to comment adversely on various theories regarding the nature and ground of punishment that are often brought forward. In these theories crime is regarded merely as an unfortunate and regrettable evil, and punishment as another evil of like character, to which society must resort in order, by frightful example, to deter others from committing crime; or for the maintenance of public safety, the protection of property, the improvement of the criminal, or the like. These theories are to be termed rather superficial than abstractly false. They are founded on considerations incidental to punishment, and which constitute its extrinsic justification, rather than on a perception of its intrinsic nature and justification. The considerations mentioned "are in their place — though mainly only in regard to the *modality* of punishment — of essential consequence," but the theories founded on them all tacitly presuppose "the previous demonstration that punishment is intrinsically just." And this is the main point. The principal question is not respecting a mere untoward circumstance (a disturbing criminal act), nor respecting this or that prospective good result (prevention, protection, improvement), but distinctly respecting wrong and right, or injustice and justice. "In our present discussion, the only essential point is that crime, considered not simply as the production of a public evil, but as a violation of right as right, is to be negated, and then to determine of what nature is the *existence* that crime has and that is to be negated; for this is the true evil that is to be abrogated, and the question respecting its nature and location is the essential one. So long as theorists are without definite conceptions on this point, confusion must reign in their views respecting punishment."

Punishment, considered as negation of a negation, or the injuring of the injurer, contains the element or aspect of retaliation. And this aspect remains ever deeply engraven on the popular conscience, which declares that crime *deserves* punishment, and that the criminal should receive *according to his deeds*. Its most literal expression is in such maxims as: "Whoso sheddeth man's blood, by man shall his blood be shed;" and "An eye for an eye, and a tooth for a tooth."

But in this sphere of abstract, or as Hegel also terms it *immediate*, right (that is, right not mediated by those forms of law which depend on the full organization of social relations in the State), the punitive negation of crime takes the form of vengeance. An act of vengeance may *in substance* be just, and in this sense ideally necessary, or beyond criticism. But *in form* such an act has the defect of apparent or possible arbitrariness, contingency, injustice. It has the air of proceeding from the subjective, particular, and unreflecting will of the avenger, — and such is indeed ordinarily its source. But the original act of wrong, or crime, against which vengeance is directed, consisted precisely in the arbitrary assertion of the particular will of the individual offender, in disregard of the true will that is universal. Formally, therefore, the act of vengeance is identical in kind with crime itself. Crime followed by vengeance is but one step removed from crime followed by crime. Accordingly, vengeance provokes second vengeance, and so on, in a false process, which may extend, if unchecked, *in infinitum*, without ever coming any nearer to the positive, permanent, concrete, and organized realization of right. With insight into the inherent contradiction involved in reliance on vengeance as a means of negating wrong and maintaining right, comes perception of the need of a justice that shall be freed from subjective interest or its appearance, as well as from the appearance of being determined by the accident of brute force, — a justice, therefore, that shall not be avenging, but strictly punitive. And what is first of all required is, that there be found in some person destined to act as ruler and judge a will that shall know and will the universal as such. In other words, there is required a will that not merely unreflectingly and spontaneously manifests itself in particular objective acts of vengeful justice, but that also reflects, — reflects upon itself, — becomes thus conscious of its universal nature, and finds therein a principle of just and unimpassioned judgment, by the application of which pure justice may be meted out. Or, still again, purely abstract right, — the sphere of will in its first, immediate, objective manifestation, — cannot logically or practically stand alone. It forces us, it forces mankind, by its own inherent defect and contradiction, forward into that stage of *subjective*, reflective will which is termed Morality.

CHAPTER II.

MORALITY.

IN the sphere of Abstract (or Objective) Right the individual was a Person, as previously defined (p. 12). Possessed of a will formally or potentially universal, he proceeded, without suspicion or without reflective consciousness of this universality and of its meaning, to manifest his will spontaneously, immediately, in particular objective acts. His fellows did the like; and the result was contradiction and discord.

In the sphere of Morality, which may also be termed the sphere of Subjective Right, or of the "Right of the Subjective Will," the Person becomes a Subject. His personality, his will, no longer exists merely for others, in a pure "state of nature," or in the form of an aggregate of purely objective acts and relations; it exists for the person himself, in the inward form of consciousness, of reflective thought, of conscience. In this more favorable soil is now planted his freedom, which thus first demonstrates itself to be more fundamentally a thing of the mind, or of the inward spirit, than of external possessions and relations.

But the merely subjective Will which is the subject-matter of Morality, and the purely Subjective Right which corresponds to and is determined by it, are still less than the concrete Will and the concrete Right, — the Will and the Right to whose fulness and completeness nothing is lacking, and in which, as the sequel must illustrate, the objective and the subjective, the particular and the universal, are united in a vital and inseparable union. The merely subjective, like the merely objective, Will " is therefore abstract, limited, and formal; " and the viewpoint of Morality is that of abstract difference and relation, or of obligation and requirement.

We may, for convenience, define an *action* as an *intentional* act, or an act so far forth as it is *intended;* and we may then say that the " Right of Moral Will" has three sides, respecting (1) the immediate relation of actions to the subjective Will of the agent, as involving objective Purpose and Responsibility; (2) their special character, as determined by the particular object of Intention, such as the Welfare of the individual; (3) their universal character, as determined by comparison, in the forum of Conscience, with the absolute aim of all will, the Good.

A. — PURPOSE AND RESPONSIBILITY.

The purely subjective Will is finite, limited, imperfect. Its finitude consists in the fact that it *presupposes,* as the condition of the actions it determines, an external object belonging to a realm foreign to and so limiting the Will, and containing in itself a variety of circumstances and relations of its own. In this realm the reflective Will conceives the idea of a change to be effectuated through its own agency. This change it *proposes* to itself; this is its *purpose*. In the change, when effectuated, the Will recognizes *its* work, for which it holds itself *responsible*.

But what is the extent of this responsibility, and what its condition? For the "change" proposed may be indefinite in its extent. The realm of external things, in which the change is to be effectuated, being one in which every part is inextricably bound up in an indefinite variety of circumstances and relations, it follows that a change introduced at any point through the interfering agency of human will may be followed by an incalculable variety of consequences. Any of these consequences which were not contemplated, and hence included, in the original purpose are, with reference to the purpose, accidental, while as determined by the objective relations of things they are also necessary. The subjective Will now claims as its right that it shall be held responsible only for those consequences which it foresaw. It claims "the right of knowledge;" it demands that the extent of its responsibility shall be measured by the extent of its knowledge, and that its knowledge shall be regarded as the sole condition of its responsibility.[1]

[1] "The *heroic* self-consciousness (as in the tragedies of the ancients, *Oedipus*, etc.) has not advanced from its primitive state of simplicity and unity to the point of making the distinction" between the objective and subjective in relation to the Will and its actions, or "between external deed or event and internal purpose and knowledge of circumstances; it makes no distinction among consequences, but assumes the responsibility for its action in its whole extent."

B.—INTENTION AND WELFARE.

It is not enough that we regard an act of subjective Will merely as a *purpose*. As such, it is only an immediate internal fact, a psychological phenomenon, a particular state of conscious knowledge or conception, of interest to us only in the point of view of its bare *quantity*, as a measure of the *extent* of responsibility. But in reality an act of Will is not simply a particular psychological *quantity;* it has also a certain universal *quality*. It is not merely one in a series of independent conscious states, the whole significance of which is exhausted when it is *measured;* it is also an active function, proceeding from a *thinking* being, and hence shares in the *universal* nature of thought, and in particular in the special character of the thought of the individual from whom it proceeds. In this point of view, an act of subjective Will is said to involve Intention.

Suppose, by way of illustration, that an act of mine consists in setting fire to a bit of wood. I have, by hypothesis, a distinct idea of my act and of its immediate consequence, in the burning up of a whole building; and so I may be said to have acted with *purpose:* I *proposed* to myself this particular act. All this may be true, and yet I may have been an idiot; in which case no one will attribute to me *intention*, whether good or bad. Being an idiot, and hence not a thinking being, I acted without conception of the universal quality of my deed; I acted thoughtlessly. But that such a deed, proceeding from one who is not an idiot, has a universal quality is made obvious through the fact that a *judgment* is passed upon it; that by this judgment the deed is subsumed under a general category, and a universal predicate is attributed to it, such as *arson;* and that, in accordance therewith, the deed is finally pronounced either right or wrong.

An action has then, *per se*, considered as an objective fact, a universal quality; and the " right of intention " is conditioned upon the agent's knowledge of this quality.

But the objective action, viewed in its universal character, is not coextensive with the whole content of the agent's intention. The agent is, by hypothesis, a conscious subject. This means that all his objective relations are, as it were, reflected in and upon himself; in him, as in a centre, they converge. His outward actions, therefore, stand in immediate relation to himself as an individual, and are performed, not merely for their own sake, but for the sake of their relation to himself. They are means to an end, or ends, in himself. It is this that gives them subjective *worth*, or constitutes their *interest*, for him.

Thus the actions that proceed *from* the subjective Will have, in turn, their ideal termination *in* the subject. It is this that constitutes subjective freedom, in the concrete sense of the term, founding "the right of the Subject to find in his action his own satisfaction."

Intention, then, includes the willing of a particular act, with conscious knowledge of its objectively universal character and of its relation to a universal

MORALITY. 35

subjective end, — the satisfaction or happiness of the agent.

The recognition and emphatic assertion of this subjective element in Right marks the turning-point between antiquity and the modern era, and is due to the influence of Christianity. The results are visible in many of the peculiar phases and principles of civilization in the Christian era, such as love, romanticism, the pursuit as a supreme aim of the eternal happiness of the individual, morality, conscience, — in principles of civil society also, in political constitutions, and in history generally, especially in the history of art, the sciences, and philosophy. A false and petty, yet far too common, result has also been that men have defined Intention with reference to its subjective element alone, leaving entirely out of consideration the objective character which, as we have seen, also belongs necessarily to it, or — what amounts to the same thing — making the objective element to be only an unessential incident of the subjective, or a mere means to the latter. Thus we have the "psychological view" of history, which seeks to depreciate all great deeds and individuals by the ostensible discovery that the main intention of the latter was, not the great work which they really accomplished, but the glory and honor, or other subjective gratification and personal advantage, which accrued to them. This is the view of the "psychological valets to whom no men are heroes, not because the latter are not heroes, but because the former are only valets." The objective element is not to be thus excluded in judging of intention. "What the individual subject *is*, *is the series of his actions*. If these constitute a series of worthless productions, the subjective Will whence they proceed is equally worthless; if, on the other hand, the series of his deeds is of a *substantial* nature, the like is true of the inner Will of the individual."

But the right to have regard in my volition to my own particular satisfaction, the right to realize my freedom in the subjective realm and form of my individual weal and happiness, is bounded by limitations similar to those which condition the purely objective realization of freedom. In this case, as in the other, freedom cannot be merely an individual property. In the exercise of my freedom I must exercise a freedom that is common to all,—otherwise, freedom quickly defeats itself by inward self-contradiction; in seeking my own welfare or happiness, I must seek also the happiness of others.

The subjective Will is therefore bound to seek, for its particular intentions, a universal and justifying form or principle,— the universal and absolute Good, the real or supposed knowledge of which will be to men their Conscience.

C.—THE GOOD, AND CONSCIENCE.

The Good is the ideal of the unity and harmony of the universal or essential Will of humanity, and of the particular Will of the individual man. In this ideal that which we have termed Abstract Right, as well as the pleasure of the individual, the vanity of

MORALITY.

private opinion, and the contingencies of external existence are conceived as subordinate to the ideal power of a universal law. They are subordinated, but not destroyed. In and through them the universal is to be realized. The Good is nothing less than the ideal of " realized Freedom, — the absolute Goal of the World."

Happiness (*das Wohl*), regarded from the point of view of the Good, has no validity as an end except in its character as *universal* happiness, — that is, as resulting from the realization of universal freedom; in other words, " Happiness is not a good without Right." On the other hand, " the Right is not the Good without Happiness: the consequence of *fiat justitia* must not be *pereat mundus*." Since the Good is that which the particular Will of the individual is under an ideal necessity of realizing, and in which at the same time it truly finds its own proper realization, it follows that in case of collision between the Good and the abstract right of Property, or the particular ends of private happiness, absolute right belongs to the former. The latter have no justification except so far as they are conformed and subordinated to the Good.

But to the *subjective*, reflective Will the Good is an abstract and as yet unfulfilled ideal, which is nevertheless in some way to be realized through the Will. In this connection the preliminary right which the Will claims is the right to know the Good, and to have its actions judged in the light of its knowledge. But, on the other hand, the Good itself has also a right of the most absolute and imperative kind, — the right and the demand to be known, and to be realized through the particular actions of the individual. In this view the Good, as an abstract universal, not yet brought into harmony with the particular forms of individual action, stands forth in the character of a vague but inviolable ideal of Duty; it is that which absolutely must be, or which has an absolute right and claim to be, realized; it is the ideal of Duty to be done for Duty's sake.

Such an abstract ideal of Duty being merely formal is devoid of definite content. The contemplation of it will give to no man an answer to the specific question, What is my duty? The nearest approach to an answer supplied in our discussions up to this point, or capable of being given from the view-point of " Morality," or of the purely subjective Will, is the indefinite one, *Do right, and seek the happiness of all men.* Accordingly, abstract moralists, like Kant, whose industry is only formal, and who do not get beyond this indefinite notion of duty as unconditioned but unspecified obligation, find insurmountable difficulties in the way of the development of the doctrine of particular *duties*. Particular duties ought to be and to appear as the necessary organic members of a living whole called Duty. In other words, Duty ought to appear and be conceived as — what it is in fact — a concrete and not merely an abstract universal, and so as an organic whole, rich in articulated details, with which it is inseparably and livingly one in thought as in fact. So a tree, for example, is a concrete universal, standing complete only as it is realized in and through the system of its members. An abstract tree would be a tree only in name; it would be at most only the conception of something that has members, without knowledge of what the members are and how they are related to each other in the tree. And he who should on the basis of such an empty conception go about to supply this missing knowledge, would resemble perfectly the abstract moralist who on the basis of an abstract conception of universal Duty attempts to determine what are the *members* of Duty, or what are particular duties. Obviously the labor of such a one must be wholly unintelligent, or can be guided, as Kant's is, only by purely formal principles, — such as that whatever is to be regarded as a duty must not stand in abstract contradiction with itself. But judged by this criterion there is no action whatever, whether good or bad, that cannot be " proved " to be a duty.

The subjective Will, then, simply arrives at the conscious recognition, under the general name and ideal of Duty, of a something unconditioned in nature and authority, which is to be realized *through the conscious self-determination of the individual.* By what means and in what form this is to be done, — this is something for the discovery and determination of which the individual fancies himself to be alone responsible. He is to trust to his own private consciousness, judgment, or conscience without dictation from another, and of course without the possibility of illumination from the purely formal ideal of Duty which he acknowledges. The *universal* — the fact of unconditional obligation —

is conceived as something objective, independent of the particular volition of the individual. It is like an empty vessel destined to be a vessel of honor or dishonor, of life or death, according to the nature of the practical content with which the individual fills it. But precisely this content — the *particular*, the detail of individual duties — is regarded as subjective, or a matter of purely subjective and individual determination.

The foregoing is the description of the subjective Conscience, which is one-sided and imperfect, and not to be confounded with the "true Conscience," or Conscience in its complete and perfect development.

The true Conscience is the consciousness and voluntary acceptance of Duty, not merely as an abstract and formal universal whose content is to be subjectively and privately determined, but as a concrete one, having a systematic and objective content of fixed principles and duties. "But the objective system of these principles and duties" first meets us at a later stage in "The Ethical World." Here, at this formal view-point of Morality, Conscience is without the mentioned objective content. It is only the unqualified "formal certainty" or conviction of a being — an individual being — having a centre of independent and responsible self-determination in himself.

From the fountain of such a Conscience — such a purely formal and subjective [1] self-consciousness —

[1] Self-consciousness, or self-knowledge, at the stage of moral development which we are now considering, is only subjective. As

it is obvious that bitter waters are as likely to flow as sweet. Being unaware of, or at all events not yet accepting as authoritative, any principles of Duty that are at once truly objective and universal, it may indeed arbitrarily or by accident adopt in a particular case, and act upon, such a principle. But it is even more likely to make caprice its law, to exalt the individual's own particular views and desires above the universal, and to act accordingly; and so to be distinctly *evil*. It is here at this stage in the development of human Will that we are to look for the " origin of evil."

The subjective Will claiming the right to determine for itself what is good, and acting in accordance with this claim, is prone to affirm the excellence of its actions on the ground of their " good intention." When this affirmation is addressed to others, it is hypocrisy; when the agent addresses it to himself, we have " the still more exaggerated extreme of subjectivity asserting itself as the absolute," or of evil.

The Good, or Duty, we must repeat, cannot be a merely abstract universal, — that is, without determinate content. And the true Conscience cannot be a merely subjective and indeterminate consciousness of an abstractly universal power and right of self-determination. The Good must, indeed, be univer-

such it is imperfect, and if persisted in becomes morbid. True or perfected self-knowledge, to which corresponds the true Will and the "true Conscience," is, as we shall subsequently see, objective as well as subjective. It is both in organic unity. It is the knowledge which man has of himself in his concrete, social, and religious relations, and in his unity with them.

sal and objective, and it must also be definitely realized through the self-determining activity of the individual subject. But the subjective Will, on the other hand, must find its own true substance, and so the motive and law of its particular self-determining actions, in an objective concrete system of Good or of duties, to which the caprice and even the so-called subjective "conviction" of the individual shall be subordinated. Objective Good, or Duty, and subjective Will must be integrated. The two must be in active organic unity. Then alone will each exist according to its true nature. And thus they do exist in the concrete Ethical World.

CHAPTER III.

THE ETHICAL WORLD.

IT is in the Ethical World,—the world of concrete social relations, such as the Family, the State, Universal History, or Humanity, and supremely Religion, or the living, willing partnership of man with God in working "the works of God,"—that the idea of Freedom is realized. It is realized as a "living Good," known and willed and embodied in actual historic existence, in and through the self-conscious activity of men. In this "ethical substance" man finds the essential basis of his own true self-consciousness, or self-knowledge, and the motive principle of his action. In brief, the ideal content of the conception of Freedom is unfolded and actualized in a present, actual world of organized human and spiritual relations, in which freedom is objectively demonstrated to be, not the attribute of "merely conscious" *individuals* (brutes are such individuals), but of beings, such as men, who are capable of finding in a consciousness of the universal the true substance of their own proper self-consciousness and the true motive of their own —that is, of all genuinely human—activity.

The realization of these relations involves neither the disgrace nor the destruction of individuality. On the contrary, individuality is maintained. It is provided with a content, a ballast of ideal substance and motive, without which it would move on quickly to self-destruction. The regulation of the individual will by a fixed or "universal" principle, — *e. g.*, by the law of one's station, and consequent duty, as member of a family, of the State, of the universal parliament of humanity, or of the "city of God," — so far from involving the annihilation of individuality, is the supremely essential condition of its true preservation, and of its becoming clothed in the garments of life and truth and beauty, essential to the concealment of its otherwise apparent and inherent nakedness. And, on the other hand, the descent of the universal — the Good, Right, Duty — from its throne of abstract, cold, and colorless authority into the hearts and into the particular actions of individual men, does not involve either the destruction or the sacrilegious violation of the universal. The rather, it is only through such descent that, from being merely potential and indeterminate, it can come to its right and be indeed actual, determinate, and effectively commanding.

The Ethical World is a system of essential relations, of essential laws, and of Ethical Powers, which govern the life of individuals. In the consciousness of these powers — of the moral organisms of which the individual is a living member — the true self-consciousness of the individual first becomes veritably actualized. Their life is his life, and their power is his power. They are, in their measure, the objective reality of that organic reason which is the essential and defining substance of the individual as a distinctively *human* — that is, a spiritual, rational, and rationally self-conscious — being. As therefore in knowing these Powers the individual, as a *human* being, is only truly coming to the knowledge of himself, so, on the other hand, it may be said that they can never be truly known and comprehended except through the development of genuine human self-knowledge (not, for example, by the way of purely objective "observation"); as also they can never exist in a form at all adequate to their nature except through the will of men, the moving-spring of whose activity is, explicitly or implicitly, precisely the rational self-knowledge in question.

Into the realm, now, of these Powers, or Moral Organisms, which constitute the Ethical World, the individual is born. He finds them existing. They exist, and in immediate relation to the individual; and the preceding paragraph indicates why they exist for him in the recognized possession of "independence in the highest sense of this term, and of an absolute authority and power, — an authority and power infinitely more positive than that of Nature." The laws of Nature — that is, the *reason* that is in Nature — he must know and respect conditionally, as far as such knowledge and respect constitute a means to the attainment of the ends of his specifically human activity. The laws of the Ethical World he must respect and obey unconditionally, for they are the laws of his own specific nature as a rational being; and in them the voice of the Organic Reason, which is the source and goal of all being, speaks in far purer and more adequate tones than in the external forms and laws of natural existence.

The laws of the Ethical World, then, are not merely formal, abstract, and dead, but substantial and living; and not merely subjective, but also objective, — they are the laws of living moral organisms. To the individual, whom as a morally indeterminate subjective entity they confront as that in which alone he can come into possession of his own true moral substance, they constitute or define a system of *duties*, binding upon his will. "The ethical Doctrine of Duties — that is, the *objective* doctrine, in distinction from the one that moralists so often attempt to build up on the empty principle of moral subjectivity, which the rather determines nothing — is consequently the systematic development of that realm of ethical necessity with which this Third Part is concerned. . . . A real and consistent doctrine of duties can be nothing else than the development of the relations which necessarily flow from the idea of Freedom, and are therefore actualized in their full extent in the State," which is nothing but the organized existence on earth of the substantial Freedom of Man, or is "the divine idea as it objectively exists on earth."

Is Duty, thus conceived, a limitation? So it appears, when regarded from the view-point of indeterminate subjectivity or abstract Freedom, or from that of the impulses of the natural Will, or of the "moral" Will, which seeks to determine the good by the light of the merely subjective and hence capricious private "Conscience." But, really,

THE ETHICAL WORLD. 47

Duty respected brings with it the liberation of the individual from the bondage of natural impulse, as well as from the inelastic sense of moral suffocation and depression which attends him to whom Duty, instead of being concrete, is an indeterminate and indefinable, though imperative, ideal. " In Duty the individual liberates and elevates himself to substantial Freedom."

The spiritual substance of the Ethical World, reflected in the individual character of its members, is Virtue; and Virtue, so far as it simply implies the conformity of the individual to the duties of his station, is Probity (*Rechtschaffenheit*). But this substance, as an immanent and universally determining principle of action in all individuals, takes the form of *Ethos* (*Sitte, mores*) or Custom — " a second nature, which takes the place of the original and merely natural will, and becomes the permeating soul" of the individual, giving meaning and reality to his existence as a human and rational being.

In the social-moral organisms of the Family and the State the ethical substance of man comes to its right, and right becomes a living and effective and moulding power. Here, too (as also and supremely in the social-moral relation with God, which both Family and State imply), the freedom of the individual is perfected. It exists, or vainly seeks to exist, no longer in purely objective fashion as in material property, nor in purely subjective fashion, as in the inner forum of indeterminate conscience, but in a realm at once objective and subjective, — a spiritual realm, which is the realized substance of freedom itself. Here duty and right are one, and man has rights as far as he has duties, and duties as far as he has rights. In Abstract Right, on the contrary, right and duty are separated: if I have a right, the corresponding duty of respecting this right belongs to another. And in the realm of Morality the ethical union of right and duty is conceived or implied only as an imperative but unrealized ideal.

The term *substance* in the Ethical World means what we express when we speak of the Spirit of a Family or of a People.

Family and People, or State, are terms in a series of stages through which the ethical substance of mankind realizes itself.

(*a*) The Family is the ethical spirit of mankind in its immediate or natural form.

(*b*) In Civil Society families and members of families go apart from each other and are re-united as independent units or individuals, for the security of person and property, under an external order, in a realm of merely " formal universality," — the " external," or visible, State.

(*c*) The invisible State, with its constitution written in the hearts as well as in the customs and laws of a people, — the State as the seat, the organ, and the self-controlling power of the public life, — unites in a more intimate and vital sense the Family and the Civil Order; it integrates and ideally completes them, by taking them up as living members into its own ideal-real organism.

Sect I. — THE FAMILY.

The immediate and active principle of the Family is love. Love is the attribute of a self-consciousness and a will which are objective as well as subjective, or which transcend the sphere of private individuality, and in their scope are, in the etymological sense of this term, *generous* (generic, *kind*-ly). Subjectively considered love is the *sentiment* of such a self-consciousness and will. As sensation is the "immediate" or naturally first term in objective cognition, so love is the like term in human self-knowledge. Love is the sentiment of an ideal social unity, and in the experience of love as the organizing and controlling principle of the Family the individual person finds a measurable fulfilment of his own true self-consciousness as a *human* being. He finds therein that his proper human existence is not achieved in abstract independence and isolation, but as the member of a moral-social organism, and that the true consciousness of himself is the consciousness of himself as such a member.

The Family, like every finite organic existence, is a process, and involves three terms: —

(*a*) Marriage.

(*b*) The Property or Fortune of the Family and care for the same.

(*c*) The Education of Children and the dissolution of the Family.

A.—MARRIAGE.

The merely physical union of male and female for the propagation of the species is a step to which other animals than man are prompted by the instinct of their species. But man is more than an animal. In him blind instinct is illuminated and transfigured by reflective self-knowledge, and the merely external union of the natural sexes becomes transformed into a spiritual one, or into self-conscious love.

Whatever the particular "subjective" origin of the personal relation that culminates in marriage,— such as a particular and unprompted fondness of the two persons involved for each other, the choice of the parents, and the like,— the objective origin of the relation is to be found in the free consent of the persons to constitute henceforth one person; to merge their natural and single personalities in a new unity; to submit, therefore, in this respect to a self-limitation, but with the exceeding great reward— since by merging themselves in this new unity they "win their substantial self-consciousness"— of gaining thereby a true emancipation. Apparently losing their lives, they in reality thus take a first and long step toward finding them. From this point of view it is to be said that it is an objective "ethical duty" of mankind to enter into and maintain the marriage relation.

Marriage is essentially a spiritual relation. The acknowledgment and maintenance of this relation is an express enthronement of the spiritual over the natural. It involves the subjection of the passions, and of the special changing likes and dislikes of the individual to the law of a common life, a common love, and a common good.

That marriage is not simply a contract relation was remarked above (p. 21, *note*). A contract implies parties who retain fully their independent personality, and is an outward relation. Marriage is an inward relation involving not only the limitation of independent personality, but even its absorption in the ocean of a larger life, in which it emerges transformed and transfigured, revitalized and essentially "a new creature." The fitting "celebration" of a marriage is therefore not the mechanical work of a lawyer, who fills out a blank form of contract which the parties concerned coolly sign, and to whose signatures the lawyer as a third party, who may be morally indifferent to the whole transaction except as he is moved by the expectation of a fee, appends his own signature as a witness. It is, the rather, a *ceremony*, whose proper witnesses are those spiritual powers the Family, the Community, the Church, and which is accomplished through the simple and significant means of spoken language, — the most spiritual form in which a spiritual reality or process can express itself.

Marriage has for the parties concerned both an intellectual and an ethical consequence. On the one hand, it solicits and elevates both the intelligence and the will of the individual to recognize their true object in something universal, something larger than the individual with his

"Miserable aims that end with self," —

namely, in a common good, a common life, a really objective and substantial end. It moves to knowledge and to action. On the other hand, it is followed by the personal consciousness of a spiritual increase, and prompts to the jealous guarding of this increase in the sphere of an interior home-life and through the patience of love. These complementary and ideally inseparable consequences are represented respectively in the active outward life of the husband, whose lovingly intelligent labor provides for the visible support and enrichment of the family; and in the wife, whose no less intelligent love is the bond and sign of its invisible and indestructible unity.

True marriage is monogamic. For, as previously indicated, an essential character of the marriage relation is that in it personality finds and is to find a substantial fulfilment or realization. In it independent individual personality loses itself in order to find itself; it merges itself in another in order thus to become more truly conscious of itself. But this it cannot do unless that other be not many, but, like itself, *a single personality*, on the part of whom and of itself there takes place a mutual and undivided giving away of single personality.

So " marriage, and particularly and essentially monogamy, is one of the absolute principles on which the ethical character of a social state rests. The institution of marriage is therefore customarily cited as one of the essential incidents in the founding of States by gods or heroes."

The Family, as constituting a single moral per-

THE FAMILY. 53

son, has its external reality — the visible sign and means of its existence — in its property or fortune (to which also the specific name of "means" is given).

B — THE FORTUNE OF THE FAMILY.

Property is a category of "Abstract Right." Under this head it was treated as the possession of the single individual, existing for the immediate satisfaction of his particular needs, and subject to the perturbations flowing from the capricious variations of his selfish desires. But a family, which has more the character of a universal and unchangeably enduring person, must and can have, not simply "property," but an enduring and sure *possession*, or a Fortune. In the labor devoted to its acquisition and the care expended in its preservation and administration, the element of individual caprice is subordinated to the thought of a common good. The labor and the care have an essentially ethical character. In the legends respecting the founding of States, or at least of social and orderly life, the introduction of fixed property appears in connection with the introduction of marriage.

The defence of the Family as a legal person against the aggressions of others belongs to the husband, as the Family's head. In his hands lie also the disposition and administration of the fortune of the Family. This fortune being a common property, no member of the Family as such is in possession of a particular property of his own, but each has a right to the common possession.

Through the marriage of a scion of the Family a new family is founded, having again an independent existence of its own. Into this new relation the individual carries with him the property which before he held only by a right subject to the executive will of his father, and as part of the common fortune of the Family.

C.—THE BRINGING UP OF THE CHILDREN AND THE DISSOLUTION OF THE FAMILY.

In children the invisible unity of married love is visibly objectified and embodied. "In the child the mother loves her husband, and the husband his wife; in it both behold their love."

The child has the right to be supported and reared at the cost of the common fortune of the family. The parents, on their part, have to remember that the child is a potentially free and spiritual being, never to be treated as a mere soulless thing. The moral education of the child has for its first and positive end to enable the ethical substance — the heart and will — of the little one to come to its first flowering and fruitage in the form of love and confidence and obedience. Its further end — a negative one with respect to the family relation — is so to develop in the children the seeds of independence and free personality, that they shall be prepared in due time to go out from the fold of the natural unity of the family.

The dissolution of the family occurs in three ways: First, and abnormally, through the complete alienation of husband and wife from each other, and their consequent separation or divorce. Secondly, and normally, through the growth and development of the dependent members, or children, into the possession of a mature and free personality as legal persons, capable of holding property and founding new families. And thirdly, through the death of the parents, and the following distribution of the common fortune among the natural heirs.

SECT. II.—THE CIVIL SOCIETY.

If the Family is, on the one hand, a necessarily permanent member of the larger Ethical World, it may also, on the other hand, be said to contain in itself that world in germ. Viewed in this way, it is a natural, organic, vital synthesis of elements, which in order to enter into the larger social unities or syntheses of State and Historic Humanity must first be separated and brought, in a measure, into the attitude and quality of mutually repellent and independent atoms. The dissolution of the Family, as we have just above seen, is its resolution into elements of this character. What we may term the natural process of the Family eventuates in the multiplication of families and of individuals, separated and opposed by differing and conflicting interests. The world of these interests becomes the sphere of Civil Society, which is "the arena for the combat of the individual private interest of all against all."

The realm of Civil Society is the realm of "particularity," or self-interest. And Civil Society itself — otherwise denominable as "the State on its external side," or as Government — is the mechanical subordination, whether by measures of constraint or of restraint, of particular self-interest to a universal law of security and protection for all.

The elements of Civil Society are *concrete persons*, as distinguished from the abstract persons of Abstract Right. In other words, they are not merely abstract and indeterminate "free-wills." Each one has come to conceive himself as an end to himself, and each is characterized by a definite set of personal needs and desires, to the satisfying of which each is moved by a strange mixture in him of natural necessity and wilful caprice. And Civil Society is an outcome from the fact that each such person can assert and satisfy himself only through the positive or negative co-operation of others, and subject to forms of law common in their application to all.

Law, or "the *universal*," is here characteristically conceived as alien and external to the will of the particular individual. The universal and the particular thus exist, or are conceived as existing, apart, — the latter in possession of the right to develop and assert itself in all directions, and the former with the right to exercise a forcible control over the particular, and to be regarded as (proximately) the true basis, the necessary form, and the ultimate end of the latter. The relation is similar to that above exhibited in the chapter on Morality, between the subjective will, with its indefinite freedom of subjective choice, and the ideal of universal and abso-

CIVIL SOCIETY. 57

lute obligation ; except that here the universal is, for the purposes of civil order, measurably and artificially defined in formal law. Law, with its formal universality, thus first confronts the individual as a task-master and as a limitation of freedom, while all its formal demands are met by outward obedience, let the inward disposition be what it may.

But if the law of Civil Society is a task-master, it is also a schoolmaster. If it imposes a limitation on formal and undisciplined freedom, obedience to it is really an education in the direction of substantial freedom.

Particularity (or individualism) seeking to be a law to itself tends to its own destruction. And even the attainment of its own transient ends and satisfactions is subject to many contingencies. Thus Civil Society, as the arena in which individualism seeks the greatest amount of unrestrained satisfaction, offers a spectacle of excesses, of misery, and of consequent physical and moral corruption.[1]

Absolute individualism is absolute civil anarchy. In order that individualism may exist at all it *must* limit itself; it must submit to law, and so take at least the outward form of universality. The individual must consent to become a link in the chain of Civil Society. If, indeed, law and society are thus to him no more than means for the satisfaction of his private interests, yet even so they exercise a tuitional influence on him. They are a brake on

[1] Hegel points out how, in the ancient States, the "independent development of particularity," resulted in moral corruption and ultimately in national extinction.

the rude unculture of natural caprice; they bring in proportion to their efficiency particular interest into at least outward agreement with the forms of universal rule, and so prepare the way for the final and saving increment of ethico-social grace, which is added when particular and universal subsist, not merely in outward agreement, but in inward spiritual unity,—when the individual recognizes that the centre and circumference of his true interest as a human being are public as well as private; and when he discovers for himself that the realm of his substantial or real freedom is not the land of his purely private wishes and whims, but the broader region of a common and public life, and of a stable and divine good.

In treating of Civil Society we have to consider,—

(*a*) The System of Wants,—the satisfaction of the needs of the individual through his labor, and through the labor and through the satisfaction of the needs of all others.

(*b*) The Protection of Property through the Administration of Justice, or the maintenance of civil freedom.

(*c*) Police and Corporations.

A.—THE SYSTEM OF WANTS.

Wants are particular needs of the individual, to be satisfied by means, first, of external things; and, second, of labor.

(*a*) *Human Wants and their Satisfaction.*—The brute has a limited circle of means and ways for the

CIVIL SOCIETY. 59

satisfaction of his likewise limited needs. Man
gives proof of his greater universality through the
multiplication of wants and means, — the multiplication taking place in part through his resolution of
concrete wants (such as the want of food, clothing,
or shelter) into single parts or sides, which then
constitute new, more special, and more abstract
wants.[1] In this process, whereby wants are specialized and rendered more abstract, consists what is
termed their *refinement*. But a refined want, by
very reason of its specialized and abstract character, has an element of generality or universality
about it. More plainly, a refined want is a social
want; it is a want which exists only as it comes to
be generally recognized, — to have a place in the
general esteem or opinion of society, or of a class
in society. In it there is built up on the henceforth
concealed basis of "immediate or natural" want a
larger "spiritual" one, the existence of which is
conditioned upon reflection and opinion. The development of social wants is thus one distinct step
toward the emancipation of man, — that is, of that
spiritual side of man's nature in which alone his
specific freedom and perfection can reside. Still, it
is only one step, where many others are needed.
The emancipation is only formal, and not substantial; for the subject of man's interest here remains,
or may remain, purely personal and selfish; and the
growth of mere luxury, unqualified by a public life
and a public will absorbed in larger interests, is

[1] Man alone, as has been said, has, or rather creates, *le besoin du
superflu.*

found to bring with it an indefinite augmentation of dependence and even of distress.

(*b*) *Labor.* — Specialized wants require equally specialized means for their satisfaction. Labor is the activity directed to the production and acquisition of these means. Labor takes the material immediately furnished by Nature, and by the most varied processes shapes and adapts it to these manifold ends. By this formative labor the means required for the satisfaction of specialized human needs acquire their worth and fitness; and so it comes to pass that *human* consumption is conspicuously a consumption of, not merely natural, but specifically human productions.

Labor has a direct relation to the development of both theoretical and practical culture on the part of man. It involves, on the one hand, not only the possession of a multiplicity of ideas, but also a peculiar facility in inward imaginative representation in the transition from one idea to another, and in the comprehension of complicated and general relations, — in short, the cultivation of the understanding in general, and so also of language. On the other hand, it contributes to practical culture, or to the training of the will, by inducing the habit first of occupation in general, and then of limiting one's activity in obedience to the nature of the material employed, and also, and more especially, in obedience to the demands of others. It is a wholesome habituation of the will to objective activities, and to the cultivation of talents having a general or quasi-public utility.

The specialization of production in conformity with the specialization of wants leads to the division of labor. In this way the labor of the individual becomes more simple, his skill greater, and the number of its products indefinitely increased. At the same time the dependence of men upon each other for the satisfaction of their multiform needs grows more absolute. Labor also becomes more and more mechanical, so enabling man in the end to substitute for the labor of the hand the work of the machine.

(c) *Wealth.* — In the manner now described, individual self-interest is converted into a ministry for the satisfaction of the wants of all. The result is what may be termed a permanent and common wealth, in which the individual by his theoretical and practical culture and skill may render himself a partaker, and so assure for himself the means of subsistence. But the possibility of such participation in the common wealth, or of amassing a private and special fortune of one's own, depends on numerous conditions. First, it may depend on the previous possession of a certain fortune, to be used as capital. Again, it will vary with one's special skill, aptitude, or ability, — points in which a great inequality exists among men, arising partly from a difference of natural endowment, whether of body or of mind, and partly from the influence of accidental conditions in rendering easy or difficult the development and use of one's endowments. This inequality, or rather difference, among men, which is an ineradicable attribute of their natural individuality, and which consequently the abstract understanding in the framing of its social ideals vainly ignores or aims to annihilate, reappears in a modified form in what may be termed the natural classes of Civil Society. Of these classes there are three, which may be termed respectively the " substantial or immediate class, the reflecting or formal, and finally the universal class."

The first of these classes is made up of tillers of the soil, and their wealth is derived from the natural productions of the soil. Being obliged to govern themselves in their labor with reference to the changing seasons, and the fruit of their labor being dependent on other variable natural conditions, they are obliged to cultivate the virtue of providence. For the rest, independent reflection and active will play a subordinate part in the life of the agriculturist, and the ethical character developed has prevailingly the quality of " immediate and substantial " (that is, natural, unbroken, undisturbed) wholeness, having its roots directly in the confiding life of the family.

With reason, therefore, have the proper beginning and first founding of States been identified with the introduction of agriculture along with marriage. For with agriculture, the formative culture of the soil, comes necessarily exclusive private possession of the soil, the exchange of the roving life of the savage for the orderly quiet of domestic law, the secured satisfaction of human wants, the regulation of the intercourse of the sexes through the institution of permanent marriage, and the consequent merging of private interest in the larger interest of the family, and of private possession in the possessions of the family. In all these results we may see the element of universality coming to the front; or, in other words, we may see in them the work of that unifying, constructive, law-instituting reason which, in one way or another, is the active principle of all existence. And so, especially, we must regard them as steps tending distinctly toward the manifestation and the actual realization by man of his own nature, as a creature "endowed with reason." We need not wonder at the agronomic festivals, images, and rites of the ancients, whereby they expressed their sense of the introduction of agriculture and of the institutions connected with it as divine acts, and so devoted to them a distinctly religious reverence.

If to the success of the agriculturist's labor Nature contributes the principal share, and his own industry a relatively subordinate one, the case is different when we come to the second of the classes in Civil Society above enumerated. This may be termed the industrial class. Its members depend for their subsistence less on the immediate beneficence of Nature, and more directly on their own labor, reflection, and intelligence, as also and essentially on the correlation of their labor with the wants and labors of others. This class is subdivided, according to the character or form of its occupation, into three classes, — the class of artisans, or manual laborers, whose work is directed to the supplying, on demand, of single wants of single persons; the class of manufacturers, who control and direct the collective labor of a number of employés in providing particular articles, for which there is a more general demand; and the commercial or trading class, engaged in the exchange of articles of demand, by means of a universal medium of exchange,— namely, money, — representing the abstract value of all wares.

In the industrial class the individual is specially forced to rely on himself; and the consciousness of this fact causes him to be among the first to demand the establishment of protecting civil institutions. It is, consequently, mainly in the cities that the spirit of liberty and civil order has first made its appearance.

To the third or "universal" class, finally, are committed the general interests of the civil association. Its members must therefore be relieved of the necessity of engaging in labor for the immediate supply of their personal needs, either through their possession of a private fortune, or through the intervention of the State, which by remunerating them provides that their private interests shall not suffer while they are wholly occupied in caring for the interests of the public.

These classes constitute (as a logician would say) the "particular" or specific differences of Civil Society. As such, they are not arbitrary, but ideally necessary. But to which class a particular individual shall belong is a matter upon the determination of which natural disposition, birth, and other accidental circumstances may have their influence, though the ultimate and essential ground of decision must lie in the subjective opinion and independent choice of the individual himself. Thus, what takes place by an inner necessity — to wit, the division of Civil Society into the classes mentioned — appears immediately dependent on private choice. To the subjective consciousness of the individual it has the form of a work of his own will; and so the principle of subjectivity receives in this sphere its due right, desert, and honor.

This is one of the points in which the difference between the political life of the Orient and the Occident, or the ancient and the modern world, manifests itself. In the former the division of society into classes arises objectively, as we may say, of itself, because it is *per se* rational, — the nature of Civil Society necessarily involving such a division; but the principle of subjective individuality is deprived of its right, inasmuch as the assignment of individuals to the respective classes is wholly left to the rulers (as in the Platonic Republic), or determined by the mere circumstance of birth, as in the Hindu castes. Thus, not being recognized in the supreme organization of society and so harmonized with it, the principle of subjective individuality, which is an essential factor of society, is rendered hostile, and either wholly succeeds in overthrowing the social order, as in the Grecian States and the Roman Republic, or else shows its fruit in the form of internal corruption and complete degradation, as was to a certain degree the case among the Lacedemonians, and as is now (Hegel was writing in 1820) most completely illustrated among the Hindus. But when the principle in question is recognized in the public order, is integrated with it, and so is maintained in its right, it becomes the all-animating principle of Civil Society, bringing with it the development of the thinking activity of men, and of personal merit and honor. Such integration of the immanently necessary reason of Civil Society and the State with the *liberty of individual choice*, is what is mainly contained in the ordinary idea of civil freedom.

The individual, now, by his own choice and by his own activity, industry, and skill, makes himself and maintains himself as a member of one of the integrant orders of Civil Society; makes provision for his own wants through this his connection with the public whole, and so acquires recognized individuality in his own sight, as well as in the sight of others. The ethical quality thus developed is that of class-honor and probity. In particular, what we have heretofore distinguished by the name of "morality" has its peculiar place in this sphere, where private reflection on one's own activity and care for particular individual wants and personal welfare occupy so prominent a place.

B.—THE ADMINISTRATION OF JUSTICE.

We have seen that the "system of wants" leads to a civil order, founded on the recognized right of individuality in the matter both of knowledge and of volition. This right is in kind universal, and is the right to liberty, but only in an abstract and consequently formal and negative sense, — the sense of freedom from outside interference. The "administration of justice" (*Rechtspflege*) is the protection of this right, particularly in the form of protection of property. The conception involved is that of a right which belongs to all men equally; a justice, which is no respecter of persons. The law protects all individuals in respect of that in which they are unequal, — their property, or, better, their properties, — whatever pertains to them as individual persons, whether in the form of material possessions, acquired talents, gifts of fortune, or what not; and it protects them all equally. All men are conceived as constituting, so to speak, one universal Person, as members of which all possess an abstract equality.

Right or Justice, then, in the sphere of Civil Society, is grounded in the notion of the abstract equality of all men. Its "objective reality" depends on, or consists in, its existing for the consciousness of men, or being known, and its being equipped with sufficient power to enable it to take and assert its place in the world of effective and objective realities, and make itself recognized as possessing a universal authority.

(*a*) *Right in the Form of Law.* — Right becomes positive in the form of law; and Law is the formal and, from the nature of the case, universal definition of Right. It is from the nature of the case universal; for definition is the work of thought, and it is the peculiarity of thought that it clothes all its objects in the form of universality. Right, or Justice, in assuming the form of Law, not only takes on the form of universality, but also then first becomes truly definite, simple, and intelligible. "Laws of custom," as they are termed, since they are laws of the custom of thinking beings, have implicitly, and so as we may say tend toward, the same form of universality; and one of the functions of legislation is to give them explicitly this form.

In Civil Society, as such, and from its point of view, right is binding or obligatory only so far as it has been defined in the form of law. The subject-matter of civil law, and the sphere of its application, are the indefinitely individualized and complicated relations and kinds of both property and contracts, as well as those ethical relations which spring up in the spiritual atmosphere of the family, so far as these involve questions of " abstract right." Morality and its commands, as being most intimately concerned with the subjective will and private conscience of the individual, cannot be made the subject of positive legislation.

(b) *The Existence of the Law.* — It belongs to the proper existence or being of civil law that it be published and generally known. It is, for example, " one and the same wrong to suspend the laws, as Dionysius the Tyrant did, so high that no citizen could read them, or to bury them in an extensive apparatus of learned books, — collections of differing decisions, opinions, customs, and the like, — and that, too, perhaps in a foreign language, so that the knowledge of what is legally right is accessible only to the learned few." The codification of law is therefore not only a benefit to a people, but an act of justice.

Abstract right takes form in the laws of Civil Society. So through the due institution and publication of the laws, what was before only the "immediate" or "natural" right of the individual acquires the attribute of being recognized, or of existing in the general will and knowledge of society. Transactions in regard to property must therefore now be accompanied by a form or formality, as the sign and condition of legal existence. Property now rests on civil contract, and on the formalities which render it capable of proof and legal.

In Civil Society, where property and individuality acquire legal recognition, crime becomes no longer a merely private but a public offence. The injury of one member of society becomes the injury of all. The inherent nature of the crime is not altered, but its external relations are. In estimating its magnitude therefore, or its gravity, it is now necessary to take into consideration the new point of view of its dangerousness to society. But this very consideration, in the case of a society firmly established, may operate to produce a sensible reduction of the severity with which crime is punished.

(c) *The Court of Justice.* — Right enters, in the form of law, into objective existence. It stands forth, independent of and superior to the particular volition and opinion of the individual, with the attribute of universal authority. The assertion and realization of this authority in particular cases is the function of the Court of Justice, whose voice (to apply an expression of Aristotle) is the voice of "intelligence without passion." To this court it is the right of every member of Civil Society to appeal, as it is also his duty to appear before it, and to accept only at its hands the justice he claims.

A right, in order to receive the approval and protection of the courts, must be provable. Legal Procedure is the name given to the steps — themselves regulated by law — by which the parties concerned are required to produce their proofs and arguments, and the judge is made acquainted with the case in dispute. The forms of legal procedure are necessary, and so are an essential part of organized right or justice itself. But as they become more minute and exact, they become indefinitely more numerous and complicated; the difficulty of mastering and following them is increased, till at last, instead of being an aid to justice, they are, in themselves or through their easy misuse, a positive hindrance. Hence the need and the duty of establishing for certain classes of cases courts with simplified methods of procedure, — courts of "arbitration," or of "equity."

The administration of justice must be public. The particular subject-matter of a case under litigation is, it is true, the immediate concern only of the parties directly involved. But by virtue of its being brought forward for legal discussion and decision, it acquires a public or general character, and the decision of it involves the interests of all. It need hardly be added, that it is the right of the accused party — a right of his "subjective freedom" — to be a witness of the administration of justice in his own case. This right is completed when the determination of the facts in his case, to which the law is to be applied, is committed to those in whose impartial intelligence he can confide, — trial by one's peers, or by jury.

C. — POLICE AND CORPORATION.

We have seen that the true relation between the Universal and Particular is one of agreement and unity; and in fact in Civil Society law is expressly established to be the universal guide and rule of particular or individual conduct. The latter is to conform to the former. The administration of justice is the enforcement or restoration of such conformity, in cases where conformity is imperilled or interfered with. But the very fact that it may be imperilled shows that the union of universal and particular is not here what it is, for example, in the realms of organic Nature, — namely, vital, concrete, inviolable. Their relation here is in a distinct degree external and mechanical; and the maintenance of conformity depends immediately on the subjective will and freedom of the individual, and mediately on the existence of an executive power, strong and intelligent enough to enforce the authority of law. Indeed, it is just because Civil Society, which is directly founded on or correlative to the "system of individual wants," is concerned only with that sphere of the public life in which law and conduct bear this relation to each other, that it is called "the external <u>State,"</u> or <u>the State</u> on its external, visible, and mechanical side. Law and conduct, or law and private interest, bearing then this external and mechanical relation to each other, it becomes possible to look upon one of them as a means existing for the sake of the other. It is thus that law is regarded in the sphere of Civil Society. It is not enough that the law should be administered through courts of justice for the punishment of actual offences against property and person; the law must also be an instrument for the actual prevention of such offences. The security and welfare of the individual must be treated as something which he may claim to have positively guarded and promoted through the administration of the law.

(*a*) *Police*. — The sphere of police regulation is the contingent actions of private individuals, each pursuing his own interest in his own way. Its first object is to provide that no one shall, by actions in themselves harmless, prejudice the interests of others or the public order. The decision of the question as to what actions are thus prejudicial must always be to a certain degree arbitrary. It will vary with varying external conditions, — for example, peace and war, — and with the changing customs, morals, and spirit of a people.

Again, the relations between producers (or dealers) and consumers involve sides that are of common and public concern. For example, the public exposure for sale of wares of daily and general use can be permitted to the individual, subject only to the right of the buying public to be protected from fraud through the examination in all needed cases, by an officer of the law, of the wares exposed. But especially the dependence of great branches of industry on foreign conditions and remote combinations, which the individuals dependent on them cannot survey in all their connections, renders necessary a degree of protective oversight and direction on the part of the civil power.

Still, when in these and other ways the civil arm has done all in its power to enable the individual to provide for his own subsistence, his success is yet exposed to many and contingent individual conditions, — skill, health, capital, and the like. And if in the first resort the responsibility in the matter of enabling the individual to meet these conditions rests on the family, yet to the Civil Society belongs the function of supplementing the efforts of the family, of supplying its deficiencies or neglects, and even, when occasion arises, of overruling its will. For the Civil Society recognizes each member of the family as an independent person. Further, it substitutes for external, inorganic Nature and the paternal acre, from which the individual originally derived his subsistence, its own artificial soil (so to speak), thus rendering the very maintenance of the family itself dependent on it, — that is, on a relative contingency. "So the individual has become *a son of the Civil Society*, which just as much has claims on him as he too upon it."

The society acquiring thus, in some true sense, the character of a universal family, has the right and the duty to see that the education of its members is not left to the capricious and uncertain determination of parents, — so far, at least, as education is required in order to fit the individual for citizenship, and is of such character that the parents themselves cannot generally and personally superintend it. In like manner it is the right and duty of the Civil Society to treat as minors, and assume the guardianship of, those who by prodigality destroy the means of their own and of their families' assured support and subsistence, — and this both for the good of society and of the individuals concerned. But the loss or absence of means of support may be due, not to wilful waste or indolence, but to accidental physical or external circumstances. In this case we have the social phenomenon of poverty, — a class of persons having all the wants which the existence of Civil Society presupposes, without the ability to provide for them. With regard to them, the "public power" is to assume the place of the family, with a view not only to the supplying of immediate material needs, but also to the correction of the disposition to idleness and the other vices that arise from such a condition, and from the feeling of its injustice.

Poverty and all sorts of human distress are not merely external "objective" phenomena. They have a subjective side, by which they appeal especially to the sympathy, charity, and love of the more fortunate. So they furnish an abundant occasion for that kind of assistance which is prompted by Morality (private or individual benevolence, and the like); and this they will continue to do, no matter how perfect the public arrangements instituted by legislation for their relief. But Hegel distinctly insists that these arrangements should in fact be made as perfect as possible, in opposition to the theory which would shift all responsibility in this matter as much as possible on the shoulders of private philanthropy, — that is, on something which by its nature is variable and contingent.

The unimpeded life of a civil society is accompanied by a constant growth in population and in the industrial sphere. The dependence of men on each other for the supply of their wants becomes more general, while industrial enterprise takes on larger forms. This tends, on the one hand, to facilitate the accumulation of wealth; and, on the other, to specialize and limit the sphere of individual labor, and so to aggravate the dependence of the laborer, — with which is connected an increasing incapacity to appreciate and enjoy the larger liberties, and especially the spiritual or intellectual advantages of Civil Society. When by an extension of this latter tendency a great mass of the population has in its means and mode of living fallen below a certain standard, which naturally determines itself as the one necessary for a member of the society, and has thus suffered a loss of that feeling of justice and honor which accompanies the consciousness of self-support through one's own activity and labor, we have the phenomenon of a proletarian class (*Pöbel*). And the existence of such a class again only increases the facility with which disproportionate wealth is concentrated in a few hands.

Now, to make the support of this class upon a proper plane of living a direct tax on the rich, or to provide for the same through public and richly-endowed foundations, would be against the principle of Civil Society and the feeling which its individual members must have of independence and honor. Or if it were sought to accomplish the same end by providing labor (the opportunity to labor), the result would only be the further increase of that mass of productions in the surplus of which, and the comparative lack of paying consumers, the evil in question consists.

So, "through this its dialectic," the particular civil society is forced to transcend itself,—that is, first of all, to seek among other peoples that lack what it has in abundance, or that are generally inferior to it in skilled industry, consumers, and thus the necessary means of subsistence. This involves a movement of great significance in its bearing on the development of general culture. It involves the use of the seas as a commercial highway. As the development of the principle of family life has its condition in the fixed earth,—in the possession of a determinate portion of the soil,—so the sea is the changing and inappropriable natural element which gives life to industry in its external relations. Searching for gain, men expose themselves and their goods to the perils of the waves. In this way they prove their superiority to motives of mere material profit. Among the results are, that the attachment of men to the soil and to the limited spheres of civil life is tempered with an element of flux, and that remote lands are brought into relations of intercourse, governed by principles accepted by all parties. Such intercourse constitutes a most important means of civilization, and commerce in promoting it becomes a factor of universal history. A further sequel is the opening up of the way for the planting of colonies, with all that this implies in the way of industrial enlargement and relief.

(b) *The Corporation.* — The Civil Society has general and particular interests. The care for the former falls within the province of what we have termed Police. The latter are organized, for their special protection and direction, in Corporations.

The Corporation is conceived by Hegel as the formal and legal union of those members of the industrial class who follow a common trade. The relations of the Corporation to its members are such that it may be called, in relation to them, a "second family." It has an ethical character. It subordinates the arbitrary action of the individual member to rules established for the common good, and cultivates in him, as an ideal regulating principle, the "honor of his craft."

But the ethical aim of the Corporation, like that of the Family, is restricted in its scope. Both *presuppose*, and by their ideal limitations demonstrate, a larger, more universal aim of man, which is, as matter of fact, organized in the State, — in which latter, as an ethical organism, and the larger world of man and of human self-realization, both Family and Corporation have their existence as constituent and subordinate members.

Under the head of "Abstract Right" we contemplated the self-developing Will of man in its purely objective aspect or relation. From this we passed under the head of "Morality" to the consideration of the same subject in a purely subjective point of view. Both of these views were found to be alike abstract and therefore imperfect. The whole and substantial and actual Will of man, which is nothing other than the intrinsic nature of man developing, asserting, and realizing itself, could be (as we saw) and is neither purely objective nor purely subjective, but both, in organic harmony and unity, and can only exist in a moral organism, of which the individual shall be a member. We next regarded the Will of man as thus existing, in a "natural" or "immediate" form, in the Family. This form, though natural and in its measure appropriate to the ideal substance contained in it, was found to be really incommensurate with the whole nature of this substance. Accordingly, we saw the members of the Family going forth from its fold, assuming the character of independent units, and forming groups of a new kind, held together in the external bonds of coercive regulation. But here, again, the end of our search is not reached. The defect of Civil Society in this regard is of the same kind as — though less extreme than — that of Abstract Right. The substantial will of man is not adequately actualized in the mainly objective sphere of the External State. The rather, the true apprehension of Civil Society, or the External State, forces us for the perfect comprehension of the latter to pass on to the

THE STATE.

Invisible State, the Nation, in which man knows and wills himself as both a spiritual and a world-subduing power. Here it is that Civil Society finds the proximate ground of its authority, its right, and its power, as well as the ideal and regulative principle of its external arrangements. In Civil Society we consider man as *governed ;* in the State, as *self-governing.* In the former case we make abstraction from human — and especially, national — character and individuality; in the latter, these are essential and all-determining.

Sect. III. — THE STATE.

The ethical idea of man has actuality in the State. The State is the ethical spirit, the manifest, self-conscious, substantial Will of man, "thinking and knowing itself, and suiting its performance to its knowledge, or to the proportion of its knowledge." This spirit exists unreflectingly in what may be termed the ethical genius of a people, and reflectively in the self-consciousness, the knowledge, and activity of the individual, who in turn finds in and through it — regarded as his own spiritual substance, as the determining goal of his own higher aims, and as the product of his own activity — his substantial freedom. The State is thus essentially a living rational value and a rational power. It is a universal or public reason, the spring of a public or national life, and the foundation of a national consciousness. This consciousness has actual existence in the particular self-consciousness of the individual. But it cannot be termed an external or mechanical addition to the latter; the rather, the "public consciousness," the "national conscience," is, in its measure, nothing but the development and completion of the particular self-consciousness of the individual considered as a rational being. It is the particular self-consciousness of the individual elevated to that character of universality which belongs to it by its own nature. Thus the individual finds in the State a revelation and actualization of his own larger and better self; its service is a ministry of freedom, and kindles in him the flame of an unselfish patriotism; its claims on him are perfect, and membership in it is a duty of the highest order.

In modern discussion the State has often been confounded with Civil Society, and has accordingly been regarded only as a mechanical expedient for the security and protection of property and individual liberty. The final end of political union has thus been viewed as the interest of individuals as such: whence the natural inference that no inherent obligation rests on the individual to accept the responsibilities of citizenship; that it depends on his own arbitrary choice, whether he shall or shall not be the "member of a State."[1] But the real relation of the State to the individual is of quite a different nature. The State being objective reason, or spirit, the individual himself has real human objectivity, true individuality, and a truly ethical quality only as he is a member of the State. Social union is, consequently, not merely a means to an end,—it is

[1] Compare, for example, Mr. Herbert Spencer's "Social Statics."

THE STATE.

itself the true end; and the nature of the individual marks him as destined to lead a universal or public life. This latter is to be at once the background and the result of all his special activities, desires, and the like. It was the merit of Rousseau that he recognized the State as founded in a principle which not only as regards its form (like, say, the social instinct, or the divine authority), but also in respect of its content, is of the general nature of thought, — nay, is thought itself; namely, the Will. But as he took the Will only in the limited form of the single Will, — the particular, private Will of the individual, — it followed that the universal Will, which as such should be the Will of man, should express the organic nature of man, and should hence be in nothing different from the rational *per se*, was understood by him merely as the *common Will*,[1] derived from a comparison of various single wills, arrived at by special agreement, and only by abstracting from all that was separately peculiar to the different wills. Hence the theory which ascribed the union of individuals in the State to a contract founded on their arbitrary opinion and volition, with all the consequences, theoretical and practical, that flow from the theory. History has already shown how baneful was the result of attempting to put these abstractions into practice.

The idea of the State (*a*) has *immediate* actuality in the individual State, — an independent organism, with its own constitution or internal polity (*Staatsrecht*); (*b*) passes into the relation of the single

[1] Compare above, p. 20.

State to other States, — external policy; (c) reveals itself as *universal* idea, or genus (specified in single States), and so as a power superior to the individual State,— reveals itself, in short, as a Spirit of Humanity, progressively actualizing itself in the process of Universal Human History.

A.— INTERNAL POLITY.

The State is the actualization of concrete freedom. Concrete freedom is the vital union of the particular interests of the individual with the universal aims of man. The former are allowed their full development, and in the system of the Family and of Civil Society their independent right is recognized. But they cannot and do not stand alone. They tend, partly of themselves, to pass over into and become identified with the interest of the universal, — the public interest; while, partly (and what is of even greater consequence), the individual comes with his own intelligence and knowledge to recognize the intrinsic need and right of such identification, — to recognize in the universal the groundwork and substance of his own spirit, and to subordinate his activities to it as to their (proximately) final end. In other words, in the State, as the actualization of concrete freedom, neither is the universal established in authority and carried into realization in abstraction from the particular interests, opinions, and volitions of individuals, nor do the latter live, as private persons, in exclusive devotion to their special interests; the rather, the universal enters concretely into their wills, and consciously determines the direction of their activity. "The tremendous strength and depth of the principle of modern States" are derived from the circumstance that the principle of subjectivity, or private personality, is allowed to be carried to its fullest and extreme development, and is yet at the same time reduced into substantial harmony and unity with, and made a vehicle of realization for, the universal Will of man.

With reference to the spheres of private right and welfare, — the Family and Civil Society, — the State appears, on the one hand, as an external and superior power, to which their own laws and interests are subordinate, and from which they depend. But, on the other hand, it also appears as their immanent end, and as having its strength in the unity of its own universal aim with the particular interests of its individual members, or in the consequent fact that the duties of its members toward it are measured by the rights which they enjoy in it.

On this last point Hegel lays the greatest emphasis. In the State, "duty and right are united in one and the same relation." In this "conception of the union of duty and right is contained one of the most important notes of the State and the inner ground of its strength. In the abstract view of duty, particular interest is overlooked or condemned as an unessential and even unworthy factor. But the concrete view shows this factor to be just as essential as its correlative (the universal one), and the satisfaction of it to be absolutely necessary. The individual in accomplishing his duty must in some way find the satisfaction of his own interest; from his relation to the State there must flow for him a *status*, such that the public affair shall become his own particular affair. His particular interest must not be left out of consideration, or even suppressed, but brought into agreement with the universal interest," so that the securing of the one shall be at the same time the securing of the other. And this is accomplished when to the relatively mechanical relation of enforced obedience or external legality, by which in the sphere of Civil Society the individual is outwardly and visibly kept in his place, there is added the inward grace of an enlightened and truly self-knowing will; when the public interest is comprehended, or at least felt, as the true private interest, and *vice versa;* when, accordingly, outward obedience becomes the natural and spontaneous garb and expression of an inward spirit, of an all-pervading *ethos*, and mere government is changed to moral and substantial self-government. In the State this end is consummated.

The State, we have said, is the actualization of concrete freedom. And this is the same as to say that the State is in its measure the actualization of the Idea of Man; that it is not simply a contingent means of human perfection, but *is* also this perfection itself; that, in brief, the State is Man, standing relatively[1] complete in that fulness and wholeness

---

[1] "Relatively," I say, in order to prevent a possible misconception. Relatively, though with an inferior degree of truth, the same may be said of the Family which, in the text, is asserted of the

THE STATE. 85

of developed being which the idea of man as a rational being implies. And it is this by virtue of a process which, just because it is rather organic than merely mechanical, has the form of a process of self-realization. To illustrate: The actual tree is such only by virtue of a process of growth. In this process the tree becomes nothing other than itself, — it realizes itself. It does this, further, by separating itself into its natural parts or members, — roots and branches. To each it allows a separate or dictinct existence, and yet holds them all together in the unity of one organic and living whole. We may say that the tree disperses or distributes itself among its members, and this as the very condition on the fulfilment of which the manifestation of its universal life and power, and the actualization of its organic unity (or the actualization of the "idea of the tree") irrevocably depend. Moreover, the tree is not an after result of the existence of the roots and branches: when they begin to exist, its existence also begins. So it is with the State. The roots of the State are families, and its branches are the institutions of civil society. Its material is individuals. These take their places under the mentioned institutions, directed by cir-

---

State. But, as we shall see later, the State itself is organic to a larger life and actuality of the human spirit, or of the "idea of man," in universal history; while universal history, again, is organic to the perfect consummation of humanity through the discovery of the true will of man in the will of God, the adoption of the latter as the inviolable *norm* of human action, and the consequent establishment of man in his spiritual perfection and completeness as a co-worker with and child of God.

cumstances, by caprice, or by personal choice. The element of "subjective freedom" has here its play. But the institutions themselves have obviously a universal or general character; and the individual in recognizing them, and maintaining himself in his own chosen place under them, recognizes and devotes himself to the service of a universal with which by his own deliberate choice he has identified himself. But the universality of the institutions has its ground in, and is the manifestation and reflection of, that ethical "universal" which we term the invisible State or Nation, or, more explicitly, the spirit of the nation, — the universal spirit of man, as it takes form and declares itself in the particular life of the nation. Thus regarded, they make up the constitution of the nation; they are the reason of the nation, developed and actualized in particular forms. They are, therefore, the "steadfast basis of the State; they immediately determine the temper of the individual citizens toward the State, and especially their confidence in it; and they are the pillars of the public freedom, since in them particular (individual) freedom is realized in a rational form; and they thus involve an intrinsic union of freedom and necessity," or are, as it were, the living and visible body of an interior, organic, and steadfast liberty.

But institutions by themselves are impersonal and unconscious. Their existence, as the above comparison of them to the branches of a tree implies, is assimilated in kind to that of a natural organism. The law of freedom, as exemplified *in them alone*, is like a natural law, inflexible, unreflecting, without shadow of turning. In particular, they contain in themselves, as thus viewed and existing, no germ of development.[1] They are the phenomenon and product of a public spirit, which they accordingly implicitly presuppose, and which must distinctly declare and develop itself in the form of clear, self-knowing intelligence and will, in order that the form of necessity under which institutional freedom existed may itself be changed to freedom. This spirit we must consider and speak of as the true substance of the State.

A subjective form or reflection of the spirit in question is what may be called the political temper in the individual,—or patriotism. But objectively the substantial spirit, or spiritual substance of the State, exists in the form of an organism of different so-called "powers" intrusted to different men, or classes of men, in whom the State, the national spirit, is particularly embodied; in whose intelligence it especially knows itself, and in whose will it wills itself, and through whom, therefore, the State may be said to "work and act in view of aims consciously known, according to principles consciously recognized, and conformably to laws which are not only laws *per se*, but also for consciousness; and so, too, as far as its actions relate to particular

---

[1] The Chinese empire is a social organism, an organism of social institutions, existing mainly in the character of a natural organism. Hence its relative fixedness and permanence, and its withdrawal from the laws of political growth and development. Cf. J. Happel, *Die altchinesische Reichsreligion vom Standpunkte der vergleichenden Religionsgeschichte*, Leipzig, 1882.

circumstances and relations, with definite knowledge of them."[1]

[1] At this point our author introduces a long digression on the relation of the State to religion. Is religion the foundation of the State? Undoubtedly it is, and the whole philosophy of the State and of history is a progressive demonstration of this truth, and of the sense in which it must be understood. The State, history, and indeed all natural existence are the gradual actualization or manifestation of an Absolute Reason, which can and must exist in its eternal fulness only as Absolute Spirit, or God. In the ethical world, in particular, we are in process of seeing how each lower grade presupposes, as its substantial foundation, proximately the next higher one, and then absolutely all higher ones. So the Family presupposes or calls for Civil Society, while the State is similarly presupposed by both. The particular State, again, the nation, with its definite national spirit, is organic to, and hence presupposes, a still larger life of the human spirit, — a life which at once takes up into itself and also transcends the limits of separate national existences, and of which universal history is both the expression and the demonstration. But man, conceived and known as the spirit immanent in universal history, as universal humanity, or *Weltgeist*, is found to be unable to stand alone. He is relative to something else, which he presupposes as his "substantial foundation;" he is not absolute. The whole historic life of humanity is organic to, and dependent on, the life and operation of the absolute and eternal Spirit, of whose thought and will it closes the demonstration, begun at the lowest grade of finite existence. When the natural and ethical worlds are comprehended as the progressive incarnation of reason in "reality," God, who is the "absolute truth," is seen to be the eternal presupposition and the omnipresent and actual condition of all existence whatever, but most conspicuously of the existence of the "ethical world." If all things whatsoever are, in their degree, the revelation and incarnation of that supreme reason in which absolute and eternal Being — God, Absolute Spirit — consists, and if it is thus true of all things that they are a present and actual revelation of divine will and spiritual being, much more obviously is this true of an ethical organism, an historic power, like the State. So Hegel declares that "the State is divine will, in the form of a present [national] spirit, unfolding itself in the actual shape and organization of an [ethical] world." The whole normal process of history,

The Political Constitution is (1) the organization of the State and the process of its organic life in relation to itself, — the inner articulation of the State and its consolidation as an independent whole; and this involves (2) the existence of the State in the form of individuality, as an exclusive unit, with external relations to other similar units.

1. *Internal Constitution.* — When is a political constitution rational? It is when the inner articulation of the State — or, as it is called, the division and distribution of powers — repeats the inner articulation of reason itself. The law of this articulation

to which all the life of man, in Family, Civil Society, and State is organic, consists in the progressive realization of concrete human freedom, — that is, of the essential spiritual nature of man, through the conscious recognition of God as the "foundation" of all the true life of the human spirit, and of the divine will as the true substance or content of the human will. In the whole process of history, or of the "ethical world," humanity is progressively learning, and showing that it is learning, that its true language is, "Lo! I am come to do thy will, O God!" And so the foundation of the State is indeed, and in the most radical and comprehensive sense, religion, which, says Hegel, has ideally "the absolute truth for its content." Upon this general truth, both in its generality and in its specific applications, our author finds occasion, as we shall see, to insist at almost every step in the development of the philosophy of history, — the spiritual story of humanity.

But when religion is otherwise regarded; when it is identified with immediate feeling, or with an intuition which claims exemption from the arduous labor of philosophic comprehension; when, accordingly, it degenerates into fanaticism and narrow dogmatism, restricting the presence of God in history within the limits of a select religious organization, and treating the State as at the best only a soulless and godless mechanism, — then the claim that religion is the foundation of the State must be rejected, or rather corrected. Then, especially, must the spiritual character of the State and its inherent right divine be emphasized.

is neither obscure nor arbitrary; it is read on every page of real existence; it is the law of the distinction of the universal, the particular, and the individual, and of their combination in a concrete and living unity; it is the law of organic and individualized unity, or of many members in one body, each of which, while having its own independent character, reflects and shares the life and character of the whole. In such a unity the members are natural, and not artificial; they flow, so to speak, in their distinction from the nature of the case, and do not exist like a clumsy makeshift, as the result of an afterthought.

Hegel remarks on the circumstance that the starting-point of so much of modern theorizing respecting political constitutions has been purely negative. Theorists have begun with the assumed fact of a general ill-will, fear, distrust, or hatred among men, and then have proceeded to set up in theory a governing power as a dike against this "natural" evil. But the governing power is conceived by them as intrinsically an evil, though a necessary one, to counteract which another power must be set up, and so on. Thus the State is conceived only as an aggregate of powers, which are not members one of another, but are inherently independent and separate, existing only or mainly for the artificial purpose of checking and limiting one another. The State is thus viewed only as a "universal equipoise, but not a living unity." It is a piece of artificial mechanism, and its ostensible growth is merely the product of an equally artificial and continued tinkering. The true criticism on all this is simply the positive science of the State as we are seeking to develop it.

The essential factors in the inner articulation of the " political State " are —

(*a*) The power to define and determine the *universal* in the form of law, — the Legislative Power;

(*b*) The power to apply this " universal " in *particular* spheres and to single cases, — the governing or *Executive* Power; and

(*c*) The power of ultimate decision, or the Power of the Prince, in which the different powers are brought together in *individual* unity. The reigning prince is thus truly the head of the State. He conspicuously stands for it as a whole, and the State itself is a constitutional monarchy.

Hegel declares that the development of the State into the form and character of constitutional monarchy is the peculiar work and achievement of the modern world. He regards the ancient division of political constitutions into monarchy, aristocracy, and democracy as superficial, and due to the fact that the State, which is a growth, had not then attained to its full development. The reverse, he holds, is now true. In the fulness of the modern time the ideal nature of the State has been historically unfolded — has unfolded itself — in the form and substance of the constitutional monarchy. In the light of this result, simple monarchy, aristocracy, and democracy appear as forms having only a temporary and accidental justification. In the constitutional monarchy, whatever is true in each of these special forms is retained: it is retained, but only in the character of a subsidiary, though organic and hence vital factor. Simple monarchy is the rule of one; aristocracy is the rule of some; democracy is the rule of many. In the constitutional monarchy all of these three sides are combined, being severally represented in the three "powers," of which the modern State is the organic union. However, as Hegel remarks, these merely quantitative or numerical distinctions lie only on the surface of the case. The main point is, that the modern State, the constitutional State, is the ideal one, because, or so far as, there is recognized and realized in it the "principle of free subjectivity," and the substantial reason of the national spirit comes in it to a condition of self-mastering actuality.[1]

[1] It will be noticed that the considerations which are decisive with Hegel are in no sense merely formal. And it is obvious that the ideal State, as he conceives it, with its three orders of powers, may exist in a republic like the American, as well as in a constitutional monarchy like that of England. It were no exaggeration to term our constitution that of a monarchical democracy (the President being the monarch, the "one" in rule), and the British constitution that of a democratic monarchy. "The President" of the United States "probably enjoys more real power than any constitutional monarch in the world" (*N. Y. Evening Post*, editorial, Feb. 1, 1886). "If Hamilton had lived a hundred years later, his comparison of the President with the King would have turned on very different points. He must have conceded that the Republican functionary was much the more powerful of the two. . . . The Constitutional King, according to M. Thiers, reigns, but does not govern. The President of the United States governs, but he does not reign" (Sir H. S. Maine, *Popular Government*, Am. ed., N. Y., 1886, pp. 214, 250). Hegel remarks, in his *Æsthetik*, i. 248, that "the monarchs of our time are no longer, like the heroes of the mythical ages, persons in whom an entire social order is concretely

THE STATE. 93

It is to be noted that the *real* existence of a constitution — in distinction from its merely *formal* existence, in the shape of a written and published document — is in the self-consciousness of the people to whom it is said to belong. A formal constitution must correspond to and express that national spirit, that spirit of the people, which as a living law permeates the customs, the consciousness, and all the relations of the individuals who compose the people. A constitution is a thing having a natural growth; it cannot be manufactured *a priori* and forced upon a people irrespective of the grade and kind of culture that the people has attained, without revolutionary and self-destructive results.

(*a*) *The Power of the Prince.*[1] — The power of the Prince represents the power of the State in its totality. It is the power of the constitution and the laws (the element of *universality* in the total conception of the State); it involves the power of deliberation (application of the universal to the *particular*); and it is the power of ultimate decision (peculiar to the *single individual*, the reigning Prince). It is by this last element that the power of the Prince is peculiarly distinguished.

The Prince is sovereign, because the State is sovereign. The sovereignty of the Prince is the sovereignty of the State; or, the *State* is sovereign in its Prince. But what is the sovereignty of the summed up, but rather more or less abstract *foci* within the sphere of an order already developed and firmly embedded in law and constitution."

[1] Hegel considers the three "powers" in an order the reverse of that in which they were first enumerated by him (see p. 91).

State? How are we to understand it? The sovereignty of the State is grounded in its organic unity. A State that lacks the characters of organic unity, lacks, so far forth, the attributes or substance of sovereignty. And a State has these characters when its various powers are neither in complete independence of one another, nor treated as the private property of particular individuals; or, positively, where organic law reigns supreme, guiding the execution of all public functions in subordination to and in harmony with the "aim of the whole," or, as it is otherwise and more indefinitely termed, the "good of the State."

But the State is also (changing the emphasis) sovereign in its *Prince*, — in a single person, the Monarch. All the attributes and functions of the State have the quality of personality. The State is itself, according to our whole development, founded in, and is the concrete realization of, universal human Will. But the will and personality of the State as a whole would subsist in a vacuum, — that is, would not concretely and effectively subsist at all, — were they not actually lodged and represented in a single individual. Only in such an individual, through whom its personal and volitional functions of self-determination and ultimate decision are in supreme and critical moments exercised, can the State attain and maintain its character as a true individual in the family of nations. The State, as a moral and sovereign personality, from being merely a thing subjective becomes objective in its Prince. The selection of the Prince, too, is withdrawn from the struggles of factions and the mutations of caprice and referred to Nature, by the rule of hereditary succession according to the law of primogeniture. The Monarch thus gives no more reason for his right to be, than does the State itself. In this, as also in the power of independent self-determination, is founded at once the majesty of the Monarch and the majesty of the State.

To the Monarch as sovereign belongs the power of pardon. The recognition and exercise of this power constitute one of the highest witnesses to the majesty of the spiritual. For offence and pardon lie supremely in the spiritual realm; and through the exercise of the power of pardon the power of the spirit is illustrated, to "render undone that which has been done, and, in forgiving and forgetting the crime, to annihilate it."

In the exercise of his power of deliberation respecting the affairs of the State, the constitutional Monarch calls in the aid of counsellors, or "ministers," who alone are responsible. For the subject-matter of responsibility is not subjective opinion, but objective facts, and the knowledge and judgment that are determined by the direction upon them of a purely objective intelligence. It is the business of the ministers, in any affair of State, to learn the exact facts in themselves and in their relations to the laws which bear on them, to circumstances and the like, and to report the same to the Monarch for his final decision.

The objective guarantee of the power of the Prince is to be found alone in the constitution and the laws, or, more definitely, in the organic unity of the different institutions and powers of the State. A State which is such a unity is made up, not of separate and constructively independent and hostile " parts," but of " members," which so consent together and so involve each other that each one, in maintaining itself, contributes to the maintenance of all the rest. But such a State is, and may be defined as, the public organization and realization of substantial freedom. Of such an organization Hegel holds the constitutional and hereditary Monarch to be an essential factor. At all events, it follows that the Monarch's throne, if secure, is so only through its organic connection with the " public freedom."

(b) *The Governing or Executive Power.* — Under this head our author comprehends the whole Civil Service of the State, including both national and local police and judicial functions. Stress is mainly laid on the need of hitting the right mean between an unorganized and merely sporadic administration, as by knights-errant, and such an extreme of centralization as was introduced into France by the Revolution. " The proper strength of States lies in the local communities," but this only when there is in them a healthy and independent political life. In the case of a highly centralized civil administration such life is wanting. The communities constitute more a confused and fermenting mass, separated from the organized and organizing life of the whole State. In order that they may really be the strength of the State, it is necessary that they should have a distinct and visible share in its power and life. Since, under the organic conception of the State, the State itself is simply public and organized self-government, it is essential that the principle of self-government should receive proportionate recognition in all departments of the civil administration.

Of the public officer or employee in the Civil Service a certain moral temper is required. He must abandon the independent pursuit of private aims, in order to serve the public interests. He is to identify himself with the public cause. That he may do this, he must receive such compensation for his services that his private interests or needs may be provided for. So his particular interest will become joined to that of the universal public.

On the right quality of the Civil Service Hegel lays a very special emphasis. Its members constitute a "middle class" between the people at large and the higher and central powers of the State. On their conduct the political intelligence and conscience of the people will largely depend. On the other hand, the character of the Civil Service will always be, in an essential measure, determined by the ethical and intellectual development of the people, as well as, also, by such considerations as that of the magnitude of the State. The point of main importance in this matter is to be aware of and strive after the realization of the right ideal.

(c) *The Legislative Power.* — Laws are "made;" Constitutions are not made, they grow. The law-making power is itself a part of the constitution, which therefore it presupposes, and which it cannot directly affect.

The subjects of legislation, as it regards individuals, are (1) their civil and political rights and privileges; and (2) their duties, or what they must render to the State. With respect to the latter point, it is to be noted that, with the exception of military service, the modern State makes no direct personal demands upon its citizens. It requires, not direct services, but their equivalent, estimated in terms of that accepted quantitative measure of all values and services which is called *money*. In other words, the State *buys* what it needs, and the citizen renders his service by paying a *tax*. In many ancient States, in the ideal State of Plato, and under the feudal régime, it was far different. The modern method marks an advance in the direction of "subjective freedom," or individual liberty.

It is of the utmost importance not to forget that in a moral unity such as the State, every member or "power" is vitally one with all the rest; a complete separation is impossible. So it is, that in the legislative power the two other main powers of the State are influentially involved,—the *monarchical* as the power of ultimate decision, and the *government* as the power specially qualified to participate in legislative deliberations through its concrete and comprehensive knowledge of the whole condition of the State in its various divisions and departments, of the practical and actual principles of executive policy, and of the special needs of the moment. Hence Hegel approves the English practice of

allowing seats in Parliament to the members of
the Government.

That element in its composition which characterizes the legislative body in its *distinction* from the other powers of the State, is the representative one (*das ständische Element*). Through it " the element of subjective formal freedom, the public consciousness as an empirical average of the opinions and ideas of the many," is made a factor in the affairs of the State. The advantage of calling a representative assembly to participate in the work of legislation does not arise from any superior knowledge which its members can be supposed to possess regarding the business and needs of the State (such knowledge belongs in much greater degree to the members of the government), but rather from their special acquaintance with the workings of government and the deficiencies of administration in those narrower circles of Civil Society which lie comparatively remote from the observation of the officers in highest position. The moral effect of such an assembly, as an organ of public criticism, need not be more than mentioned.

But the most important thing to notice in this connection is that the legislature, or parliament, as a representative assembly, exercises the organic function of mediating between the government on the one hand and the mass of the people on the other. In this point of view, it is obvious that its members are required to have no less what may be termed the political temper, or the spirit of the State and of its government, than an eye for the interests of particular classes and individuals. Through the exercise of their mediatorial function the royal power is prevented from taking on the appearance of mere arbitrary despotism, while the conflicting and disordered aims and wishes of particular classes and of the masses are reduced to harmony, receive articulate expression, and, instead of being left to eventuate possibly in a brute and blind insurrectionary resistance to the State, are organized into the quality of willing, healthful, and helpful membership in the State. That view of a representative legislative assembly, therefore, which regards it primarily and essentially as a power antagonistic to the government is extremely superficial.[1]

It is the *particular* classes of society, the "substantial" and "formal," in distinction from the "*universal*" one,[2] whose representation in the legislative body gives to the latter its distinctive character. The "substantial class" has by itself, and without election, its independent place in parliamentary representation. Like the royal element in the State, this class is constituted as if by nature

---

[1] "A Constitution," says Hegel, "is by its nature a system of mediation. In despotic States, where there are only princes and people, the latter works, if at all, merely as a destructive mass, in opposition to all organization. . . . In despotic States the ruler spares the people, and expends his fury on those who are in his immediate environment. In such States, too, the people pay comparatively few taxes, while in a constitutional State taxes are increased through the very fact of the political intelligence of the people, which leads them to appreciate the needs of the State and voluntarily to make provision for them. In no country are so many taxes paid as in England."

[2] See p. 62.

on the basis of the family principle and of an independent and inalienable landed possession. At the same time its needs and rights are those of the other classes of society. Thus it is qualified in a peculiar way to exercise a mediatorial office between prince and people, and to be "at once the prop of the throne and of society."

The other element in parliamentary representation is derived from the more mobile and flexible side of Civil Society, which, both on account of its numerousness and still more necessarily on account of its nature and occupation, can participate only through selected delegates in the work of general legislation. But whom and what, precisely, do the delegates represent, and on what theory are they selected? Is it that all men, taken singly and individually, being members of the State, and the affairs of the State being therefore the affairs of all, all have an equal abstract right to make their knowledge and will felt immediately in the direction of the State's affairs; and that then, because it is practically impossible for all directly to exercise this right, they, as an unorganized mass of independent individuals, and on the basis of indiscriminate or universal suffrage, convey this right, with instructions as to how it shall be used, to a person or persons, selected by a — possibly accidental — majority of votes? This view is recommended by nothing but its abstract simplicity. But this which constitutes its apparent merit is the source of its real defect. It is true that all have, abstractly, an equal interest in the affairs of the State; but it does not thence follow that all have that political intelligence which qualifies them equally to exercise a determining influence in the direction of those affairs. Nor is representation a right that belongs to unorganized, unclassified masses. The "concrete State," as has above been repeatedly said and shown, has the character of an organic whole. As such it has its quasi-natural members, which are themselves relative wholes, made up of particular individuals. The individual is thus a member of the State only as he is a member of one of these members of the State. It is thus alone that the individual acquires the right to representation. It is not the individual as such, but the individual as member of one of the natural classes or divisions of society, that has the right to be represented in legislation. So the representative is chosen to stand in the parliamentary assembly for the interests of his class, community, or corporation; and yet not for these interests alone, but for these in harmony with and subordination to the interests of the whole State. That he will do this, the body which he represents must trust in his good-will and his intelligence; he must not be hampered with minute instructions. The guarantee of such good-will and intelligence is to be found in the previous life and practical experience of the delegate.

How now, and with what advantages, the two main elements in representation constitute two legislative branches, — these are points on which we need not enter into details. A few words only may be added respecting the relation between representation and "public opinion."

It is not the view of Hegel that a State is or can be conducted by public opinion. But neither is it his view that public opinion is to be ignored. In fact the representative legislative assembly, with its public proceedings, is precisely the point at which, and the vehicle through which, public opinion comes in determining contact with the State and its affairs. Its function is not to take the place of government, not to put its reason in the place of the final reason of the State, but to aid and strengthen the government by bringing to it an increment of special knowledge derived from the fresh contact of its members with the varied special interests of their constituencies. As it does this, the more universal relations, interests, and purposes of the State are in turn laid before it; and in this way public opinion itself receives a needed increment of substantial instruction.

For public opinion is indeed a two-faced affair. On the one hand, it has its foundation in a public conscience, which takes the form of ordinary " common-sense," is grounded in the peculiar substantial *ethos* of a people, and " contains the eternal substantial principles of justice, the true content and result of the whole constitution, of past legislation, and of the public situation generally, as well as a sense of the veritable needs and true tendencies of the actual present." But this conscience is, in the first instance, only instinctive. Hence, on the other hand, since the instinctive is not converted into the form of explicit, conscious, and adequate knowledge all at once, but only as the result of a prolonged and specific *process* of practical education, the form in which its contents are constantly coming forward in the consciousness of this, that, and the other individual, whose voices all go to swell the chorus of public opinion, is a contingent, superficial, and often even a perverted one. With such persons the more singular an opinion (of their own), the more important does it often appear to them. But the singularity, or peculiarity, of an opinion is a sure sign of its worthlessness.

In different senses therefore, and equally, public opinion deserves to be respected and despised, — the former with reference to its essential basis in the public conscience, and the latter with reference to its accidental, superficial expressions. The State cannot be abjectly dependent on it and at the same time prosper. "Independence with regard to it is the first formal condition of the accomplishment of anything great and reasonable in the world of practical actuality, as well as in the world of science." And when any such thing has been accomplished, public opinion is among the first to applaud it, and to adopt it as its own.

The State being the organized Will of a people, and Will involving necessarily the side of "subjectivity" (subjective knowledge, conviction, assent, intention), it is essential that this side should receive its rights, or its natural and full development. The growth, expansion, and influence of public opinion, with its liberty of expression, in the modern State is a movement in the direction named. But mere public opinion, variable, uncertain, mistaking the accidental for the necessary, the apparent for the true, would, if left uncontrolled, lead to the dissolution of the State. It would be inconsistent with true individuality in the State, which implies a "subjectivity," a knowledge that is fixed, sure of itself, consistent with itself, and "identical with the substantial will" of the State and people. It is such a subjectivity which, by hypothesis, is lodged in the head of the State, the constitutional Monarch,[1] and enables the State (among other things) to take and assert its place in a family of nations.

2. *External Sovereignty.* — True individuality is not bare, separate existence. It is, in the technical language of Hegel, ("existence for self.") In its most perfect forms, it is existence *plus* the knowledge of one's existence, in a character inwardly known and consciously willed. Such existence then is "exclusive;" it is in *relation* to the existence of other individuals, but is independent of them. Political independence is the independence of a national individual; it constitutes the foundation of a people's liberty and its highest honor.

Further, every existence which is to maintain in any degree a healthy and positive individuality must do so by an active process described by Hegel as "negation of negation." It is this principle, in a certain phase, that modern biology expresses by the phrase, "The struggle for existence." Individual existence affirms itself, secures and preserves for itself affirmative and positive being, only through the active negation, repulsion, and overcoming of

[1] Or President.

resistant and rival forces. The form and circumstances under which these forces are encountered may appear accidental; but that they should in fact be encountered and conquered is a necessity flowing from the nature of the being whose self-affirmation or preservation is in question. So we may accept it as a law for all finite existences that "it must needs be that offences come." The case of a national individual, or State, constitutes no exception to this law. The oppositions of States (or wars) have a natural and necessary part to play in the development and maintenance of national individuality. And since a nation is a moral individual, we must recognize in war an ethical factor. This it is not difficult to do. A nation conquering or defending its independence in war gives to its own people an instructive and important lesson regarding the true relations of ethical values. It then requires the sacrifice of, or the readiness to sacrifice, all private and particular interests, including property and its rights, and even life itself, that the independent and sovereign life of the State may be preserved. It teaches, by a severe object-lesson, the relative vanity of purely finite and selfish relations, and that their ethical worth is wholly contingent on and subordinate to the maintenance of relations which in comparison may be termed infinite and universal. It teaches that the true individual is inseparably bound up, not alone with his accidental and changeable private interests, but with the individuality of the moral whole of which he is a member, and with its interests. In times of prolonged peace this lesson is apt to be forgotten. Men forget the whole through the complete absorption of their attention in the part; the universal is obscured for them by the particular. All things remaining with them as they were at the beginning, they come to deify, as it were, the world of their petty and personal relations; its horizon comes to bound for them the moral universe. The result is moral petrifaction, or corruption. War makes an end of all this; it is to nations what winds are to the sea,—it preserves them from stagnation and putrescence. Further, the energetic and successful maintenance through war of the sovereign individuality of the State in its external relations, is found to exert a conservative influence on the internal relations and sovereignty of the State.

The readiness to make sacrifices for the sovereign individuality of the State is a part of the essential, or "substantial," moral attitude of all citizens or subjects. It is a universal duty. Like other universal relations, it requires to be represented in a particular class,—the army,—whose animating principle is bravery. Bravery, as here understood, involves the union of the extremest opposites. Its motive lies in the apprehension of the sovereignty of the State as the true and absolute end; and the realization of this end, as the work of bravery, depends on the sacrifice of personal individuality, even to the point of counting life itself as nought. "It implies complete obedience, suspension of personal opinion and judgment, and in this sense *absence* of a mind of one's own, and yet the most intensive and comprehensive and instantaneous *presence* of mind and determination, the most hostile and personal warfare against individuals, and at the same time a completely indifferent or even kindly disposition toward them as individuals."

The external relations of a State are founded in its moral personality, its true individuality. ' The direction of the State in these relations is therefore a function of the "princely power" to which it belongs, "immediately and alone, to have command of the armed forces of the State, to maintain relations with other States through ambassadors, etc., to declare war, and to conclude treaties of peace and other treaties." When war is declared and entered into, not on the ground of that knowledge of the nature and demands of the situation which the executive power alone can have, but in obedience to a purely popular impulse, injustice and disaster are among the results sure to follow. "In England the whole people have repeatedly insisted on war, and in a measure compelled the ministers to enter into it. The popularity of Pitt arose from his recognizing and carrying out what the nation at the time demanded. It was only later, when the popular excitement had cooled off, that the fact that the war was useless and unnecessary, and had been undertaken without counting the cost, was brought to consciousness. For the rest, the State is involved in relations, not only with one other State, but with many States; and the complications of these relations become so delicate that they can only be treated by those who stand at the head of the State."

B. — EXTERNAL POLITY.

External Polity (*Das äussere Staatsrecht*) is grounded in the relation of independent States. It involves, for the single State, the existence of neighbors and the recognition by them of its independent sovereignty. Such recognition is the first absolute and inherent right of the State, and is essential for the complete establishment of its character as a true political individual. Just as the single human being is not an actual person except in relation to other persons, so the State cannot be an actual individual without relation to other States.

How the State shall be constituted, what and what form of government it shall acknowledge, — these and similar questions are indeed primarily to be settled by the State itself and its people, without foreign intervention or dictation; this is the first note of the independence of the State. But the second note, no less essential than the first, is that the State receive the recognition of other States, — and this depends on the opinion and the will of the latter. From a State that is to be recognized, for example, there is to be required a guarantee that it will in turn duly recognize the States that recognize it; in which point of view it is plain that the constitution and internal policy of a State demanding recognition cannot be a subject of indifference to those on whom the demand is made. For mutual recognition implies a certain degree of moral identity or likeness.

Since States confront each other, in the first instance, with the claim of separate and unqualified independence, the special relations among them depend on their respective and arbitrary wills, and are hence clothed in the form of contracts or treaties. The universal principle of international law is that treaties should be respected. But independent States recognize no power superior to themselves, authorized and able, in the case of a dispute arising from the alleged violation of a treaty, to render a decision and to enforce the same. The only way, therefore, to reach a decision when worst comes to worst, is by war.

In the conduct of war, as well as in the direction of all their affairs, separate States are guided by considerations relative to their separate and particular welfare, or advantage. So a national spirit is, after all, a particular and limited one. The universal spirit of man does not come to its total realization in any one State. But it arrives at a fuller manifestation of itself and of its power in Universal History; to which individual States are organic and subordinate, and which is, to apply the poet's word, the "world's tribunal" to pronounce and execute judgment on them.[1]

[1] Hegel's "Philosophie des Rechts" ends with a number of paragraphs on the logic of Universal History, which is also the subject of the independent work, to the exposition of which the remainder of this volume is devoted.

Part Second.

THE PHILOSOPHY OF HISTORY.[1]

CHAPTER IV.

INTRODUCTORY IDEAS.

THE concluding paragraph of the preceding Part points to the Philosophy of History as a sequel to the Philosophy of the State. The former is a continuation of the Philosophy of Man begun in the latter. It is another chapter in the spiritual story of Man.

The material of the Philosophy of History is universal history. In the philosophical view of universal history mankind is one vast society of nations, — "The individuals of universal history are nations." What is the law of this society? What is the grand argument of human existence, regarded from the view-point of universal history? Such are the questions to be considered here.

It is obvious that the Philosophy of History in seeking to answer these questions must do more than take into consideration the separate military

---

[1] G. W. F. Hegel's *Vorlesungen über die Philosophie der Geschichte*, vol. ix. of the complete edition of Hegel's Works. English translation by J. Sibree, M. A., in Bohn's Philosophical Library (Hegel's Lectures on the Philosophy of History, London, 1861.)

and political careers of national "individuals" *plus* their merely external relations to one another. The lesson of history does not lie on the surface of human events; nor, because this lesson is not merely superficial and external, is it anything essentially arbitrary and subjective. The Philosophy of History is not a "pragmatic" application of historic occurrences to point a passing, arbitrarily chosen moral. It is necessary, not to abstract from, but to look through and beneath, the outward story of the nations, till we find the inward story of which the former is the visible sign and language. "The history of man," says Goethe, "is his character." We are to see in universal history a drama, in which nations are the actors. The theme of the drama is human character. The narrative histories of different epochs and of the deeds and fortunes of different peoples constitute what may be termed the analytical table of contents of the drama. The Philosophy of History undertakes to pass in review the drama as a whole, to discover its final cause, to demonstrate its motive, to indicate its total significance. Of separate human events History may be called the artificial memory; the Philosophy of History is the comprehension of their logic.

In the wide and free perspective of universal history the nature and significance of the *rôle* played by each nation become more evident; here each one displays its special character, its individuality. And the *rôle* played is more than merely and narrowly political; it is not simply the *rôle* of a

INTRODUCTORY IDEAS. 113

"monarchy" or "aristocracy" or "democracy," of a roving people or of a nation of stay-at-homes, of conquerors or of those conquered,—it is truly the *rôle* of national individuals, having each, as our author says, its "definite spirit," which manifests itself not only in the political constitution, but also in the religion, the art, the philosophy, and the whole life of the people, with all which indeed, in the higher sense, the political constitution is organically one. Moreover, this "spirit" stands in definite relations to natural conditions of geography, climate, and the like. How wide and even all-inclusive the scope of the Philosophy of History is, as involving attention to all these matters, is obvious. Equally obvious are the extent and thoroughness of the preparation to be demanded of any one who would undertake an independent treatment of it. To Hegel, all the studies and labors of his life were directly or indirectly a preparation for his lectures on this subject, which was the last one among the various philosophical disciplines that he ventured to take up. Not until he was fifty-two years old, and had already lectured—and in some cases appeared in print—on the subjects of Logic, Philosophy of Nature, Philosophy of Spirit, Philosophy of Right, Philosophy of Religion, Philosophy of Art, and History of Philosophy, did Hegel in the winter semester of 1822–1823 first lecture on the Philosophy of History,—or, in the language of Thaulow,[1] not until he "had in his studies gone through

[1] Hegel's *Ansichten über Erziehung und Unterricht*, 2. Theil, 1. Abtheilung, p. 55. Kiel, 1854.

the whole of human knowledge and the totality of all sciences, and had systematically expounded them." Dr. Thaulow adds: "Consequently it is obvious that all the other works of Hegel are presupposed by his Philosophy of History."[1] In this sense we must, with Thaulow, assent to the assertion of Professor Michelet, that Hegel's Philosophy of History is "the crown of all" his works. But if it thus presupposes all the other works of its author, and therefore in a sense requires a previous knowledge of them on the part of him who would fully comprehend it, yet it also in turn throws a new light on many of them, and it has qualities which have led many of the best judges to regard the study of this work as the easiest introduction to the Hegelian Philosophy.

The drama of history is essentially a development. The subject of this development is Man. External visible Nature constitutes the stage-setting of the drama and its locality in the literal, but here superficial, sense of this term. Its true location is in the inward realm of human will and knowledge. And the true subject of development is especially the human spirit. The function of the human spirit is to think, to know, to will. An essential incident in the accomplishment of this function is the reaction of human thought, knowledge, and will on external Nature, followed by a growing mastery of Nature and reduction of her to human uses. But the thing

[1] Hegel's works on History of Philosophy, Philosophy of Religion, and Philosophy of Art are all — and especially the last two named — important studies in the Philosophy of History.

of main importance is not man's transformation
and subjugation of Nature, but his transformation
and subjugation of himself; not his reaction upon
Nature, but his reaction upon himself; not his
thinking, knowing, and willing of that which at
first appears, and is accordingly usually regarded,
as only objective and foreign to man *per se*, but his
thinking, knowing, and willing of himself. The progress of human history is a progress in self-knowledge
and self-mastery. But in self-knowledge and self-
mastery consists the very substance of the freedom
of a spiritual being, or, indeed, of all real and positive freedom,— since freedom, in the positive sense,
is only a spiritual attribute ; and freedom, as thus defined, constitutes the very essence of spiritual being.
Accordingly, we may say indifferently that the fundamental subject of the development of history is
the human spirit, or is human freedom, and especially
the spirit or freedom of the race of mankind as a
whole. " The spirit, viewed according to its essential
nature, as defined in the notion of freedom, — this
is the fundamental subject of Universal History, and
hence also the guiding principle of development; . . .
as also, conversely, historic events are to be viewed
as products of this principle, and as deriving only
from it their meaning and character. . . . Universal
History is the unfolding of spiritual being in time, as
Nature is the unfolding of the divine idea in space.
. . . History is progress in the consciousness of freedom." The end of history is " the consciousness
of spiritual freedom, and therewith the realization of
this freedom." The history of the world, at the

head of which man marches, is an aspiration and an advance — marked by many irregularities of movement, many stumblings, many temporary failures, and yet a real advance — toward an ideal, which is eternally realized in Him who is the absolute principle and end of all finite being and doing, and whom the Hebrew Psalmist characteristically addresses as a "free Spirit." The goal of history is resemblance to God. Nay, more, without departing from the spirit and intent of Hegel's work, we may say that the whole labor of history (*Laborare est orare*), including the "groaning and travailing" of the whole creation, is an inarticulate repetition of the supplication of the Psalmist, "Uphold me by thy *free Spirit*."

But this inarticulate prayer is more unconscious than conscious. It is not Man, the subject of human history, but God, who sees its end from the beginning. "It is not in man that walketh to direct his steps." And to him who looks on human affairs, having in view only the immediate thoughts and purposes of men, it may well appear that "man walketh in a vain show." It is plain enough that "man proposes," but not so immediately evident to man that "God disposes." And yet God does dispose; and the Philosophy of History is the comprehension and demonstration of this truth. "God," says our author, "rules the world: the substance of His rule, the execution of His plan, is the world's history. This plan it is the aim of Philosophy to grasp," — not, it may be added, through any absurd pretence of power to fathom the divine mind

INTRODUCTORY IDEAS. 117

per se, or apart from its actual manifestation in the world and history, but only as it is revealed in these. The divine idea or plan "is no mere ideal;" it is an historic actuality. The thought of God is the immanent, constitutive, and executive reason of all existence; and the true action of "reason" (*Vernunft*) in man consists in the "recognition [*Vernehmen*] of the *divine* work."[1]

God, not apart from history, decreeing its results from afar, but in history, working hitherto and still working, revealing and showing himself in His work, — this is the one essential side of the case. And the other is, Man a co-worker with God, — sometimes unconscious of this divine partnership, sometimes blindly or even wilfully rebelling against it, yet on the whole growingly obedient to the guidance of his Father's hand, and finding in the present knowledge of Him, and in vital, willing, and active union with Him, the perfection of his true or spiritual nature and of his essential freedom. So the "progress in the consciousness of freedom" is a progress in man's

[1] The "divine work," in its relation to the affairs of men, is popularly termed Providence. It is particularly thought of as "special" and relating peculiarly to the fortunes of individuals. "But," says Hegel, "in Universal History we have to do with individuals that are peoples, and with wholes that are States: here, therefore, we cannot stop short with this small-trade faith in Providence (so to express it); and just as little can we rest in the merely abstract, indefinite faith which only goes so far as to admit the general proposition that there is a Providence, without recognizing its presence in definite acts. We must, the rather, in all seriousness, seek to recognize the ways of Providence, the means it employs, and the manifestations it makes of itself in history, and to connect these with the divine Spirit as their universal principle."

consciousness of God. The historic working out of
the problem of self-knowledge is, in its essential
degree, a solution of the problem of the knowledge
of God. And the progressive accomplishment of
the Will of humanity becomes a progressive demonstration of the truth that the substance or motive of
the perfect Will of man is identical with the substance or motive of the Will of God; that the service of God is perfect freedom; and that man first
truly knows himself and is free when he can say,
in all sincerity and with full conviction, " Lo, I am
come to do thy will, O God!"

"Man proposes," — or, more accurately, men,
individuals, propose. The successive outward phenomena of history are the immediate results of
their proposing. The differentiating mark by which
an historical phenomenon is distinguished from a
purely physical one, is that there has passed upon
it the transforming breath of the active interest and
the personal agency of individual men or classes of
men. It is to the thoughts, purposes, passions, and
volitions of individuals that historical events are
traced as the immediate, determining cause of their
existence. And yet — such is the allegation of philosophy and the proverb — "God disposes." The
particular historic event exists by the grace of the
particular volition of a particular human being; it
is immediately what the individual intended, and
is explained by his intention, but by the grace of
God it acquires a character beyond what was intended, requiring a deeper and broader explanation.
The results of human action are not only launched

INTRODUCTORY IDEAS. 119

upon the face of a physical universe that has its laws, which condition *pro tanto* both the form and the ulterior nature of the results, but they also enter into — nay, they are accomplished within — the realm of a spiritual cosmos, whose imperative law is the nature and will of God, — the free, absolute, self-conscious Spirit, — and whose empirical law is that of the growth of man in spiritual stature and spiritual freedom. While, therefore, man " works out," it is God who "works in" him " to will and to do according to His good pleasure." But not arbitrarily. God is not to be conceived, according to the mind of our author, as though he were simply a second " non-natural" man, interfering with laws of Nature and of human action, which are capable of subsisting by themselves without God, and in that sense making the course of events to be different from what it would have been had God kept quiet; on the contrary, the thought is that without God and his constant and omnipresent, creative and sustaining, agency no laws of Nature and no course of human events would be possible. It is the laws themselves that reveal God, and not supposed infractions of them.

What, then, is the state of the case before us? We have the thought of history as the scene, sign, and changing result of a spiritual process which gives to history its fundamental meaning. This process, being a spiritual one, takes the form of an evolution or development. The subject of development is man as a spiritual value, a spiritual being. As being a development, and occurring therefore in time, the process has a beginning, a middle, and an end; it is a progress from the potential to the actual, from the implicit to the explicit. At the beginning of the process man is, in potency, all that in the sequel he is destined to become in developed actuality: but only in potency. At the outset, man is a spiritual being only *per se*, or in kind, and of course perfect in his kind; the spiritual nature exists in him, at best, only in the form of a perfect, unbroken, and uncorrupted instinct. Then begins the "eternal story" of the "fall of man" from this state of innocence, through the commencement of reflective knowledge. This is the beginning of the process of history, which can be regarded as destined to reach its termination, as a development, only when the scope of knowledge shall have become commensurate with the whole potential content of the original instinct; that is, when knowledge shall have become complete spiritual self-knowledge, and the latter (involving necessarily, and as its most important element, the knowledge of God) shall become the determining ground of all human activity. Meanwhile, on the way toward this goal, man appears as a creature having within him the instinct of his true and spiritual self, — as it were, the seed of God and the present power of God within his own breast, — an instinct in varying degrees helped or hindered by the changing state of his knowledge. The immediate, subjective ground of his actions is therefore, in general, composite. Partly, it is a generic and universal instinct, the results of which appear conspicuously in the organic construction of an " Ethical World " (domestic and public,— Family, Society, State) and in religious conceptions and activities; and, partly, it is the individual's actual knowledge, his empirical consciousness of his immediate environment and of himself in his relation to the same, with all the personal interests, the passions, desires, and purposes of the hour which result therefrom and furnish a direct occasion of action. In action wholly conformable to the instinct and determined by it, — though not by it as a mere or blind instinct, but by the instinct transformed and elevated into the quality of knowledge, and of self-knowledge (knowledge of principle, of the universal, of the essential self; that is, of essential *humanity* as a spiritual image of the divine Spirit, and perfected by voluntary conformity to and vital union with the same), — in this action mankind would be truly free, and the goal of history would be reached. This would be "substantial freedom."

It follows, on the other hand, that in action determined wholly in view of empirical considerations, with complete indifference to law, and only in the spirit of "doing as one likes" without rendering any reason, there would be no true, substantial, or proper freedom. This would be what is understood as the "liberty"— that is, the irresponsible independence — of the individual : a "liberty of choice," or "of indifference," which from the point of view of the Universal or Essential Man (the Man which each individual should embody, and must embody, in order to claim with full right the name of a man) is essential bondage. Such liberty as this (as we have seen in an earlier part of this volume) is only, and is rightly called, subjective and formal; it is not objective, also, and substantial. The attempt to assert subjective and formal liberty, *purely and simply*, in action is the root of all sin. Nevertheless, looked at from this point of view, it is undoubtedly true that "there is no man that sinneth not;" "all have sinned and come short of the glory of God." The "liberty" in question, taken by itself and asserted by itself, far from being, as is so often supposed, the most valuable of all human possessions, is rather the most fatal of all. On the other hand, taken not "by itself," as though it were the all of freedom, but in its relation to the whole economy of free action, it appears in its true light as only a formal, though necessary, condition and dependent factor of substantial freedom. The realization of *freedom* in history at large, and in any individual, consists in the reduction of the formal "liberty of choosing" to its true condition as an adjunct and servant of substantial freedom. The individual, for example, in the exercise of his liberty of choice, is to determine himself to conduct obedient to law; which being done, he finds that he has "obeyed" only his own better and truer self,—the self of humanity within him, and the voice of God,—and so is truly free.

The ethical requirement, flowing from analysis of the generic spiritual nature of man and of freedom, is, that the individual should actively direct his intelligence to the apprehension and comprehension

INTRODUCTORY IDEAS. 123

of the laws of spiritual freedom and perfection, and that he should order his choices, and consequent actions, conformably to these laws, — and yet not mechanically, so that the laws appear as a power foreign to the man, either restraining or constraining, but the rather in such manner that the action, as an outward form or phenomenon, shall have the character of an unconstrained and spontaneous expression of the law as its own inward substance and vitalizing principle: the man in obeying the law must be consciously, spontaneously, joyfully "enacting himself" (in the language of Professor Green). This ideal is but indifferently realized in the life and conduct of the average man; but in proportion as it is realized, it is plain that the *means* by which this end is reached — the means whereby true freedom is realized — are to be found in the immediate subjective choices of individuals. And now we are prepared to understand the statement of Hegel, when he says that the means whereby the process or purpose of history is accomplished are the passions of men, their individual interests, and the actions by which they seek to secure them, — or, in short, their subjective choices; and not only these passions, interests, or choices in conscious and voluntary subjection to the law of freedom or spiritual development (such subjection is as uncommon, comparatively speaking, as are the developed knowledge and the trained will which it implies), but in all their blindness and "finiteness." The whole interest and thought of the individual may be practically confined to his immediate personal aims and restricted plans. Beyond them he may not consciously see; to aught besides them he may be indifferent. But the sequel shows them to have been the material for the accomplishment of a plan of history, which is none other than the realization on this planet of self-conscious and self-mastering spiritual existence, — man possessing himself through knowledge and control of a natural world of which he is the crown, and through knowledge and love of a God who is the intimate ground and the eternal goal of all the travail both of Nature and of Man. Thus God makes even the wrath of man to praise Him.

But this end, by these means, is not accomplished without moral and psychological friction. The field of history is not a garden of pure happiness; on the contrary, it has often the fearful appearance of a "slaughtering-block." The plans and purposes on which individuals and nations have concentrated all their energy often come to nought; men are cut down and wither in the midst of their proudest achievements, and their achievements perish with them. This is "the tribute of existence and of perishability" which the particular pays to the universal, self-interest to the universal interest, formal freedom to substantial freedom. But this tribute is not wholly lost; it does not go simply to swell the moral waste-heap of human history; it has its place in the spiritual economy of historic progress. The only way in which the true universal can be established is through the successive assertion — self-assertion — and negation of the particular; the

INTRODUCTORY IDEAS. 125

only way in which substantial freedom can be realized is through the assertion of formal, subjective freedom and its negation. Thus the human failures of history are divine or providential successes. The apparent evil is partly good in the making; it is the "cunning of reason," which allows selfish interest to have its own way, and yet makes it ministrant to the ends of reason.

Human progress, as a development, proceeds by fixed steps; it does not repeat itself. Each new step leads to a new level, which could only have been reached by the way of the preceding ones; and each level, once attained, is attained only to be in its turn left behind. When a certain definite level has been once fully reached, the time is already ripe for its abandonment. The ideal character of any historic epoch is the "spirit of the time." The great man, the leader of his people, is the one who comprehends the spirit of his time and makes himself its organ; and if the great man is a revolutionist, it is because he sees that his time is ripe, that its fulness has come, that its fruit is ready to be plucked, and that the seed-time of a new historic era has arrived.

So, gradually, the thoughts of men are widened, and with their thoughts their interests, and the scope and character of their volitions. The spiritual instinct of man, which has prompted him originally to seek in the life of the Family, the State, the Church the attainment of a common good, comes by degrees to know and consciously to will itself in all its fulness. Humanity comes increasingly to know itself as one, and to will its unity. And it approaches this end by a process at once of self-discipline and providential guidance. The guidance was not arbitrary and artificial; it did not take the place of human endeavor, — it was the unchanging condition of all human endeavor. Nor did it prejudice human freedom; the rather, it was the rock by which human freedom climbed out of the slough of blind and particular self-interest, in which it had like to have been fatally buried, into the light of a steadfast liberty, and in being firmly planted on which alone its permanent security depends.

In the Introduction to the Philosophy of History Hegel includes, along with considerations like the foregoing, a brief view of history in relation to its geographical conditions. This relation is not superficial. The view upon which we are to proceed in our treatment of the whole subject before us is, indeed, that history presents us with a logically progressive series of national and human types, corresponding to the natural order of the successive stages by which spiritual existence advances from the condition of an unfulfilled potentiality to completed, self-conscious, and self-mastering actuality. With reference to this process, the natural environment of a people is, abstractly considered, purely external. But it is not indifferent. It is in nature and natural environment that the progressively self-realizing spirit of humanity has, so to speak, its footing. The "geographical basis" is therefore essential and necessary. Moreover, this basis is not uniform the world over. Different geographical localities have their different natural characters, or types; and the natural type of a locality stands in intimate correspondence with the type and character of the people which has issued from it.

It is important that we should have a just view of this matter. "We must neither overestimate nor underestimate the influence of Nature. The soft sky of Ionia certainly accounts for much of the grace of the Homeric poems; but it alone can produce no Homers. It does not always produce them; under Turkish dominion Ionia has had no singers." Environment, speaking somewhat loosely, may be said to determine the natural colors, the *nuances*, of national character (with what colors should character paint itself except with those the materials for which it finds at hand in its environment?), and it is an instrumental condition for the self-developing activity of character; but it does not create character.

But while Nature cannot take the place of the human spirit and do its work, it may more or less effectually hinder it. This it does in the arctic and tropical zones. Man, we must remember, begins his career in the closest union with Nature; his first conscious reaction on Nature, which is the beginning of the process whereby he distinguishes himself from Nature and raises himself above it, gives rise to wants — first of all, physical wants — for the supplying of which he reduces Nature to his service. It is only, as Aristotle has observed, when the pressure of want has been relieved that man turns his attention to what is universal and superior. This pressure, in the zones of extreme heat and cold, "can never cease and never be removed: man is constantly forced to direct his attention to Nature, to the glowing rays of the sun, and the icy cold. The true arena of history is therefore the temperate zone, and especially the northern portion of it, where the earth is distributed in continents, and has, as the Greeks said, a broad breast."

Historians and geographers divide the world into the "old world" and the "new." The New World, including North and South America and Australia, says our author, is such not only in view of its late discovery by Europeans, — it is essentially new, "as regards its whole physical and spiritual character." It is not an original factor in the world's history.

The centre of Universal History is the Mediterranean Sea. It is a bond of union to the three continents of the Old World, whose shores it washes. "For streams and seas are to be regarded as means not of separation, but of union. . . . On the Mediterranean lies Greece, that point of light in history. Here too is Syria, with Jerusalem, the centre of Judaism and Christianity. To the southeast lie Mecca and Medina, the original home of the Mahometan faith, while to the west are Delphi and Athens, and, still farther west, Rome. Alexandria and Carthage too are on the Mediterranean Sea. Thus the Mediterranean is the heart of the Old World, — as it were, the conditioning and animating principle of that world. Without it the world's history

INTRODUCTORY IDEAS.

could not be conceived; it would be like ancient Rome or Athens without the forum, where all things centred.

The geographical footing of the human spirit, in the historic march of the development of the latter, varies. The most important variations, or geographical differences, are the following: —

1. The arid upland, with its great steppes and plains.
2. The valley plains, intersected and watered by large streams.
3. The coast region, in immediate connection with the sea.

These differences correspond with leading differences or *stadia* in the development of the "ethical world" of history.

1. The upland is the home of patriarchal life. Here men lead a comparatively careless existence, united in large families or groups of families. The soil is generally unfruitful. Men subsist by their flocks and herds, and not by agriculture. They lead a roving life. Established legal relations are wanting. Existence is in the main peaceful; but the peace is the peace of indifference, — of men not having developed relations with one another. At times, however, some accidental impulse may bring them together, setting them in external and united movement. Then "like a devastating torrent they fall upon the people of more cultured lands, and the revolution which they introduce has no other result than destruction and desert waste." Examples of such uplands are to be found in Central Asia, and

of such movements in the exploits of the Mongolian tribes led by Genghis Khan and Tamerlane.

2. In the valley plains, intersected by great streams, to which they owe all their fruitfulness, agriculture begins, and with it the founding of great States. Agriculture involves labor definitely regulated by the order of the seasons. With it come property in the soil and the legal relations thence resulting,—"that is to say, the bases and substrata of the State, which is first rendered possible through the establishment of such relations." Examples of such valley plains are "China; India, intersected by the Indus and Ganges; Babylonia, where the Euphrates and Tigris flow; and Egypt, watered by the Nile."

3. If it is in the valley plains that the foundations of historical development are laid, it is in the coast region that this development is carried forward.

First, it is necessary to repeat that streams and large bodies of water form a far less effectual barrier to the extension of human relations than do great ranges of mountains. Since the discovery of America and the East Indies Europeans have remained in constant relations with these lands, but into the mountain-girt uplands of Africa and Asia they have scarcely penetrated.

"The sea raises the idea of the indefinite, unlimited, infinite; and when man receives the impression of this infinite, his courage is stimulated to quit the scene of his terrene limitations. The sea invites man to conquest, to robbery, but also to the search

INTRODUCTORY IDEAS. 131

for gain: the land, the valley plain, attaches him to the soil. He thus becomes involved in multifarious forms of dependence, from which the sea furnishes him an avenue of escape. The aim of seafarers is gain, profit; and yet the means employed are in such manner incongruous with the end aimed at that they involve the risking of property and of life itself. The character of the means is thus the opposite of the character of the end. This it is, precisely, which raises gain and business above itself, and gives it a quality of bravery and nobility. Courage must now enter into and leaven the calculations of trade, and bravery must be joined with prudence; for bravery in facing the sea must at the same time be crafty, since craft is pre-eminently the attribute of its opponent the sea, the most uncertain and deceitful of all natural elements. The ocean's boundless surface is absolutely yielding, for it resists no pressure, not even that of the breath of air, and it looks infinitely innocent, complaisant, friendly, and inviting; and it is exactly this appearance of pliability that renders the sea the most dangerous and violent element. To such deceit and violence man opposes only a simple piece of wood. He relies on his courage and presence of mind, and so goes forth from the firm land upon the supportless sea, taking with him his manufactured ground. The ship — this swan of the sea, cutting across the billowy plain, or describing circles in it with agile and swelling motions — is an instrument the discovery of which redounds with greatest honor as well to the boldness as to the intelligence of man.

This deliverance of man, through the sea, from the limitation of the land is something that is wanting to those gorgeous political structures the empires of Asia, even when they border on the sea, — as, for example, China. For them the sea is only the end of the land; they hold no positive relation to it. The activity to which the sea invites is altogether peculiar; whence it is found that peoples occupying coast-lands mostly separate themselves from their neighbors of the interior, even though connected with the latter by a stream. So Holland has become detached from Germany, and Portugal from Spain."

Considering, now, the three continents of the ancient world with reference to the above-mentioned geographical differences, we observe that the northern coast-land of Africa is to be joined, in the reckoning of history, with Europe. The great valley of the Nile is similarly connected with the history of Asia. Africa proper lies south of the Desert of Sahara, and is an immense and mainly unknown upland, with narrow borders of sea-coast. This is the land where men are children, — "a land lying beyond the daylight of self-conscious history, and enveloped in the black color of night." Its inhabitants, the negroes, represent the "natural man" in all his untamed savagery. The principle of their life is, not liberty, which is law, but license; the sense of anything fixed and universal, like law or God, engaging their will and mirroring to them their own higher and spiritual nature, is wanting to them. Their religion is of the most elementary kind,

INTRODUCTORY IDEAS. 133

and consists rather in that negation of religion which must first be, and then be negated, in order that the positive substance of religion may itself be developed.[1] Religion begins with the consciousness that there is something higher than man, on which man is dependent. To the African negro this consciousness is wanting; his "religion" is sorcery and fetichism. Sorcery involves no idea of a God, nor any other distinctively ethical belief; it implies that the highest power is Man, and that he may successfully command the powers of Nature. As for the fetich, it is any object — an animal, a tree, a stone, a wooden image — arbitrarily selected to be regarded as a "genius." It may well be arbitrarily selected, for what the negro contemplates in it, considered as a "genius" or fetich, is, not God, nor his own better and spiritual self, but simply the principle of his own arbitrary caprice; it is the "contingent will of man," viewed as superior to Nature, and having power to control it. Herein lies indeed the recognition of the elevation of man above Nature, but not of man above himself,[2] and still less of God above man. In consequence of this, man has here no reverence for himself. The eating of human flesh and the selling and being sold into slavery excite no horror. If death is not feared, it is because life, being deprived of all spiritual dignity, is

---

[1] We have previously remarked that positive development begins, as well as goes forward, by a movement which may be termed, according to Hegel's usual statement, "negation of negation."

[2] "Unless above himself he can
Erect himself, how poor a thing is man!"

incapable of being prized. Legally constituted ethical relations are here, therefore, impossible; they are incompatible with the "state of Nature" in which the African negro lives; the "light of the spirit" has not yet begun to rise. With this brief mention we must dismiss Africa proper, since it only lies before the threshold of the temple of history, with no power to enter.

In Asia we find immense mountain-girt uplands, followed by great valley-plains, or, as they may better be termed, river-regions; while in western Asia, including Arabia, Syria, and Asia Minor, all three of the chief geographical differences mentioned above are united, and the bridge of transition to European history is constituted. On the whole, the striking feature of Asia is the large contrast of contiguous upland and valley-plain, — of patriarchalism, with its restless nomadic life, and the civil order of peoples devoted to agriculture and domestic commerce, and thus inviting by their example their neighbors of the upland to take the first step forward in the direction of political progress. The rise of all religious and political principles belongs to Asiatic history; their development is the work of Europe.

The geographical contrasts of Europe are milder than those of Asia. Details in regard to them may here be omitted.

History begins when the daylight of a spiritual consciousness dawns upon man. This dawn occurred in Asia. The first main division of our study will accordingly be the Oriental World, the scene of

INTRODUCTORY IDEAS. 135

History's childhood. Here first begins the recognition of freedom as a spiritual attribute, though only in an inadequate form,— the form of an *abstract universal*, which as such can be lodged only in one subject or substance. The Oriental World, therefore, admits that *one* is free. This one, politically, is the monarch, who is the substance of the State, of which his subjects are the accidents. This conception in the political order is of just the same kind as, in the religious order of ideas, is the pantheism so characteristic of the Oriental faiths.

The Grecian world will constitute our second division, representing, as it may be said to do, the second age in the life of History,— the age of youth. Here, though spiritual freedom is not yet recognized as a *concrete universal*, and hence as the property of all men, yet it is no longer ascribed solely to one. In other words, in the Grecian (and Roman) world "*some are free.*" In Greece "individualities are developed." The ethical spirit or substance of the community or race lives in and through the free, spontaneous volition of individuals, constituting what may be termed a "realm where freedom has the form of beauty."

History attains its age of manhood in the Roman world. It is the age of painful labor. Individuality is brought under the yoke of abstract and "dead" law, receiving however, as a partial compensation, the formal recognition and definition of its legal status in the possession of specific "personal" rights.

Finally, with the Germanic world, and under the inspiration of Christianity, we come to the age of full maturity, whose mission is to comprehend and carry out the truth that freedom is the birthright of all men.

CHAPTER V.

THE ORIENTAL WORLD.

HISTORY must begin for us with the establishment of political relations in States or Kingdoms. History is prosaic; and prose is the language of a consciousness so far developed as to be able to recognize fact as *fixed* fact, — that is, as *regulated by law*. More especially, the subject-matter of the prose of history is law established to be the guide of human conduct, and recognized and obeyed as such.

The content of such law is, as we have heretofore seen, the Will of man. Its character is distinctly and essentially ethical. The ethical is whatever flows from and agrees with the universal ideal substance of human will, — which is the same thing as the essential, and therefore spiritual, nature of man, considered in itself and in its spiritual relations to Nature and to God. We may say, therefore, that the ethical is the true essence of humanity; and that the whole labor of history, so far as this has any significance for us, is a labor to render this essence, at first only abstract and merely potential, concrete and actual in the established order of a real Ethical World.

The Oriental world presents us with a view of the first definite beginnings of this process. Its special historic principle, says Hegel, is "the *substantiality* of the ethical." By this is meant that the first great step here taken by mankind in the direction of spiritual self-development consists in the abstract recognition of the ethical, expressed in the form of political and religious laws and guiding conceptions, as having such characters as science is accustomed to ascribe to the supposed *substance* of a thing in distinction from its *accidents*, — *e. g.*, permanence, immutability, indestructible and inalterable being. The substance of a thing is, in this view, to its accidents as a fate which holds them together, — a truly *existent* law, which abides though the accidents change and perish, and to which in their own uncertain lease upon existence they are irrevocably subject. Such, generally considered, is in the Oriental world the relation between law, political or religious, on the one hand, and the voluntary activity and obedience of the individual on the other. The subject in obeying is not conscious of rendering obedience to himself. The law appears to him as the objectification not of his own will, but of a will completely foreign to his. What is absolute and free, fixed and substantial, is the will of the ruler; to it the will of the individual is as a dependent accident. When, as is here usually the case, the will of the ruler is identified with the will of God or of divine powers, it is not thereby sanctified to the subject; it does not thereby receive the consecration of conscious identification with his own true will. For God in his conception is no nearer to him than is the earthly ruler; He is even farther away.

Such is the generic character of the Ethical World in the Orient; a character most perfectly illustrated in the empire of China.

A. — CHINA.

China is the oldest of existing historical empires; and yet it may be said to have had no history. Many things have indeed occurred on Chinese soil during the long centuries of the existence of the Empire: there have been changes of dynasties, feats of arms, the construction of monumental works, varying forms of expression of religious and ethical belief and opinion. But there has been no essential progress. The ethical principle, speaking broadly, of the national life has remained fixed, in the form of a "substantial" law of belief and conduct immediately and invariably determining the "accidents" of action. The factors of historical development, — that is, of true ethical and spiritual progress, — here mainly exist in immediate unity, in the merely abstract and potential form in which the elements of a developed organism are contained in an unfructified germ. Progress requires that this unity should be disturbed; that the individual should become conscious of his subjective freedom and responsibility; that the "substantial" universal — laws, regulations, beliefs — should become to him a subject of free and deliberate reflection, and should finally acquire its authority and power, as a moving and controlling principle of life and conduct, through the individual's recognition in it of the native content of his own true will, as a human and above all a spiritual being. Then it will be indeed an active, moving, historic principle, and not merely a dead and rigid "substrate." It is because in China and also in India this process has never begun, that both of these countries may be even said to lie beyond the pale of the world's history; they are nevertheless to be included in our view of that history, because, in the sense above suggested, the basis of their ethical, political, and religious life contains in undeveloped germ the essential factors of historic progress. In this sense they represent the necessary "pre-supposition" of history.

In an earlier chapter (Chapter III.) we saw that the elementary form of existence in the Ethical World was that of the Family. The Family represented the factors of spiritual existence in their still undeveloped "natural" unity. It is this type which is repeated in the whole political and religious constitution of Chinese life. In China, the duties of "family piety" are most carefully and minutely defined, and are performed with scrupulous exactness and in a thoroughly unquestioning spirit of obedience. The State, on the other hand, is to the Chinese simply the Family "writ large," in which the relations and the temper of the lesser family are but repeated on a larger scale. As the father of the family to the little child stands as it were in the place of a God, — the embodiment not only of all power and authority, but also of all goodness and wisdom, — so the Chinese Emperor is to his subjects as a "Great Father," who cares for them in all things well, whose power is unlimited and whose authority is unquestioned, and who is at once, not only a civil and military ruler, but also the "ruling chief of religion and science."

The Chinese Emperor is the object of the greatest reverence to his subjects. As a paternal ruler, he is required to take personal cognizance and direction of the affairs of the realm. Yet little space is left in this regard to his merely private caprice; everything is done in accordance with old established maxims. The education of the imperial princes, both physical and mental, is most carefully conducted under the oversight of the Emperor, "and they are early taught that the Emperor is the head of the realm, and must in all things appear as the first and the best. . . . So it has come to pass that China has had rulers of the most conspicuous excellence, of whom the wisdom of a Solomon might be predicated. . . . In Europe, Solomons are impossible. In China they are necessary, inasmuch as the maintenance of justice, welfare, and the general security depends on the single impulse of the supreme link in the whole chain of the political hierarchy."

Of a "constitution" of the Chinese empire we cannot properly speak, but only of its *administration*. A constitution would imply individuals and corporations having independent rights, partly in relation to their particular interests, and partly in relation to the whole State. "In China is the realm of absolute equality, and all distinctions that exist are possible only in the department of administration, and are to be obtained only through personal demonstration of superior merit. Because in China equality, but not freedom, prevails, despotism is here the necessary form of government." The government is exercised by the Emperor through a hierarchy of officers or "mandarins," who are in complete subordination to the Emperor. Mandarins are of two classes, scholars and military officers, and the former outrank the latter. The Council of the realm consists of the most learned and talented men. From their number the heads of the other councils are selected.

The administration in China follows a fixed routine, uniform and regular, like the course of Nature. The ever-watchful and self-directing soul of the administrative mechanism is (actually or constructively) the Emperor. The officers are as cogs in a wheel, held to their responsibility not by their own conscience or honor, but by external command and rigid supervision.

With reference to the jurisprudential side of the Chinese administration, three things are to be noted:

1. The principle of government being here patriarchal, all subjects are treated as minors. Conduct in all relations is hence strictly regulated by fixed rules. How the different members of a family are to feel towards one another, even, is formally determined by the laws. Freedom of sentiment, and in general what we have previously (Chapter II.)

termed the "standpoint of morality" are *pro tanto* excluded.

2. The family relation is made to be of such an external character that it turns almost to slavery. "Every Chinese husband buys his wife, and may sell his children."

3. Punishments are mostly corporal. "To us this would be peculiarly disgraceful; not so in China, where the feeling of honor is undeveloped." The Chinaman is constructively a child; the blows which he receives are more for discipline than for punishment. Punishment implies that the recipient of it possesses proper, independent, conscious responsibility. No subject in China is too exalted to receive stripes. "Once, when an English embassy was being escorted by the princes and their retinue from the palace to their own quarters, the master of ceremonies, in order to clear the way for them, lashed the bystanding princes and other dignitaries wholly without ceremony." The equality of all before the Emperor means that all are equally degraded. From the consciousness of this degradation the passage is easy to such extremes of immorality as are actually prevalent among the Chinese. For example, "It is notorious that the Chinese will cheat whenever they can."

Pass now to the religious side of the Chinese State. Religion, as we understand it, implies the self-conscious freedom of the spirit that is in man. This freedom in the Chinaman is undeveloped. In this regard, as in others, a mere child, he remains in respect of his religious consciousness a dependent accident of the State, or of the Emperor as representing the abiding substance of the State. Chinese religion is essentially "state religion." Religious functions belong primarily to the Emperor; he is the priest of the whole nation. The religion of the Chinese is to be classed among the "religions of Nature." God in their speech is "Heaven," and "Heaven" here means simply "Nature." Only the Emperor is privileged to make religious approach to "Heaven," not individuals as such. To the realm of Nature belong numerous Genii, or Spirits of Nature, on whom the welfare of individuals and provinces is supposed to depend. These Genii are subject to the laws of the Emperor, who yearly assigns to them the persons or regions over which they are to preside, and deposes them on occasion of misfortune due to their alleged ill-will or neglect. There is thus a manifest element of sorcery in the Chinese religious system. Soothsayers and conjurors have among the Chinese an open field. The Chinese are incredibly superstitious; a thing not to be wondered at, for the basis of superstition is inward immaturity, — the opposite of spiritual freedom.

The same lack of inward development declares itself in the character of Chinese science and literature. The great extent and antiquity of the writings of the Chinese, the high honor in which they are held, and what is done by the Government to promote literary and scientific accomplishment are matters of common notoriety. The Emperor himself may be styled the ruling chief of literature. Notwithstanding all this, the literature and science of the Chinese, not being planted in the soil of true mental freedom, lack the peculiar scientific interest. " There is here no free ideal realm of the spirit, and that which may be termed scientific is of an empirical nature, and is controlled essentially by the conception of what is useful for the State and its needs, and for the needs of individuals." The histories of the Chinese, for example, "include only the narrative of particular facts, without any opinion or reasoning upon them. Their works on jurisprudence, in like manner, are simply a collection of actual and particular laws, and their ethical writings contain an enumeration of particular duties without regard to their intrinsic reason and justification." The same empirical and scientifically undeveloped character belongs to such knowledge as they possess in mathematics, physics, and astronomy. The Chinese have indeed a philosophy, the fundamental ideas of which are very old; but these ideas are abstract and comparatively contentless. They have not, for the Chinese, the value of real germinant principles of truth and of scientific comprehension; and those who specially devote themselves to philosophical studies fall into much extravagance and mysticism.

Such, then, are the Chinese, — a nation of grown-up children, without developed spiritual individuality;, as it were, natural fixtures of the soil. "They treat Europeans as beggars, because, as they reason, the latter are obliged to leave their own homes and seek their support elsewhere than in their own land. On the other hand, we may say that the Europeans, just because they have inward spiritual development, are unable to imitate the external, perfectly natural *technique* of the Chinese. For in the preparation of their varnishes, the working of their metals, and especially in their art of casting them extremely thin, as also in their manufacture of porcelain, and many other things, they remain unequalled."

B. — INDIA.

In China the governing principle of human life in all its forms was external and foreign to the individual. The ideal deficiency of such a state of things was sufficiently obvious. It is necessary that the government of man, in all senses, become self-government. That which in China was thus external only, must therefore become also internal; what was objective must become also subjective. The obedience that was forced by a power without, must also proceed from an enlightened conviction and a consenting will within. Further, the accomplishment of this result will involve the setting of what was above termed the "accidental" in a new relation to the "substantial." The former, instead of being left in helpless separation from and mechanical dependence on the latter, must become integrated with it. Unity must not be abstract, excluding variety, but concrete, including it.

We meet with the first steps in the direction of these changes in contemplating the historic character of the Hindus; but only the first steps. The spiritual condition and the historic character of the Hindus are as elementary and undeveloped as are those of the Chinese. But the leading characteristics of the former stand in complete and complementary contrast to the characteristics of the latter. Over against the thoroughly prosaic mind of the Chinese we find set the dreaming, unregulated fancy of the Hindus; the unimaginative realism of the former is confronted by the fantastic idealism of the latter. The dead level of Chinese society meets its opposite in the social differentiation of the Hindus into a number of castes, separated by irremovable barriers.

I. The general mental attitude of the Hindu is characterized, if we say that he lives as if in a dream. The human spirit in India is a "dreaming spirit." The peculiarity of the dreaming condition is, that in it the individual has no consciousness of the separation between himself and the objects of his knowledge. He has no proper sense of his own individuality; he is practically, in his mental attitude, one with his immediate, finite, and sensible environment. Failing thus to make this spiritual distinction between himself and his surroundings, he also neglects to distinguish clearly between the latter in their external and single character, as immediate objects of the senses, and in their universal and essential nature; in other words, he confounds these two aspects of existence, passing from the one to the other without intervening distinction. So the dreaming Hindu identifies himself with everything that we are accustomed to term finite and individual, and also with what he regards as divine. The Hindu "philosophy" is therefore pantheistic; and, in particular, it is "a pantheism of imagination, and not of thought." The pantheism of thought would idealize the sensible, finding in it simply the beautiful form and the pliant means of expression of a universal spiritual life. The pantheism of the dreaming imagination, on the contrary, remains unaware of this distinction between sensible form and spiritual or ideal content; if secretly prompted to think the infinite and absolute, it obeys the prompting by simply extending the sensible beyond all limit or measure, and the "divine" is thus rendered merely bizarre, monstrous, or fantastic. "The dreams of the Hindu are not, to him, pure romances, — a play of the imagination, in which the spirit, without losing the mastery of itself, simply disports itself. On the contrary, the spirit becomes lost in its own reveries; they represent to it its own and all reality, — as they change, it changes. The spirit is made subject to its own finite fancies, as to its Lords and its Gods. So, to the Hindu, everything is a God, — sun, moon, stars, the Ganges, the Indus, beasts, flowers. Finite objects, thus divinized, lose, of course, their fixed and constant character, and all understanding of them vanishes; while the divine, rendered thus changeable and inconstant, is reduced to a form at once corrupt and absurd."

II. If, in the development of all organized rational existence, the first ideal requirement may be said to be unity, the second one, of equal necessity for the perfect State, is variety, — difference. We have seen how China stands in history as the representative and illustration of the first of these abstract and elementary requirements. India stands for the second one. The unity of China was a despotic one, levelling before it, as we have seen, all natural differences. India, in spite of its political inferiority to China in other respects, exhibits this mark of essential advance; namely, that despotic unity is limited by the existence and recognition of fixed differences. These differences are the Hindu Castes.

Every true State is so far like a living organism that it involves an internal differentiation. The products of such differentiation are diverse classes, which are the necessary members or organs of the State. In the free and developed State the assignment of the individual to a particular class or service is made by no power or authority foreign to himself. The final responsibility for the place and condition of the individual is placed upon himself; he is presumed and required to exercise his own " subjective freedom."

In the Platonic Republic the separation into classes was to be under the direction of the rulers, who were themselves to be guided by ethical considerations; while in China such distinction as any individual may acquire is subject to the will of the Emperor.

The peculiarity of the caste distinctions of India, — a peculiarity which marks the very elementary or undeveloped character of the social condition in that country, — is that the will of man has nothing to do with them. Like geological formations, they exist and are perpetuated as if they were the product of the impersonal agency of Nature; and like those geological formations, these human formations, as they may be called, are petrified, fixed, with no avenues of transition from the one to the other.

III. We are accustomed, properly, to regard all special rights and duties belonging to particular men or classes of men as flowing from and subject to the universal rights and duties belonging to all men, as such, without distinction. Not so with the Hindus. They know no rights or duties but such as pertain to a particular caste. Under these circumstances, a sentiment, for example, of universal human brotherhood is impossible. "Benevolence on the part of a superior caste toward an inferior one is absolutely forbidden, and it would never occur to a Brahman to render assistance to the member of another caste who was in danger." The "duties" of the several castes, and especially of the higher ones, consist mainly in a great number of purely ceremonial observances, many of them, according to our notions, being simply bizarre, absurd, and even inhuman. They are most numerous and carefully defined for the Brahmans, the highest caste; but once accomplished, everything else, no matter how immoral, is permitted. "It is characteristic of the humanity of the Hindu that he kills no animals, and founds and maintains rich hospitals for them, especially for aged cows and apes; while in the whole land not a single institution (founded by Hindus) for sick and decrepit human beings is to be found. The Hindus will not tread upon ants, but a poor wanderer they will with perfect indifference allow to perish."

All these things, which characterize the social state of the Hindus, stand, of course, in essential relation to their religion. The religious caste, especially, is the Brahmans; and the Brahmans are so named from Brahma (neuter), the Hindu name for universal and absolute being. Brahma is the "substantial unity" of all existence. Brahma is pure being, one and (*per se*) undifferentiated. It is the *being* alike of all things, whether of gods or men or natural existences. All things *are* only so far as they are Brahma, and not in virtue of that which constitutes them, to our view, separate existences. To Brahma, as thus conceived, no prayers are offered, but only to gods, natural objects, and idols, which are regarded peculiarly as incarnations of Brahma. The Brahmans themselves, in comparison with the other castes, are regarded as peculiarly such incarnations; they are, to the members of the lower castes, as "present gods to finite men." The members of these castes may indeed rise to the dignity and quality of Brahmans, but only through prolonged acts of renunciation, torture, and penance, which flesh can scarcely endure. This is wholly logical. For Brahma is a pure abstraction; the notion of it is arrived at only by making complete abstraction from all that characterizes, or seems to characterize, individual things. To become Brahma, therefore, and thus truly to deserve the name of Brahman, one must, so to speak, practise or carry out this abstraction upon one's self. One must, while still existing, seek the negation of (individual) existence. The body must be mortified and the feelings stupefied, and "the will to live," or to be aught but Brahma, — that is, pure, unqualified, undifferentiated being, — must be quelled. Those who are Brahmans by birth do not indeed practise this logic upon themselves; but it constitutes an essential part of the notion of the religious cultus, and reappears in a peculiar and specially interesting form in the doctrine of Buddhism.

IV. On the basis of such an abstract conception of what is highest it is obvious how slender must be the chances of the development of positive ethical conceptions, of art and science, and of a solid political structure. Where the absolute Being is not conceived as positively spiritual, self-conscious, and free, there man too lacks the knowledge of himself as possessing the like attributes; and this lack is fatal to the existence of the State, with all that it implies. India is "only a people, not a nation." It is the home of despotism and tyranny, which can flourish only where men are too destitute of spiritual self-knowledge, and consequently of self-respect, to feel the degradation which such misgovernment implies.

One part of the Hindu cultus, Hegel remarks, consists in the benumbing of consciousness in a wild frenzy of sensuous excesses. Politically and socially it is, or was, a part of the usual régime of the Hindus to live involved in the frenzied turmoil of a multitude of petty and warring despots, against whose excesses the accepted laws of caste alone furnished a partial barrier.

To his account of the place of India in history Hegel appends a few pages on Buddhism, dealing more especially with that development from Buddhism which is termed Lamaism, and which, like an Oriental Papacy, exercises an extended temporal power in the Mongolian world. Further reference to this subject may here be omitted.

C.—PERSIA AND THE PERSIAN EMPIRE.

Under the above caption are included, along with ancient Persia and the Persians proper, all the lands and peoples of Hither Asia, once united under Persian dominion. These include the Assyrians, Babylonians, Medes, Syrians and Phoenicians, Jews and Egyptians. These all, taken together, constitute the connecting link between Asiatic and European history, and also the line of transition and of advance from the former to the latter. This they were adapted to do, not only in consequence of their geographical situation, but also in virtue of their racial affinities with the peoples of Europe. And the key or password to the inner historical significance of all these ancient nations is found by our author in the fundamental conception of Persian thought and religion, — the conception and the worship of Light.

If we look at China and India, the occupants of Farther Asia, in the point of view of the spiritual principles that mark their place in the historical development of mankind, we may well speak of them as nations that "sit in darkness." The vivifying sunlight of an ample spiritual self-knowledge has not burst upon them; they therefore have not in themselves a principle and power of historical development; "they remain unprogressive," as Hegel remarks, "and lead a natural, vegetative existence to the present day." In Western Asia, on the contrary, the light of the spirit, which is the light of a truly human self-knowledge, begins positively to dawn. The Persians adored the light; they were called "fire-worshippers," or worshippers of the sun. The meaning of this tale is, not that the sun was to the Persian what his fetich is to the brutish savage, but that it was to him an expressive symbol; in the physical light the ruling power of the universe was revealed to him. The natural light animates; it sets in activity all the processes of organic growth and development; it combats and chases away the darkness, in which nought but evil and destruction can thrive. Moreover, it shines and sheds its blessing equally upon all things. It may be called a "universal," but is not a jealous one, envious of the very being of the particular objects that share its benefits, like the Brahma of Hindu philosophy; on the contrary, they all are allowed and enabled by it to develop their own individualities, or individual characters, each in its own kind and way; particular objects, bathed in the universal light, at once reveal its glory and attain their own proper good. So Light, the most universal reality of the physical world, symbolizes and declares for the Persians the supreme Power of the Universe as a spiritual power, whose essential attribute and nature is Good, and whose office is to fight and conquer Evil; the law of whose activity is the ideal law of human conduct, and whose ready help may be secured by all without distinction of persons. These statements indicate the complexion of that conception of the Absolute which begins to dawn in the Western Asiatic world: how different it is from the blank metaphysical and naturalistic conceptions of Eastern Asia, and in particular how much more spiritual and ethical it is, are matters immediately obvious. Especially important is the circumstance that the conception in question involves the notion of opposition, of struggle, and of consequent possible progress and victory, — the opposition and the struggle between light and darkness, good and evil. This notion enters, however inadequately, into the conception which the Persians, and in general the peoples composing the Persian empire, had of themselves; it defines for them, *pro tanto*, the nature of human life and of its mission, and constitutes in them a "principle of development" such as is not to be found in the national conceptions of the Chinese and Hindus. Accordingly, Hegel declares that "with the Persian empire we first enter into the real web and woof of history. The Persians are the first historical people;" and the proof — a paradoxical one, apparently — is that "Persia is the first empire that has passed away." Except the seed cast into the ground perish, it can bear no fruit. The seed sown by Eastern Asia in the field of the world's history did not fulfil this condition; it has remained unchanged, and therefore unfruitful, to the present day. Western Asia actually began to have a sense of the problem of human progress, of human self-realization, and of its solution through a contest between the natural and the spiritual, ending in spiritual self-conquest. It was as a voice in the wilderness of history, calling on men to become "children of the light." The voice vanished, but its echoes were not lost till they had awakened and set in activity the germinant forces of a higher civilization in the European world.

We have now briefly to consider the different pre-existing national elements, out of which the Persian empire was first built up, and then that empire itself, with all that it further included.

I. *The Zend People.* — What concerns us here is the fundamental conceptions of this people as laid down in the scriptures attributed to Zoroaster.

Now, the first point to be noticed in connection with the views of the people who accepted Zoroaster as their spiritual interpreter is, that the Absolute was so conceived by them that man's relation to it was distinctly a positive one: the last term of thought and human aspiration was not merely negative. Negative it had been in the minds of the Hindus. Man, as we saw, became fully blest and achieved his highest possibility, according to them, only through "negation of existence." Brahma was the darkness and the emptiness of pure abstraction; it was the pure being, in which all the apparent differences of finite existence vanished, — or, to apply a phrase employed by Hegel (in another work) in a different connection, " the night, in which all cows are equally black." To the people whom we are now considering, on the contrary, the Absolute, or God, was not darkness, but light. The essential function of supreme being was, not to conceal and destroy, but to reveal and protect. The doctrine in view is that above intimated,— of Light and Darkness, Good and Evil; of their active mutual opposition, and of the victory of the former. In the theological or mythological language of Zoroaster, the Good is Ormuzd; the Evil, Ahriman. "Ormuzd is the Lord of the realm of Light, of the Good; and Ahriman, of Darkness, or of Evil." The dualism thus postulated is not satisfactorily comprehended or accounted for in Zoroastrianism. Still, the postulating of it constitutes a fundamental merit rather than defect of the Zend doctrine. For the antithesis in question is real; and, moreover, the principle of dualism as such belongs to the very conception of spiritual existence, which can realize itself only by the recognition and overcoming of difference, of opposition, within itself.

The directions given by Zoroastrianism for the attainment of moral perfection all set before man a positive end, which might, it would appear, be summed up in the command, "Be ye pure, even as He is pure;" "The end of each individual is to keep himself pure and to spread this purity about him." And again : Men "are required to conduct themselves as becomes members of the kingdom of light; the general direction therefore is, as already mentioned, to observe spiritual and bodily purity."

This requirement, further, is not merely negative, or given in the spirit of asceticism; socially or practically interpreted, it does not simply mean, "Live and let live," — it has a positive and practical application. "The Persians were specially enjoined to protect living things, to plant trees, to dig wells, to irrigate deserts, that life, the positive, the pure, might everywhere flourish and the kingdom of Ormuzd be extended in all directions." So it is that in the days of their extended empire the Persians, as Hegel in another place remarks, did not seek to exterminate the nations whom they conquered, nor even to abolish their customs and laws; each people was allowed to retain its own individuality and the conditions on which such individuality depended, subject only to a general loyalty to the Empire.

Such was the "higher, spiritual element" which the Zend people contributed to the Persian empire.

II. *The Assyrians, Babylonians, Medes, and Persians.* — It was Assyria and Babylonia that brought to the Persian empire "the element of external riches, luxury, and commerce." The legendary history of these empires extends backwards into the earliest times; the fame of their great cities, of their wars and conquests, and of their brilliant material culture has gone into all the world. Their geographical location, in the great plains of the Tigris and the Euphrates, favored the development among them of agriculture and trade, and then of the arts.

The Medes, on the other hand, were mountaineers,

dwelling to the south and southwest of the Caspian Sea, as far as to Armenia, and having for their principal characteristics "fierceness, barbarism, and warlike courage." Among the six tribes constituting the Medes are mentioned the "Magi." Indeterminate as is the sense of this name ("The Greeks termed all Oriental priests without distinction Magi"), yet from all the data it is evident that a somewhat close connection existed between the doctrine and practice of the Magi and the Zend religion. "Xenophon says that Cyrus first offered sacrifices to God after the manner of the Magi; the Medes were therefore an intermediating people for the propagation of the Zend religion."

Under the Persian tribe, not only Assyrians, Babylonians, and Medes, but the whole of Hither Asia, were united in one empire and brought into direct contact with the Grecian world. We find the Persians in earliest and closest relation to the Medes, the transference of authority from the latter to the former making no essential difference with them, as Cyrus was himself a relative of the Median King, and the names "Medes" and "Persians" were united in a common expression. It was as the leader of the Persians and the Medes that Cyrus made the conquest of Lydia and of its King Crœsus. The Greek colonies on the western coast of Asia Minor, a home of art and poetry, became with Lydia subject to the Persian dominion. "Of the war against the Lydians Herodotus remarks that it taught the Persians, who previously had been only poor and uncultured, the conveniences of life and civilization. Cyrus next subdued Babylon, and with it came into possession of Syria and Palestine. The Jews he released from captivity, and permitted them to rebuild their temple. Finally he marched against the Massagetae and attacked them in the steppes between the Oxus and Jaxartes, but was defeated, and died the death of the warrior and conqueror. The death of the heroes who have marked epochs in the world's history is always agreeable to the character of their mission. So Cyrus died, occupied with his mission, which was the union of Hither Asia in one dominion, without any further special aim."

III. *The Persian Empire and its Component Parts.* — The Persian empire resembled an empire in the modern sense, such as the former German empire, or the great empire of Napoleon, — consisting of a multitude of States, all indeed dependent, but retaining their own individuality, customs, and laws. "As the light illuminates all things, communicating to each a peculiar vitality of its own, so the Persian authority extended over a variety of nations, leaving to each its own particular character." All three of the principal geographical distinctions before mentioned (Chapter IV.) were united in this empire, — the high lands of Persia and Media, the valley plains of the Euphrates and the Tigris, and also of the Nile, where agriculture, trade, and the sciences flourished, and finally a sea-coast in the possession of peoples accustomed to brave the dangers of the sea, — the Syrians, Phœnicians, and the inhabitants of the Grecian colonies and coast-cities of Asia Minor.

(1) *Persia.* — Under this head Hegel draws for us a picture of the Persians as a free people of mountaineers and nomads, retaining, in their newly acquired rule over more cultured and luxuriant lands, on the whole the characteristics of their old accustomed manner of life. At home, the King is as a friend among friends and equals; elsewhere he is a master, to whom all are subject and pay tribute. The Persians remain loyal to the Zend religion, devoting themselves to practices of purity and to the pure worship of Ormuzd. The nucleus of the Persian army consists of a corps of Persian cavalry under excellent discipline and of well-proved valor; about this are assembled the forces of the various tributary lands, no attempt being made to bring all under a common discipline, but the troops of each country being allowed to move and to fight according to its own method: the movement of the whole army resembles a vast roving expedition, the men being accompanied by their families. Into countries like Egypt, Scythia, Thrace, such a multitudinous and motley force could advance without successful opposition; but the small armies of Greece, excellently led and disciplined, and above all animated by a single purpose, were able to withstand it and overcome it. The education of the princes, and especially of the heir to the throne, is very carefully conducted. From the seventh year on they are trained in riding, shooting, and the like, and in speaking the truth. Among the royal advisers — " free men, full of noble loyalty and patriotism " — are found representatives of the Magi. The gov-

ernment of the provinces is of necessity intrusted to viceroys, or "satraps," whose conduct was often characterized by arbitrariness toward their subjects and by hatred and jealousy toward each other. Still, their functions were properly only those of chief overseers, and they had the merit of generally leaving the kings of the subject lands free to live and to exercise their authority according to their peculiar and accustomed ways. "Thus the rule of the Persians was in no way oppressive, whether in secular or religious regards." The only exception to their rule of religious toleration is perhaps to be found in occasional iconoclastic outbursts against the worship of graven images; "they destroyed Grecian temples and broke in pieces the images of the gods."

(2) *Syria and other Semitic Nations.* — Its western coast-lands were an especially important part of the Persian Empire as the source of its naval forces.

The number and wealth of the sea-coast towns of ancient Phœnicia, as well as the great extent of their maritime trade, are familiar matters of history. Here "the most beautiful works in metals and precious stones were executed, and the most important discoveries — such as of glass and purple — were made. Here, too, written language received its first development, the need of which necessarily made itself early felt in view of the commercial relations of the Phœnicians with the people of various lands." The Phœnicians were the first to discover and venture upon the Atlantic Ocean. Cyprus and Crete, Africa

THE ORIENTAL WORLD. 163

and Spain, Britannia and the Baltic, were the scenes of their colonizing and industrial activity. In the picture of such a life we are brought face to face with a new spirit, a new germinal principle of human development. It is the spirit of venture, of bold reliance on human wit and skill to overcome the greatest of natural obstacles in the search for means wherewith not only to support, but also to embellish and dignify, the life of man. It is the courage of cool intelligence, and not of unthinking savagery, that alone prompts and sustains such labors.

Passing now to the region of religious ideas, Babylon, various Syrian tribes, and Phrygia are described, especially in the Hebrew prophets, as the home of a vulgar and sensuous idolatry in marked contrast to the Persian cultus of purity. Regarding the Phœnicians, on the contrary, we are told that at Tyre Hercules was worshipped. This is highly significant. Hercules, according to the Greek notion, with which no doubt the Phœnician substantially coincided, was the type of human valor and virtuous toil, — qualities by the strenuous exhibition of which he raised himself to a place among the gods. Another point, of greater speculative significance, is gathered by our author from a consideration of the worship of Adonis. The Adonis cultus was a cultus of grief for the fair youth too early dead, and of rejoicing over his resurrection. The important point is, that here human pain and sorrow, in which man has the most intense feeling of his own subjective personality, become an element of the general cultus, and more especially that the element of negation is admitted into the conception of divinity, the story of Adonis being the story of a god. Death, the most extreme negation, and the victory over death are by implication treated as incidents in the career of Absolute Being. This is a step decidedly in advance of any taken by the mind of Eastern Asia. It is essentially a movement in the direction of the conception of the Absolute, the Divine, not simply as a spiritual abstraction, but as concrete Spirit, as true God. For there must needs be included in the concrete conception of Spirit the element of extreme distinction, of opposition, of "infinite negativity," and of power to overcome and transcend the same in the process of an absolute life. So the functions thought and love, in which pre-eminently man achieves spiritual reality for himself, involve, the one the absolute distinction and opposition of subject and object, of universal and particular, and the reconciliation and unity of these contrasted terms in a process of actual conscious knowledge; and the other the like antithesis between the loving, self-centred agent, with personal interests all his own, and another whose personal condition may be one of abject need, and whom the former, by a practical paradox, puts in his own place, treats as himself, and so first truly realizes his own better and truer self.

To the consciousness which man has of God correspond the consciousness which he has of himself and the necessary practical fruits of the latter in the advancing movement of human history. Hence the importance of these "speculative" or "theological" considerations in the philosophy of history.

(3) *Judæa.* — The other Semitic people of Western Asia, belonging to the Persian empire in its widest extent, was the Jewish.

With the Jews we meet again a people having "scriptures," — in the present case the "Old Testament," — in which the basal ideas of their faith and life are set forth.

A current and real distinction, amounting to complete contrast, is that between the "natural" and the "spiritual." When man fails to make this distinction in regard to himself, and consequently like the beasts leads a purely natural existence, his condition is one of barbarism or essential inhumanity, and no thread of the web of really human history can be woven. It is of the utmost importance, therefore, for the solution of the problem of human self-knowledge and for the consequent evolution of the drama of human history, that man should come clearly to conceive himself in his spiritual character, in its contrast with and superiority to the merely natural side of his existence; but to this end, according to the principle above laid down, it is necessary that the like conception should be had of the transcendent spirituality of Absolute Being, or of God. To this height we find the Jewish race rising in its religious notions. The theological ideas of all the peoples hitherto considered were naturalistic. Brahma was but the Universal Being of Nature, conceived, to boot, in such abstraction that it constituted no definite object of consciousness. To the

Persians the Absolute was less abstract; still, it was viewed as an object of sensuous consciousness, or as the universal physical light. The Phœnicians, too, in the story of Adonis saw not merely the symbol of a spiritual truth, but rather the description of a natural solar process. In all these notions the determining and fundamental element was a naturalistic one. In the Hebrew theology all this is radically changed. The break, in this regard, between the East and the West is completed. First in the order of being, and alone absolute, is Jehovah, — God, the pure Spirit; and Nature is His dependent creation. It is not strange that in holding this conception the Jews were conscious of their distinction above the nations that surrounded them. In their mind their God alone was true God; all other so-called "gods" were false. In knowing and worshipping Him, and in being visited with His favor, they were manifestly a "chosen people." Jehovah was not only the one true God, He was also the exclusive God of the Jewish people, "of Abraham and of his seed." In this way the contribution made by the Hebrews to the development of the spiritual consciousness of mankind was preserved, for the time being, from the degradation that would have followed a compromise with the naturalistic notions of the rest of the ancient world.

The Hebrew conception of Jehovah-God is sublime. Nature, in her measureless immensity — "the heaven of heavens" — cannot contain Him; she exists to declare, not her own glory, but only the glory of her Creator; her specific character is to be external, not divine. In the cultus of the nations whose theology was naturalistic the sensuous and immoral had even a privileged place. With the Hebrews this was impossible; for to them the Truth was no longer Nature, but Spirit, — not the Sensible, but the Non-sensible. Thought had thus become radically free from sensuous bondage, and true morality and righteousness were rendered possible; for it was only by righteousness that Jehovah as a spiritual being could be honored, while on the other hand it could be said that the essential rectitude of man as a spiritual being could and did only consist in "walking in the way of the Lord." On such rectitude temporal prosperity was recognized as depending, — as we read, "that thou mayest live long in the land," etc. Here, too, we meet what may be termed that prosaic state of mind which is requisite in order to the taking of a properly historic view of things and events: it is the mind to which the finite, definite, limited is just what it is thus described to be, its outlines not being washed away by the waves of an undisciplined sensuous imagination. "Men are treated as individuals, not as incarnations of God. The sun is regarded as simply the sun; mountains are viewed merely as mountains, and not as having in themselves spirit and will."

And yet the Jewish conception of God as Spirit was an imperfect one, by reason of its restriction to the very point which was above noted as its distinguishing merit; for while it is indeed necessary, in order rightly to form the notion of spiritual being, that the opposition between such being and merely natural or sensible existence should be sharply apprehended, this is not enough. A notion thus formed still remains only negative and abstract. Spiritual being has a positive as well as a negative relation to natural existence; and it is only when this latter relation is comprehended, — in a way in which this was not done by the Jews, — that the notion of Spirit becomes positively concrete and true. It is only then that the Apostolic assertion, "The Spirit is truth," acquires its full meaning, exhaustive of the whole realm of truth; and that the knowledge of this truth has power to render to man the priceless gift of concrete, spiritual self-knowledge, and to make him fully free. The content of the Hebrew conception of God is pure, non-sensuous thought; the relation of the individual to this being is a relation to pure thought. In such an object the individual, concrete, spiritual being does not find the mirror which faithfully and fully reflects the ideal perfection of his own nature; in his relation to it — his service, his worship — he is not spiritually free. The religious service which the Jew was called upon to render was accordingly a severe and hard one; it was a service of ceremony and of the law. The Jews confessed themselves as owing whatever they were to the one God, Jehovah; thus the individual, whether person or race, lacked the consciousness of independence, freedom, worth. Hence, adds Hegel, we find among the Jews no belief in the immortality of the soul. But the family here possesses the independence that the individual lacks; it is to the family that, so to speak, spiritual substantiality belongs. The worship of Jehovah is a worship rendered by the family. The State, on the other hand, is foreign to the principle of Jewish life and to the legislation of Moses. The true king is Jehovah, the God of Abraham, Isaac, and Jacob, who led them out from Egypt and gave them the land of Canaan.

When the Jews, in spite of the divine warnings to the contrary, had established over themselves an earthly king, and had then fallen apart into two separate kingdoms, both of these latter, equally unfortunate in external and internal wars, became finally subject to the Assyrians and Babylonians. By Cyrus the Israelites were permitted to return to their own land and live under laws of their own.

(4) *Egypt.* — The Persian empire is a ruin. Its fairest and richest cities — such as Babylon, Susa, Persepolis — have completely perished, with but few remains to indicate their ancient location. Egypt, the last to be mentioned among the countries composing the Persian Empire, may be called pre-eminently the " land of ruins," as it is also a " land of wonders." To the ancients, even, it was a wonderful land, while in modern times it has been the object of the greatest interest.

As to the place of Egypt in the philosophy of human history, — the story of man's labor to comprehend himself and his world, — we may say that in Egypt there are brought together the various ideal elements which met us singly in our contemplation of the other parts of the Persian empire; they are brought together as elements of a problem, which demands solution. The elements in question — not to recapitulate in more minute detail — are Nature and Spirit, sense and pure thought. The problem is to combine these, to comprehend them in their harmonious unity; or, more concretely, it is the problem of human self-knowledge, — to know man as a spiritual being distinctly transcending Nature, and yet as part and parcel of Nature: as it were a true birth of Nature, and so, while not abstractly identical with it, yet truly one or in harmony with it. This is the riddle; and Egypt represents the human race in the throes of an effort, mainly instinctive, to solve it. "Among the figures peculiar to Egyptian antiquity is one that is especially to be remarked; to wit, the Sphinx, — itself a riddle, an equivocal form, half beast, half man. The Sphinx may be regarded as a symbol of the Egyptian spirit: the human head, looking out from the beast's body, represents the spirit of man, as it begins to rise from the realm of Nature, to tear itself loose from it, and to look more freely about itself, without however being able as yet wholly to emancipate itself from Nature's fetters." The memorials of Ancient Egypt furnish a multitude of symbols or types, all expressing the same character; we recognize in all of them a spirit under the stress of an inward impulse to apprehend and manifest itself, — and indeed doing this, though only in sensuous forms.

Passing over the details of the political history of Egypt, let us look at some of the special sides of this riddle of Egyptian character.

The wisdom and practical ability of the Egyptians were objects of envious admiration to other ancient nations. In mathematics and its applications they led the ancient world. The spirit of mathematical and mechanical order would appear to have entered into their political or governmental arrangements; so that we find Diodorus of Sicily remarking that Egypt was the only land where the citizens had no care for the State, but only for their own private affairs. Such a condition of things, adds Hegel, could not but be especially surprising to Greeks and Romans. And yet it would be quite incorrect to think of the Egyptians as a spiritually stagnant people, whose national existence was irrevocably fixed in an iron mould, restrictive of all growth or change : the mind busy with the "riddle," fermenting, seeking to objectify itself, is still there, and gives account of itself in a series of prodigious creations.

Removed in the main from embroiling relations with other nations, yet bordering on the Mediterranean Sea, — "that grand *locale* of the display of nationalities," — the Egyptians occupied what might almost be termed a peculiar and separate natural world of their own. The valley of the Nile was the universe of the Egyptian, and the course of the Nile — its rise and fall, corresponding, and as it were one, with the movements of the sun — was to him the course of Nature. Nature thus had for him a very definitely marked individuality; as it was the immediate basis of his life, so it determined the form of his religious ideas. "Dispute arose even in ancient times respecting the sense and meaning of the Egyptian religion. Chaeremon the Stoic, who lived in the time of Tiberius and had been in Egypt, gave it a merely materialistic explanation; the Neo-Platonists went to the other extreme, finding in everything the symbol of a spiritual meaning, and so turning this religion into a pure idealism. Each of these views is one-sided." The religion of the Egyptians is at once materialistic and idealistic, or naturalistic and spiritualistic. Natural and spiritual powers are here not separated in conception; the course of Nature, as it appeared in Egypt, and the process of the divine life are viewed as one and the same thing. In the consciousness of this people the spiritual meaning is not set free; the Nile, the sun, and Osiris are one; the rise and recession of the river and of the heavenly body are the birth and death of Osiris. The natural phenomenon and the divine change are each equally symbols of the other; they are also symbols of human life and the sources of all that sustains and enriches it. Thus the most heterogeneous elements are combined in one conception, and in a confusion that contrasts very unfavorably with the rounded clearness of Greek ideas. But this confusion is not that of mere and utter mental helplessness; the mind therein involved is brooding and breeding, fermenting and putting forth as it were spiritual tentacles, "feeling after God, if haply it may find Him." The result may be artistically ugly, but to its meaning we cannot be indifferent.

The characteristic element in the cultus of the

Egyptians was their veneration of animals. Odious as such veneration may appear to us, we are not at once to set down those who indulge in it as the spiritual inferiors of the worshippers of sun and stars, but rather the reverse: the world of animal life, with its wonderful and mysterious instincts, offers to human intelligence a problem of a much higher order than do the heavenly bodies. The Egyptians, in viewing this world, felt themselves peculiarly in presence of that riddle which their whole life and all existence propounded to them, if not also of its solution. For the rest, it was but natural that the dull and undeveloped self-consciousness of the Egyptians, not yet opened to the idea of human freedom, should incline them to sympathize with animal life, and to worship the secret and singular type of psychical existence which belongs to it. We need not dwell on the brutish and inhuman extremes to which this worship was sometimes carried; it is more important to recur to the signs that reveal what we may term its spiritual drift or significance. These are to be found in the Sphinxes above referred to, — bodies of lions, with heads of maidens, or sometimes of bearded men. What the mind divines and seeks begins here to venture forth and find distinct expression: the human head crowning the body of the beast is the Spiritual tending to emerge from the merely Natural, and to assert its right of command. But, on the other hand, we also find in the products of Egyptian art the human form disfigured by the addition to it of the face of an animal: individuality of expression, which the art of the

Greeks was able to attain through spiritual characterization in forms of beauty, the Egyptians were helpless to render, except through the use of animal heads and masks. But thus, too, we see that where they were naturalistic in their conceptions they took the natural object for more than what it was according to the first appearance, seeing in it the symbol of an inner and hidden sense and spirit. Indeed, the Egyptian spirit is to be recognized as pre-eminently "the symbolizing spirit." The secret of this spirit was an inward impulse toward self-comprehension. It was this impulse, and not any motive of mere display or recreation or pleasure, that prompted the immense artistic industry of the Egyptians. In the products of this industry they sought, as it were, to find out what they were by showing objectively what was in them. So far as these works were and still are riddles, they but truly express what the Egyptian spirit was to itself. Of these works, constituting, as Hegel remarks, an empire of artistic achievement comparable for its might to the political empire of the Romans, — an empire of works of art "whose ruins demonstrate their indestructibility, and are greater and more astounding than all other works of ancient or modern times," — our author mentions as most remarkable those devoted to the dead. "These are the immense excavations in the hills along the Nile at Thebes, with passages and chambers wholly filled with mummies, — subterranean habitations, as large as the most extensive mines of modern times; then the great Field of the Dead in the plain of Sais, with its walls and vaults; further, those wonders of the world, the pyramids, — enormous crystals, as they might be called, in regular geometrical form, destined — as Herodotus and Diodorus of old reported, and as the investigations of modern times have anew demonstrated — to serve the purpose of tombs; and finally, the most astonishing thing of all, the Tombs of the Dead, one of which has been opened in this century by Belzoni."

It is of particular consequence that we notice what were the ideas of the Egyptians concerning the dead. From them we may most certainly learn what, in their view, was the essential character of man. Now, what is most distinctive and remarkable in this connection is the circumstance that, according to the declaration of Herodotus, the Egyptians were the first who expressed the thought that the soul of man is immortal. To hold the immortality of the soul is to hold that the soul is something other than Nature, and has an independent spiritual character; it is, further, to ascribe to the human individual an infinite worth. This doctrine, then, we find the Egyptians beginning to hold, but in an undeveloped and largely naturalistic form. The soul appears to have been conceived by them in atomic, physical fashion, and as capable, *per se*, of being housed indifferently in any sort of body, whether of man or animal; for the Egyptians believed in the transmigration of souls. This was, however, in their view, a degradation and punishment, from which only those souls were exempted that had remained faithful in their earthly lives to

Osiris. The Egyptian practice of embalming the body appears as a means of bearing witness to the immortality of the soul that had inhabited it. The soul after death was judged; if favorable judgment was passed upon it, it was received into the kingdom of Osiris. The deeper meaning of this was that the individual had become united with Osiris: on the covers of sarcophagi we even find a deceased person represented as having himself become Osiris. Thus the perfect human and the divine are united in one conception.

Recapitulating all that has been said regarding the peculiarities of the Egyptian character, we may say that it is the expression of a spirit still immersed indeed in Nature, yet travailing under the secret and but partially comprehended impulse to seek its own emancipation. There is accordingly the union of the most contradictory traits, — on the one hand, features of savagery and wild sensuality; and on the other, marks of cool, reflecting intelligence and of a hopeful spiritual fermentation. The problem is to bring these two sides — the natural and the spiritual — into concrete, harmonious unity; a unity in which Nature shall become simply the scene and the soil for the manifestation of the spirit. This problem the Egyptians could not solve; it remained to them their "riddle."

(5) *Transition to the Grecian World.* — The inward ideal transition to the spiritual principle, as we may term it, of the Grecian world is made through Egypt. Egypt is or becomes part of an Oriental empire; it is allied to the Oriental spirit, but it

faces also toward the dawn of a new and higher spirit in the Western world. If Asia, as a whole, represents the stage of spiritual childhood, Egypt is boyhood, inwardly impatient of the weakness and limitation that mark the earlier stage, and feeling out after that independence, that clearly conscious self-mastery, which is exhibited to us in what we may term the early manhood of the world in Ancient Greece. In Eastern Asia the human spirit is sunk in Nature and, as it were, in a torpid identity with it. In Western Asia this same spirit breaks with Nature; while in Greece it attains the first and simplest, and perhaps fairest, form of harmony both with itself and with Nature.

The outward historic transition occurs through the coming in contact of the Persian with the Grecian world. Here, indeed, there confronts us, for the first time, a real historic transition, — Persia as an empire perishes, and her supremacy is transferred to Greece. The Persian empire had to perish; and the fact of this necessity furnishes the proof that Persia stands for more — for a higher principle — in the development of human history than an apparently indestructible but petrified empire like that of China. (Mere duration is never a proof of superior excellence. "The imperishable mountains are not to be rated higher than the rose, whose leaves quickly fall and whose perfumed life is but for a season.") In Persia the protest of the spirit of man against a mode of existence purely natural begins. The evidence of the efficiency of this protest is found in the circumstance that the historic existence of the Persian empire was of short duration. "The principle of separation from Nature comes in with the Persian empire, and it therefore stands higher than the other Oriental empires. The necessity of progress is thus disclosed; the bud of the spirit has opened, and must go on to its mature development. The Chinaman first counts for something when he is dead. The Hindu deadens himself, sinks himself in Brahma; is dead-alive in the condition of complete unconsciousness, or is, by the mere fact of his birth, present God. Here no change, no progress, is possible; for there can be no advance except where the spirit is conceived and asserted as in its nature independent. With the 'light' of the Persians begins spiritual perception; and in this, spirit takes its leave of Nature." Hence, as Hegel here again remarks, the Persians respected the freedom and individuality of the various peoples included under their empire, by leaving each in possession of its own riches, constitution, and religion. This, indeed, became the weak side of Persia as compared with Greece, and the immediate source of her fall. For the Persians left the "particularity" of the different members of their empire to that degree undisturbed that the empire itself lacked organization; it was more a loose aggregate than an organic whole; it was not effectively animated by one spirit. The Greeks were the first people who, while respecting national or tribal individualities, succeeded in bringing them all into organic harmony with each other and with a universal spirit, — the spirit of Greece, which thereby became free.

CHAPTER VI.

THE GRECIAN WORLD.

HEGEL, in his various works, often repeats the remark that man, in order properly and fully to exist as man, must undergo a second birth,— the "birth of the spirit." Of this birth we witness the progressive labors in the history of Asia; in Greece we become aware of its full and definite accomplishment. Our path in Asia is from darkness to approaching dawn; in Greece we are flooded with the light of the actually risen spirit. But there is a difference between the spirit fairly born and the spirit in the plenitude of its mature development. The sun just risen does not display all the glories of noontide. Greece is the fresh morning of human history, not its noontime nor its closing day; it is like the morning sun, rejoicing to run its race. Before the race of the human spirit in history shall have been fully run, many hard and serious labors are to be accomplished, which the joyous Grecian world neither comprehends nor can execute. We are to look in Greece only for that which Greece presents, and that is the "joyous view of the youthful freshness of spiritual life." First, it is a freshness of *youth*. "Grecian life is a veritable achievement of youth. It begins with Achilles, the poetic youth, and is brought to an end by Alexander, the real youth; both appear engaged in a contest against Asia." And, secondly, it is the freshness of a *spiritual* life. The spiritual is indeed not here in abstract and rigid opposition to the natural; it seeks not to suspend itself as it were in a vacuum above the actual natural world; it lives in the sensuous present; it is not disembodied, but embodied, and it both finds in and lends to its sensuous environment a spiritualized significance. But the more important point is that here the spirit has come to such maturity that it is able, in some true sense, to have itself for the object of its knowledge and of its volition. The result, as it appears in the Grecian world, is the emergence of what we may term beautiful spiritual individualities; they are individualities conscious of no opposition between the ends of the State, the Family, Law, and Religion, and their own ends, — conscious, the rather, that only through the former can spiritual individuality itself exist.

We have now to consider in Grecian history three periods, — the period, first, of development; secondly, of independence and conquest; and thirdly, of decline and fall.

A. — FIRST PERIOD: THE ELEMENTS OF THE GRECIAN SPIRIT.

The reader, recalling what has been said respecting the abstract, unindividualized "substantiality" of the spirit of the Asiatic world, will the more readily appreciate, by contrast, the force of Hegel's characterization of Greece as the home of "spiritual individuality." The geographical environment of Greece corresponds, in its way, with this characterization. Here is no large stream, with vast plains, adapted to be the scene of the vegetating and unprogressive existence of a homogeneous people. Greece is a collection of islands, together with a portion of the mainland that is itself almost an island, and is indented by numberless bays; it is a land of mountains, narrow plains, and little valleys and streams, "corresponding perfectly to the heterogeneity of the Grecian tribes and the mobility of the Greek spirit."

This heterogeneity of the original elements of the Grecian people is an important circumstance. No nation that has played a weighty and active part in the world's history has ever issued from the simple development of a single race along unmodified lines of blood-relationship; there must be difference, conflict, a composition of opposed forces. So the Romans sprang from a *colluvies* of the most diverse national elements; and so the early history of Greece exhibits to us the wanderings and comminglings of numerous different tribes, partly native and partly of foreign origin, — Attica, in particular, where Grecian culture was to bear its richest fruits, being especially a place of refuge for races and families the most unlike. What the history of Grecian civilization begins with is thus the existence of independent individualities, and from the outset whatever bond unites them is not one of Nature, but of will and spiritual character. Of the rudeness of the early conditions in Greece,— the unrest, insecurity, robberies, — Thucydides gives us a picture: it was the Athenians, he says, who first laid aside their weapons in time of peace. The place occupied by foreigners in the beginnings of Grecian history is particularly conspicuous. Athens, according to the legends, is founded by Cecrops, an Egyptian; and Thebes by Cadmus, of Phœnician origin, to whom also the introduction of the alphabet is ascribed; Pelops, of Phrygia, gives his name to the Peloponnesus. In brief, Greece is colonized by people of an older civilization. The result, however, is not — as in the case of the contact of the English colonists with the North American Indians — the supplanting of the natives. It is a new growth, in which both the foreign and the indigenous are combined.

By the foreigners fortresses were established and royal houses were founded, from which, as centres, went forth the first fixed radii of an associated life in Greece. Massive remains of the "Cyclopean" walls of these fortresses are still found. The authority of the princes who inhabited them was neither patriarchal nor despotic; nor was it sanctioned and controlled by civil laws: it rested on superiority of wealth, of possession, of arms, of personal valor, of intelligence and wisdom, and finally of lineage and ancestry, for the princes being "heroes" were regarded as belonging to a superior race; and obedience was rendered to them simply under a sense of the general need of a bond of social union, in single-hearted loyalty, without jealousy and without ill-will. On the whole, the princely authority is personal, resting on individual merit: it is the authority of the individual "hero," and is subject to such limitations of extent and permanence as this circumstance involves. Customs and manners, in this period, are very simple: the princes prepare their own food; Ulysses builds his own house. In the Iliad of Homer we see a "king of kings" the leader in the great national enterprise which the poem celebrates; but his supremacy over the other leaders is as little absolute as is that of these latter over the people who follow them. Such also, precisely, is the relation in which, in the Homeric Olympus, Zeus, the King of the gods, stands to his fellows.

The royal families perished, partly through individual acts of violence, partly by natural and gradual decay. The people were not involved in their ruin, owing to the looseness of the moral connection between them and the princes. "This relation between the people and the royal houses is exhibited to us also in Grecian tragedy. The people are the Chorus, passive, inactive; it is the heroes who accomplish the actions and bear the responsibility. There is nothing in common between them; the people have no power to pass and execute judgment, but appeal simply to the gods. Hence such heroic individualities as those of the princes are conspicuously adapted to be employed as the subjects of dramatic art; in all their resolutions they act independently and individually, not guided by universal laws, binding on every citizen; their deeds and their destruction are individual."

After the decline of the royal houses, Greece was left in a more settled condition. The earlier incessant wanderings of tribes is at an end, and men make their homes in cities. Commerce flourishes, and the growing population overflows in colonies, — in Ionia, in the islands of the Mediterranean, in the Italian peninsula, in Sicily. In some quarters the growth of excessive wealth breeds tyrants. Finally, with the time of Cyrus we reach the period of special interest in the history of Greece; it is the period of the ripening development of the characteristic Grecian spirit in religion and civil polity.

In seeking to give an account of the essential elements or rudiments of the Greek spirit, it is of the first consequence that we consider the relation in which it stood to Nature. We have already spoken of the correlation which may be observed between the face of Nature in Greece and certain conspicuous features of Grecian character. There was no danger that Nature should here stupefy the mind by her monotony, or terrorize it by the mere blank immensity of her forms; man's companionship with and dependence on Nature in Greece would be, the rather, conducive to mental alertness. The characteristic attitude of the early Greek mind toward Nature was a wondering, listening, divining one. It was, in the nobler sense, an attitude of curiosity, — of curiosity permanent and serious and not merely idle and casual, relating to Nature *in toto* and in all her parts, and not simply to occasional phenomena marked by apparently extraordinary features. The existence of Nature was not to the Greek, as to modern science, a mere bloodless *fact* and nothing more; it was a spiritual excitant, it was full of voices and meanings, it invited interpretation; and the meaning which it had for the Greek was precisely the meaning that it had *for him*, not a meaning that belonged to it *by itself*, or apart from *thinking men*. The wonderful and characteristic thing is that the Greek was thus able to find in Nature the expressive language of his own thought, of his own inward being. Such an attitude of mind toward Nature, such a treatment of Nature, is of course purely poetic; it is the work of fancy, not arbitrary and artificial, but spontaneous. It is, in the main, wholly without superstition; artlessly and without effort it simply reads into the immediate sensuous fact a spiritual sense:[1] the murmuring of the waterfall is, in the language of the objective fancy of the Greeks, the voice of the Naiad. But the ulterior — inner, human, subjective — meaning of this "interpretation" is made evident when we reflect that from the Naiad, in the further development of the Grecian mythology, springs the Muse, — the subjective, spiritual power that inspires this and all other fancies. So the effect of his contact with Nature is to bring the Greek to a consciousness of himself, of his own powers, and in general of those ethical forces by which man is governed, and self-governed, so far as he attains to spiritual freedom.

[1] The Grecian spirit transforms "das Sinnliche in Sinniges." Hegel here employs a singularly happy and significant expression, for which it is hard, if not impossible, to find in English an equally happy equivalent.

The Gods, the first conception of whom takes its origin in connection with the perception of natural objects and phenomena, come to denote characteristically these powers. "In the beginning of the Iliad, Achilles breaks out in wrathful indignation against Agamemnon, and is about to draw his sword, but checks the movement of his arm and restrains his anger, mindful of his relation to Agamemnon. The poet interprets this, saying, that it was Pallas Athene (Wisdom, Reflection) who held him back." The poets were thus the ethical teachers of the Greeks. Such, above all, was Homer.

In the investigation of the sources of the Grecian mythology account must indeed be taken of something more than the inward and outward promptings felt by the Greek mind in the first-hand presence of Nature. It is well known that both in religion and art the Greeks early received ideas from Eastern nations, and notably from the Egyptians. Herodotus says that Homer and Hesiod created for the Greeks their mythology; he also says that Greece received the names of its gods from Egypt. The contradiction here is only superficial. The Greeks receive a name, but they transform and spiritualize the conception. Hercules, as a foreign conception, is the sun, accomplishing its journey through the twelve signs of the zodiac: to the Hellenes he represents the spiritual in man, rising by its energy — its "twelve labors" — to Olympus. So the Greek received from others, but transformed what he received, and gave it a new character according to his own spirit.

THE GRECIAN WORLD.   187

Summing up, now, our view of the elements of the Grecian spirit, we may say that it stands in the mean between two extremes. The one of these extremes has confronted us in the Asiatic world, where man is without spiritual independence,— all that is spiritual and divine being as yet undistinguished from purely natural modes of existence; the other is illustrated in the subjective idealism of modern times, where thought rejects any other ultimate basis than the pure certainty it has of its own reality, admitting nothing except upon the authority of the consciousness of the thinking, personal Ego. The freedom of the Grecian spirit is, therefore, certainly not a freedom in complete ideal independence of Nature. The activity of the Grecian spirit finds its instigating occasion in Nature; Nature is the alphabet of the Greek, Nature is his language. The use and meaning of this language his own spirit determines; on the other hand, no "meaning" is conceivable for him which has not its natural expression or embodiment. So the Grecian spirit is essentially artistic. It is the spirit of the plastic artist, who fashions the block of stone into a work of art. To the artist the stone does not remain mere stone, to which form is added from without; the rather, even against its nature it is made to become the expression of a spiritual conception, — it is not simply formed, but *trans*formed. On the other hand, the artist too *needs* for the expression of his spiritual conceptions the stone, colors, sensuous forms; out of relation to them he can neither become conscious of his own idea, nor communicate it to others. The Egyptian, too, was a worker in the raw materials that Nature offers; but in the products of his workmanship we see the natural not yet brought into subjection to the spiritual. . . . In Grecian art the sensuous is only a sign, expression, envelope, in which the spirit manifests itself."

Finally, in the artistic results of his transforming spiritual activity the Greek becomes conscious of his freedom; "he is their creator, and they are the so-called works of man's hand." But, on the other hand, what he has expressed in them is not his accidental, but his universal and better self; not worthless eccentricities of individual fancy, but "the eternal truth and powers of the spirit as such, so that it may as well be said that they are not as that they are his creation." Thus he can reverence in them the manifestation of what is absolute and divine, as well as of that which is highest and most distinctively human in man. "The glory of the human is merged in the glory of the divine."

We return to the point from which we started out. Spiritual individuality is the essential note of Grecian character. By way of more definite characterization we may now add that this individuality is in form distinctively beautiful, artistic. All the products of the Grecian spirit are works of art. For the purposes of our present survey they may be summed up under the three heads of the Subjective work of art, or the culture of man himself; the Objective work of art, or the fashioning of the world of divine beings; and the Political work of art, or the form of the social constitution and the status of individuals under the same.

B.—SECOND PERIOD: THE CREATIONS OF THE GRECIAN SPIRIT.

I. *The Subjective Creation.* — He who first invented a tool gave one of the most demonstrative, and doubtless also one of the earliest, proofs of the superiority of man over Nature. By his tools man turns Nature against herself, and forces her to become subservient to his needs. A tool is the product of the activity of mind, and is to be regarded more highly than a natural object. The pleasure which the Greeks took in contemplating their various tools and implements, and the objects constructed by means of them, is well illustrated in Homer. The honor of human inventions for the subjugation of Nature is ascribed to the Gods.

Man also employs Nature for purposes of personal adornment, the sense of which is to show what a man is and has, and has made of himself. Even the Homeric Greeks in this point of view showed a very developed interest in the matter of personal adornment. The immediate subject of adornment is the human body, which to be worthy of this distinction should actually be informed, and not merely idly inhabited, by the spirit which it was created to serve. An elementary, though oft neglected, essential of human culture is that man (as Hegel elsewhere remarks) should " take victorious possession of his body," bringing it into subjection and rendering it a perfect organ of his will. This he must do, not only for the sake of the uses which the body may thus be made instrumentally to serve, but also in justice to his body and for the plenitude and dignity of his higher spiritual life. This the Greeks, in the youthful freshness of their spiritual self-consciousness, took a naïve and keen delight in doing. And herein lay the *subjective* beginning of Grecian art. "The Greeks first made of themselves beautiful forms, before they sought to express the like in marble and in paintings." It was, notably, in their games that they thus "took possession of their bodies," making of them real "works of art," and innocently exhibiting them for the admiration of their fellows and for the honor of the Gods. With the athletic exercises were joined music and the dance.

Developed human song requires an objective content, whose genesis is in the realm of thought, and which takes form (in poetry, first of all) as an *objective* work of art.

II. *The Objective Creation.* — The absolute and essential content or subject-matter of song, says Hegel, is religious. In song man declares and celebrates that which he regards as highest. What we have to consider under the present head is, therefore, the religion and mythology of the Greeks.

The Greek Gods correspond, in conception, to what we have recognized as the peculiar character of the Grecian spirit; they are, so to express it, spiritualized natural beings. The contrast is great between the Grecian and, say, the Hindu conception of divinity. In the latter, the central idea is that of some impersonal natural force, to which the human form, in which the imagination clothes it, is purely accidental. In the former, the main element is spiritual and personal, and the naturalistic element is transformed and elevated into harmony therewith, — just as the Greek himself transformed and elevated his own natural body into harmony with the beautiful soul within him. We may say decidedly that the Greeks worshipped God as a Spirit; though with the immense limitation, that they did not have the developed and purified conception of God as the one, absolute, and free Spirit, but admitted in their pantheon many Gods, each having a restricted individuality, existing under human limitations and in dependence on external conditions. The Gods of the Greeks are to them eternally beautiful individualities.

We have already spoken of the spiritualizing treatment given by the Greeks to the naturalistic mythological conceptions introduced among them from other lands. In the mythology of the Greeks this whole process of the reduction of Nature, in human conception and religious regard, to a position of dependence on and subservience to the spiritual, is most naïvely and distinctly expressed in the legend of the war among the Gods, ending in the overthrow of the Titans by the race of Zeus. Nature is cast down from the supreme place, but the new Gods still retain in themselves naturalistic elements and a definite relation to particular powers of Nature. So Zeus, while he is the political God, the guardian of morality and patron of the rights of hospitality, is also the one who has the lightning for his messenger and the clouds for his chariot.

The Gods of Greece, we must repeat, are individualities. They are not allegories nor symbols; they are (in conception) personal. The spiritual nature, in all its many-sided fulness, is not conceived as resident in any one of them; each is a particular character, having one among the many different attributes of a spiritual being as his special possession (wisdom, courage, or the like). All ethical and spiritual attributes are thus wholly distributed among the different divinities. The unity, under which Greek thought was compelled to consider all of them as placed, could therefore only be unspiritual and abstract; it was the unity of "Necessity,"— blind, shapeless, contentless, irrational. "The higher truth, perceived when this unity is known as God, the One Spirit, was not yet known to the Greeks."

The "anthropomorphism" of the Greeks, in representing their Gods in the form and character of human beings, is often criticised as a defect; on the contrary, it constitutes a relative merit. It is by virtue of the spiritual human element in them that the Greek Gods are raised above all Nature-Gods and all abstractions of the one "pure Being," such as we have contemplated in Eastern Asia. On the other hand, there are others who, like Schiller, see in this anthropomorphism of the Greek religion a mark of superiority over Christianity, which, it is said, excludes man from its conception of divinity.

"When," says the poet, "the Gods were more human, men were more divine." In reply to this we must insist that "the Greek Gods are not to be looked upon as more human than the Christian God. Christ is much more man; he lives, dies, and suffers the death on the cross, which is infinitely more human than the man of Grecian beauty." The Christian view of the union of the divine and human nature is higher and more perfect than the Grecian, because with Christianity there came a more ample conception of the true character of spiritual life and freedom.

III. *The Political Creation.* — The "subjective" and "objective" creations of the Grecian spirit hitherto considered, furnish the ideal factors of the animating and organizing principle of the "Political Creation," to which we now turn. The national spirit of Greece, on its universal side, is the same which the Greeks sought to render objective to their imagination in their conceptions and representations of the Gods. With this universal the individual spirit of the separate citizen is organically united in a patriotic, public self-consciousness, which each practically recognizes as constituting, not the accidental, but the substantial and essential side of his own existence. The individual is here nothing, and less than nothing, without the State.

To this spirit and this State the democratic constitution was alone adapted. It was just as necessary that in Greece government should be the self-government of all the citizens, as that in the Orient it should be the despotic rule of one man.

A democratic polity is not patriarchal, nor founded on ignorant submission to an arbitrary ruler; it implies a diffused ethical consciousness, and laws having in this consciousness their basis and sanction. Moreover, it implies that this consciousness shall be not only universally diffused among the citizens, but also permanent and, as it were, a second nature. To the Greeks it was their first nature. The public conscience was immediately identical with the conscience of the individual citizen; the public life, the general interest of the State, of the "city," were as intimately one with his own private life and interest as is, for example, in man's bodily organism the advantage of the whole body with that of each one of its members. The individual in the spontaneous exercise of his own freedom wrought the will of the whole ethico-political body of which he was a member; it was in the like spirit that he participated in the making and administering of the laws. So, just as the beautiful of Grecian art has in its express and essential relation to a sensuous form a naturalistic element, the laws of the Grecian democracy exist in a fashion that imitates or suggests natural necessity.

Thus the living ground from which Grecian democracy sprang was an ethical one, — was spiritual, but was also one of what would be termed moral innocence; and from this ground nothing but such a democracy could spring. To the existence of what is ordinarily understood as "morality" there is needed a peculiar kind of reflection, the exercise of private judgment, proceeding on the assumption that the private opinion of the individual may possibly have better grounds in reason, and so be worth more, than the dicta of the public or common consciousness. The individual then comes to profess responsibilities and convictions and to have intentions that are all his own, the obligation or right to pursue which he regards as superior in sacredness to the social will as actually expressed in the laws of the community. That the introduction of such reflection must needs occur in the spiritual development of mankind; that the moral crisis that follows it must needs be passed before the condition of spiritual maturity (to know the universal True) can be fulfilled, so that it may become to the individual as a second nature to will the same, — of this there can be no doubt. Just as little is it to be doubted that the introduction of such reflection (notably by the Sophists) into the moral world of Greece was the entering wedge for the destruction of Grecian democracy.

We note, in connection with this subject, especially the three following points: —

(1) Democracy as it existed only in Greece involved and was connected with the belief in Oracles: if a colony was to be sent out or a battle to be fought, inquiry was made of the Oracles. In order to undertake the independent decision of practical questions of this sort there is needed, of course, a trained and self-reliant intelligence, able to perceive and to be determined by the weight of reasons. This is a species of "subjectivity of will" (as Hegel terms it), to which the Greeks, at the time

when the democratic polity first declared itself as the only one natural to them, had not attained. Later, indeed, this was not the case. In the most important affairs it was not the Oracles, but the particular views of the popular orators, that determined the decision. But then, too, the corruption, ruin, and constant tinkering and changing of the political constitution had begun.

2. The conditions of life in a Grecian democracy involved of necessity the maintenance of a class of slaves. The life of the individual citizen was the public life; the public affair was his special private affair. In order, therefore, that he might be free to lead his proper life as a citizen, it was necessary that the labor for his daily bread should be done for him by others. These others could not be citizens, — they must therefore be slaves; for freedom and citizenship meant the same thing. The Greeks had indeed advanced to the notion of the *equal* freedom of all citizens; they had not gotten so far as to recognize in freedom the necessary attribute of man, as such. *Humanity* is a universal notion, implying an advanced degree of moral reflection. But the ethical status of the Greeks was, as we have seen, marked relatively by the absence of such reflection, being expressed in and bounded by local habit and custom. Such appreciation of the rights of man as man, as would have led them to abhor slavery and exclude it from among their institutions, was therefore not to be expected from them.

3. We have to note that such democracies as those of Greece are only possible in small States,

not exceeding by much the compass of single cities. "In the time of Pericles, at the beginning of the Peloponnesian War, the whole population of the Athenian territory took refuge, on the approach of the Spartans, in the city." It is only in such cities that there can be a sufficient community of interest for a successful democracy; whereas in great empires a variety of local interests exist in conflict with each other. The citizen of a democracy requires to have a plastic, undivided character. His participation in public affairs must not be abstract, remote, partial, but concrete and complete, involving "the passion and interest of the whole man;" he must move and be moved by the living, warming power of the voice, of audible speech. The French in the time of their Revolution had the people in the different communes hand in their written votes, and counted the results; but they did not thus succeed in etablishing a democracy, and "tyranny, despotism, raised its voice under the mask of liberty and equality."

We pass now to a brief review of the political history of Greece in this its second period.

(*a*) *The Wars with the Persians.* — The second period in the history of any nation is the one in which, after a previous first period of unobserved growth and preparation, it comes in contact with the people next preceding it in the march of civilization: it is then that the nation first shows what it is, and asserts and defends, as a new factor in human history, the principle that itself embodies. This the Greeks first did in their wars with the Persians.

It is unnecessary to enter descriptively into the details of these wars; it is enough to know that the Persians threatened the liberties of Greece, which liberties the Greeks successfully and gloriously defended at Marathon and Salamis. Greater battles than these have unquestionably been fought; the bravery and genius of the Grecian soldiers and leaders have elsewhere been equalled; yet these battles have a peculiar immortality in the memory, not only of the fortunes of nations, but of science and art, and of all that gives to human life nobility and ethical worth,— for they were victories of and for culture and the power of the spirit. The interests involved in all other military engagements have been of a less universal order. "The Greeks are justly entitled to their undying glory, on account of the exalted cause for which they successfully fought. . . . The interest of universal history here lay in the balance. The opposing parties were, on the one hand, Oriental despotism,— that is, a world united under one master,— and on the other, divided States, of limited extent and means, but animated by a spirit of free individuality. Never in history has the superiority of spiritual power over mere mass, and that too over a by no means contemptible mass, been so brilliantly exhibited. This war, and the following development of the States which took the lead in it, fill up the most brilliant period of Greece. Everything that was contained in the Grecian principle was now unfolded and displayed.

The lead in the wars against the Persians was taken by Sparta and Athens. When the wars were over, the specific contrast in the characters of the two peoples proceeded to emphasize itself. The Athenians continued their career of conquest for a long time, and advanced to opulence; while the Lacedemonians, having no naval force, displayed less activity. The antithesis of Athens and Sparta has furnished a favorite theme of historical discussion. Argument for the purpose of proving the superiority of either of these States over the other is idle; the one thing needful is to comprehend how each was in its own way a necessary and worthy product of the Grecian spirit. Before speaking of the Peloponnesian War, in which the jealousy of Sparta and Athens came to a violent expression, we will consider separately the fundamental characters of the two States.

(*b*) *Athens.* — Athens is peculiarly the home of free individuality, developed in forms, in personalities, worthy to be called living works of art.

We have already had occasion to mention Athens as an asylum for the inhabitants of the other parts of Greece, and thus acquiring a very heterogeneous population. Legislated for by Solon, and educated to the habit of order and peace, and obedience to the legislation of Solon, by Pisistratus and the Pisistratidæ, we find them, under a constitution constantly growing more democratic, at last and at the crowning point of their history united under the leadership of Pericles the statesman, — himself a free and great individuality; the Zeus, as Aristophanes termed him, of Athens. It was in his individuality that his power and authority over the

Athenians was founded, — in the well-grounded conviction he was able to produce in them that he was a thoroughly noble man, with an eye single to the welfare of the State, and superior to others in mind and knowledge. No other statesman can be compared with him in respect of power of individuality. For the rest, a democratic constitution, more than any other, is favorable to the development of great political characters; for it not only tolerates individuality, but invites individual talent to assert itself. On the other hand, such assertion can succeed only when the individual is able to comprehend and conform to the mind and opinion, as well as the passion, of a cultured people.

On the whole, we may say that the leading elements in the Athenian character were individual independence and culture animated by the spirit of beauty. It was for the Athenian people that, "under the direction of Pericles, those immortal works of sculpture were produced, the sparse remains of which are the wonder of posterity. It was before this people that the dramas of Æschylus and Sophocles were represented. . . . To this people the orations of Pericles were addressed, and it was from the midst of this people that there sprang forth a galaxy of men, who are classical existences for all the centuries; for among them are to be classed, in addition to those just named, Thucydides, Socrates, Plato, Aristophanes." The most truthful characterization of the Athenians is that which Thucydides places in the mouth of Pericles. Love of the beautiful, as distinguished from the merely showy; devotion to philosophy, though not in that form or degree which leads to inaction ; boldness and daring, without unthinking foolhardiness, — such, according to Pericles, are the marks of the Athenian.

(c) *Sparta.* — In this State the leading idea is political virtue. But it is a virtue of a rigid, abstract kind, calling for a life in such wise merged in and subordinate to that of the State that energy and freedom of individuality are repressed. The practical ideal is rather a dead equality than free movement.

The Lacedemonians were of Dorian origin, and the Doric character is expressed in their political constitution. Themselves intruders in the Peloponnesus, the Dorians reduced the indigenous Helots to a slavery of the most abject sort. While the slaves of the Athenians were regarded more as friends and members of the household, the Spartan Helots were treated as public enemies. By Lycurgus, according to Plutarch's narrative, the land was divided into equal parts, for distribution among the Spartan inhabitants of the city and the Lacedemonians, or Periœci ; and the private sale of land was forbidden. This provision, intended to secure equality in the ownership of land, was frustrated in its effects through frequent intermarriages, whereby in the end all the land fell into the possession of a few families, — " as if," says our author, " to show how foolish it is to aim at a forced equality in landed possessions, all attempts to maintain which, besides being ineffectual, are directed against liberty in one of its most essential conditions ; namely, the right of free disposition of property." Further, by forbidding the use of any other money than iron, a substantially prohibitory check was placed on foreign trade. Add to this, that the Spartans were without a naval force to support and favor commerce: when for any other purpose they were in need of such a force, they applied to the Persians. Still another device for securing social homogeneity among the Spartans was their eating at public tables, thereby putting the family life in the background. With the Athenians, eating and drinking were, as they should be, a private affair; and when on exceptional occasions, as at banquets, larger numbers came together at the table, this was not mainly in order to eat and to drink, but for the enjoyment of reason's feast.

The political constitution of Sparta, though democratic in its foundation, differed little from an aristocracy, or oligarchy. Government followed more the lines of custom than of written law, and its powers were finally exercised with a tyranny resembling that which was practised by Robespierre and his followers for a time in France.

The State thus organized left little or no place for intellectual culture. Art and science were not at home among its citizens. To the rest of the Greeks the Spartans appeared coarse and awkward, without mental flexibility and practical tact. In their dealings among themselves they were in the main honest, but with others, unscrupulous.

Thus the leading feature in the Spartan character is political; the "virtue" of the Spartan is a political virtue. But it is of a rigid, ungraceful type, not leavened, as in the case of the Athenians, by a genuinely humane consciousness of the beautiful and true, and so not rendered fruitful in the realization of the higher glories of the associated life of man.

(*d*) *The Peloponnesian War.*—The Peloponnesian War was the sign and result rather than the cause of Grecian ruin. In it we witness no longer the positive working out of the constructive spiritual principle of Grecian civilization, but, the rather, the demonstration of the ideal limitation and imperfection of that principle.

It was impossible that the whole of Greece should be united in one common political body without detriment to Grecian freedom; for Grecian freedom was peculiarly freedom of individuality, and imperatively required the division of Greece into small States and concentration of men in cities, where, as before observed, there could be a substantial community of interests and likeness of mental development. And yet union of some kind and leadership were matters of controlling necessity, when all the States of Greece were threatened by a common Asiatic foe. The hegemony fell to the Athenians, who retained it and were enriched by it during the years of their greatest prosperity. In the Peloponnesian War the Athenian leadership was contested and brought to an end by Sparta. The "absolute gain of humanity" from this war is, not any contribution to the direct progress of human civilization, but Thucydides's "immortal" history of the greater portion of the war. The story of

Sparta's treasonable appeal for Persian intervention, and of the brief period of Theban supremacy, may here be omitted.

The theme offered us for consideration by the Peloponnesian War is the ruin of Greece.

Note, first, the brevity of the period of the highest and fairest bloom of Grecian civilization, which lasted only some sixty years, or from the Persian Wars to the Peloponnesian War. It could not be of long duration, in view of the character of the spiritual principle of which it was the fruit and the expression.

We have recognized the spiritual in man as that which constitutes him essentially and distinctively human. The "philosophy of history" is to us simply the story and the comprehension of the growth and manifestation of the spiritual character of man. But spiritual growth has its inherently determined order; it has its earlier and its later stages, at none of which, before the end of full development is reached, can it be permanently detained. Now, when we speak of the "spiritual principle" of Greece, we mean the human spirit at a determinate stage and in a peculiar form of development. The stage in question is here a comparatively early and unripe one; and just because it is really a stage in a growing existence, it must quickly pass away and give place for the more and better yet to come.

The Grecian spirit in its youthful freshness undoubtedly affects us with an impression of soundness and wholeness. But this soundness and wholeness are such as may be witnessed in a swelling but as yet unbroken germ, or in the short-lived blossom of the fruit-tree; the germ must burst, the flower must fall to the ground, before the full-grown tree or the ripened fruit can be in existence. A fundamental condition of spiritual maturity is what may best be termed rational self-consciousness. By this is meant chiefly a reflective, conscious, and confirmed knowledge of the truth, — the holding of the truth as a distinct and inalienable subjective possession of the individual; and then the consciousness of the truth as the true spiritual substance and foundation of the individual, the content of his will, and the motive power of all his conduct. The way to this end lies through the depths and dangerous quicksands of inward feeling, doubt, reflection. The child who in his infancy feels heaven immediately near him must submit to the pain of seeing it recede from him into the viewless distance, and must then find it again and take its kingdom as if by violence, before he can finally and permanently live in the full and assured glory of its light. Truth is indeed the very nature of the spirit; it is its first nature. But the human spirit never comes to live in the truth, and so according to its nature, until by an active independent labor it has conquered and taken possession of the truth, and thus conquered and taken possession of itself, causing the life in and according to the truth to be to it as a second nature. The Grecian spirit was as that of the youth who is not yet conscious of the serious labors, the cares and distractions, and also the victories of ripe manhood. The individual Greek, as we have seen, was born into a moral atmosphere, which he did not stay to analyze, but was content simply to breathe and to thrive upon from his birth till his death. He had not the reflective vanity to count himself for a possible something apart from the social-moral organism of which he was a lucky member; he was immediately one with this organism and in harmony with it. His Grecian morality was to him as a first and sufficient nature; his thought was unbroken by a sickly reflection; his highest conceptions of the divine and the beautiful clad themselves in those first and immediate forms of intelligence which sense supplies. These characters, which mark the fresh and healthy beauty of the Grecian spirit, were also the signs of its limitation and the seed of its ruin. It is not enough that a morality be unconsciously and spontaneously accepted; it must also be consciously and deliberately adopted. What I am to admit as right and good must approve itself within me, by the witness of my spirit. From that beauty which presents the true in a form adapted to sensible perception, I must go on to the absolute truth of an inward and supersensible world and to the beauty of holiness. And the way to this consummation (once more) lies by the untried paths of the inward individual spirit, — the paths of doubt, of "private judgment," of thought.

We are now perhaps prepared to understand Hegel's statement that the decay of Greece had its principle in the freer development of subjectivity. The signs and fruits of this development are witnessed in many ways. The Grecian religion of beauty is threatened by subjective thought: the political constitutions and laws are threatened by the passions and caprice of individuals. In brief, the whole ethical fabric of Grecian life is menaced by a conscious individualism that grows and manifests itself in all directions. "Thought thus appears here as the principle of corruption, — the corruption of substantial morality." Thought questions what was held to be unquestionable, and insists on general principles. "Parallel with the progress of the development of religious art and of the political condition goes the strengthening of the limbs of thought, their enemy and destroyer; and at the time of the Peloponnesian War science had already reached an advanced stage among the Greeks." If it was with the Sophists that the practice of questioning accepted beliefs and the authority of existing institutions began, it was Socrates who first declared to his fellow-countrymen the one thing needful for their fuller spiritual health. And this was, that they should not merely actually will and do the things that are right, but that they should do this knowingly. Moral intelligence, conviction, must be the decisive ground of action. The immediate result of such teaching was to set up a rival of the authority of fatherland and custom, and to make of the "subject"—the conscious, thinking, responsible person —an oracle, in the Grecian sense. Socrates, it is well known, actually professed to be guided by an oracle within, which made itself known to him in the form of a warning "daemonic" voice. So "through the rising inner world of subjectivity occurred the break with the world of immediate actuality." The principle that Socrates enunciated was true; it was the next higher truth to which the undeveloped principle of the Grecian world pointed. The acceptance and working out of the new principle could not but carry with it the destruction of the Grecian world in that which was most characteristic of the latter, — its serene beauty, its joyous freshness, its youthful wholeness. From the old-Grecian point of view, the sentence pronounced against Socrates was just. But Greece soon perceived that in condemning Socrates it had condemned itself. The new principle had widely taken root; the disease was widely spread and was no longer to be arrested. In the midst of the process of national decay the Athenian spirit still appeared noble and charming. It had indeed acquired irretrievably the propensity freely to ask and answer questions on all subjects; but it did not part with its well-poised cheerfulness and self-respect. In Sparta, on the contrary, the *contre-coup* of national decline was private corruption, with the moral vices of extreme individualism, — selfishness, avarice, venality.

(e) *The Macedonian Empire.* — The ultimate, deciding voice in Greece, which all were bound and accustomed to respect, had been that of the Delphian Apollo. The final death-blow was dealt to Grecian unity when the temple at Delphi was desecrated and plundered by the Phocians. It was natural that the next step to be taken should be the substitution of a single human will in the place of the divine will thus dethroned; and this substitution was accomplished by King Philip of Macedon, who, entering Hellas under pretext of avenging the injured honor of the Delphic deity, succeeded in establishing there the supremacy of the Macedonian kingdom. The great distinction of Philip is, that he prepared a kingdom for his illustrious son and successor, Alexander the Great.

The early education of Alexander was intrusted to Aristotle, the profoundest and most comprehensive thinker of the ancient world, and was conducted in a manner worthy of him who undertook it. Alexander was made acquainted with the deepest problems of metaphysics, — with the result that his natural disposition was completely refined and liberated from the ordinary fetters of mere opinion and intellectual crudeness and vanity. Aristotle, says Hegel, left this great nature in all its original untrammelled simplicity, but impressed on it a deep consciousness of that which is the True: he made the gifted spirit plastic, "like an orb floating unhindered in its own ether."

Such was the education of the man who undertook to avenge upon Asia its former insults to Greece. In carrying out this purpose, he repaid the Orient for the elements of culture that it had earlier lent to its Western rival, by extending over it the high and mature culture of Greece, and stamping as it were with an Hellenic character the lands conquered by him. The magnitude and interest of this work were in keeping with the genius and the peculiar youthful individuality of the conqueror. The direct fruits of Alexander's undertaking are traced by Hegel in the numerous Grecian or Grecian-Oriental dynasties and empires that followed in its train; but notably in Egypt, which became a great centre for science and art, and whose chief city, Alexandria, not only led the ancient world in commerce, but also became a meeting-place for Oriental custom and tradition and Occidental culture.

It was, in the view of our author, not only the good fortune of Alexander that he died young, — it was an ideal necessity. As the last representative of the Grecian world, — the world of spiritual youth, — it was needful that he should stand out in history, for posterity, only as a youth. "Just as Achilles, to repeat a previous remark, begins the Grecian world, so Alexander ends it; and these two youths not only give us the most beautiful impression of themselves, but also furnish a thoroughly complete and finished image of the Grecian character." In addition to Alexander's devotion to the sciences, it is to be noted that, next to Pericles, he is celebrated as the most generous patron of the arts.

C. — THIRD PERIOD: THE DESTRUCTION OF THE GRECIAN SPIRIT.

Under this last head we can well afford to be brief. Greece in its best days had been a collection of independent political individualities. The independence was now lost, but not the memory of it, nor the disposition to affect the airs of independence and to meditate on the possibilities of its recovery. The state of affairs brought to the front in Greece a series of individuals great and distinguished indeed, but exercising rather the gifts of diplomacy and eloquence than of military leadership. But the noblest intentions and the most skilfully laid plans could not restore that which was irrecoverably lost; namely, that ideal, ethico-religious bond of unity which had been the basis and fruitful condition of the healthful and independent development of the separate States, each according to its particular character. The sense of unity was no longer founded in solid reality; it was only an abstraction, and could oppose no successful barrier to the destructive floods of mutual jealousy and hatred.

The outward emancipation of Greece could not be accomplished without a previous work of inward emancipation, in a victory of the Grecian spirit over itself. What Greece could not do for itself, no foreign power could do for her; though the "liberation of Greece" became a common formula to express the object of the ambition of foreign kings and nations. At last the Romans turned themselves to this task, and the result of their contact with Greece was the immediate and objective demonstration of the hopeless inward dismemberment of the Grecian spirit and of Grecian life. "Over this individualism of passion, this disunity, which involves good and bad in a common ruin, there rises a blind fate, an iron power, made to reveal all the infamy and impotence of this condition, and to deal out miserable destruction, — for healing, amelioration, and comfort are now out of the question. This destructive fate are the Romans."

CHAPTER VII.

THE ROMAN WORLD.

IF Grecian civilization was like a perfect unstudied poem, the civilization of Rome has rather the character of reflective prose. Greece is a beautiful spirit, in a beautiful body; it is a richly endowed inward character, existing in all the undisturbed wholeness and freshness and sanity of youth, spontaneously manifesting and actualizing itself in the forms and instrumentalities of the natural world, as if the latter were its native element. The Grecian spirit, because inwardly unrent and outwardly spontaneous, is artless; and so, despite the verbal paradox, it achieves its own existence in the form of a work of art, and in the midst of a world of its own artistic creations. In Rome, on the other hand, " it is all over " (in Hegel's phrase) with this *natural* spontaneity and wholeness of spiritual existence. Rome is the practical spirit of early manhood, which has forgotten or learned to despise the happy dreams of youth, and finds life full of stern and sombre realities, of immediate, definite, practical problems, to cope with which it must limit and specialize its activities, must learn a rule, or rules, and force itself to walk thereby. Instead of bounding with natural and unconscious grace over the solid earth, it must learn, as it were, to walk artificially, on stilts, through mire. Its activity is not artistic, but mechanical; not spontaneously creative, but laboriously constructive. It withdraws those tentacles of the spirit which in youth reach out into the infinities, and finds its sphere in the prosaically finite and particular. It is definitely reflective; and the result of its reflection exists in the form of rigid, abstract, general ideas, — rules, laws, civil and military forms, and the like. The " abstract universal," which is as a Procrustean bed to the " particulars " subsumed under it, — that is the rule, that is the principle, of the Roman world. In accordance with this is the political ideal of the Romans, which is realized in the form of a universal dominion, whereby nations of the most diverse individuality are all brought under the yoke of a uniform rule or law. The results of this same principle are observable in the further character of this law itself, which in its relation to individuals has not regard to the concrete nature of individuality, with its uncodifiable rights, but is founded on the abstract notion of personality (see Chapter I., pp. 13 *et seq*), — the notion of formal freedom as the common note of every human individual, carrying with it, chiefly, the right to possess property, and to have this right maintained.

We consider the history of the Roman world in three Periods, analogous, in their relation to one another, to the three periods of Grecian history.

A.—ROME TILL THE SECOND PUNIC WAR.

I. *The Elements of the Roman Spirit.* —The signs of artificiality, of mechanical forcible construction, belong to Rome from the very beginning. The city itself sprang up in nobody's land, — in an angle, where three different districts, namely, those of the Latins, Sabines, and Etruscans, came together. Nor did Italy constitute geographically such a natural unity as is found in the valley of the Nile; still less were the tribes originally inhabiting the country joined by the bands of a homogeneous culture, — as was the case among the native tribes of Greece. The first community of Rome was a community of robbers, or of predatory herdsmen, — that is, it was a community having force for its main foundation-stone; there the criminal rabble from all quarters was welcomed. It was by an act of religious deceit, backed by violence, that, according to the tale, they first supplied themselves with wives.

In this story of the founding of Rome we must see the essential basis for the peculiarity of Roman life and discipline. A State founded on force must be held together by force. Of such a beginning the natural fruit is, not a spontaneous, ethical, liberal connection of man with man, of citizen with fellow-citizen, but a constrained condition of subordination. And the further relation of this to the peculiar character of Roman "virtue" is equally obvious. Roman *virtus* is valor, not merely personal but essentially corporate, or founded on the connection of the individual with his fellows in the bonds of the State, — which connection, born of necessity and cradled in violence, as it now appears as the best and most useful of things, is also regarded as the most sacred, for the maintenance of which any sacrifice on the part of the individual may be commanded and the most violent means may justly be employed. Every citizen was by original necessity a soldier.

The founders of the Roman State were not men living in the bonds of a tender and humanizing family relationship. We have alluded above to the deceit and violence which they employed in securing for themselves their first wives; so, in general, among the early Romans we find the family not grounded in a free relation of love and mutual confidence, but resting on a basis of despotic authority and severity on the one hand, and of complete dependence and subjection on the other. The wife was one among her husband's formal possessions, the civil form of the marriage ceremony being borrowed from that of a bill of sale. The power of the head of the family over wife and children resembled that of a Roman owner over his property; more nearly did it resemble the power of the State over the citizen, who, if he was a despot in his own family, was himself subject to the unqualified authority of the State. And this, adds Hegel, is the foundation of Roman greatness, the peculiar note of which was unrelenting inflexibility in the union of the individual with the State, and with its law and mandate. This is the prose of Roman life, in contrast with that turbulent poesy of the Oriental imagination, which instead of comprehending finite relations and reducing them to order simply inverts them and turns them topsy-turvy, and with the artistic, harmonious poetry and the perfectly poised freedom of the Grecian spirit. The consciousness of the Roman is definitely fixed and confined upon the finite, as such; his thought moves along the lines of the abstract understanding. What he grasps and fixes is the abstract notion and relations of legal personality, stripped of its rich garment of individual character and feeling, and of its potentialities reaching out into infinity; and in the place of ideals he puts a number of present and finite utilities.

It is to this bloodless and heartless understanding that Positive Law owes its origin and development. In the Oriental and Grecian worlds law was immediately one with religion, custom, ethical temperament; it could not segregate itself, so as to become an abstract, impersonal, inflexible form. Such a form the Romans made of it. Because the gift with which the Romans thus endowed human civilization is not to be regarded as the final embodiment of all wisdom and reason, it does not follow that its greatness need be underestimated. The Romans, as the authors of positive civil law, provided that formal mechanism of the civil State which is indispensably necessary for the secure existence and development of human freedom.

The like formalism and utilitarianism pervade the religion of the Romans. The poetic gods of Greece transferred to Roman soil become very prosaic affairs. When we hear the Romans talk of Jupiter, Juno, Minerva, we are impressed in much the same way as when we hear these names pronounced upon the stage. Their peculiar deities are abstractions (Peace, Care, Plague), or useful arts. The greater gods have their useful specialties. Juno, for example, among other things, is *Ossipagina*, the "Bone-fastener, or the goddess who causes the bones of children to become firm and solid." The Romans had no lack of "*sacra*." Almost every action and condition of life, whether private or public, had its appropriate ceremony, in the formal accomplishment of which the Roman was extremely conscientious. The joyous imagination and freedom of the Grecian worshipper, and the tender moral susceptibility of the Christian were lacking.

II. *History of Rome till the Second Punic War.* — The first development of social order among the Romans takes place under the leadership of Kings. Within the body politic, as determining factors of its growth and final character, Patricians and Plebeians are distinguished, through whose mutual conflicts and their solution Rome acquires the organic strength, under the leadership of elective Consuls in a republican polity, to enter into successful rivalry with the leading historical power next preceding it. We gather further from the legends that Rome at the first was constituted simply as a military community, religious ceremonies being introduced only later, under Numa, the second king. This feature is in striking contrast with the history of other peoples, whose religious traditions date from their earliest times, and antedate the development of civil institutions. In Rome the highest sacerdotal functions belonged to the political chieftain, or King.

The fact of leading importance in this first period is the gradual advancement of the Plebeians to the position of independent landholders, accompanied by the right to participate in the higher honors of the State. The earliest constitution of Roman society was strictly aristocratic; citizens distinguished for wealth, or otherwise, formed a body of "Fathers" (*Patres*, whence "Patricians"), or Senators. This was the first distinction within the State. Then the internal organization of the State was advanced by the recognition of different families (*gentes*) or classes, each distinguished by its specific part in the religious ceremonies. The division of the people into classes is ascribed to Servius Tullius, who also especially aroused the anger of the Patricians by wiping out a portion of the debts of the Plebeians and assigning to the poorer among them a portion of the public lands. The tendency of the Kings (who were almost all of foreign origin) was generally to curb the pretensions of the Patricians, and to cultivate the favor of the people. The final banishment of the Kings was the work of the Patricians, and not of the Plebeians. It is worthy of remark, in passing, that the immediate occasion for this action was found in an offence committed against the sacredness of the marriage relation. However deficient family life may have been among the Romans in the flowers and fruit of sentiment, these people were the first to see in the foundation principle of the family—the relation of man and wife—something absolutely sacred and inviolable. This followed of necessity from that which we must regard as the essential and defining character of the Roman spirit; namely, the respect for abstract personality, for the formal freedom and right of the individual will, or, as Hegel terms it, the "principle of subjectivity." We find the recognition and maintenance of the principle of monogamy following among the Romans, as an apparent matter of course. The same feeling, in its general character, that prompted the revolt of the Patricians against the Kings, led to subsequent risings of the *Plebs* against the Patricians, and of the Latins and their allies against the Romans; till finally the equality of private persons throughout the Roman dominion was established as a principle to be, not simply respected, but actively maintained by the despotic authority of the State.

The banishment of the Kings inured wholly to the immediate advantage of the aristocracy. A republican form of government was instituted, at the head of which stood two Consuls, elected for the period of one year; but the Plebeians were excluded from power. The details of the long contest, which ended by rendering them eligible to all offices and dignities, must here be omitted; special mention may be made, however, of the agrarian laws, by the passage of which a limit was placed upon the amount of landed property that might be vested in a single owner, and a share in such ownership was secured for the Plebeians.

The conclusion of these long contests left Rome provided with a political organization and a stock of national energy that enabled it to enter upon the career of war, and finally of universal conquest, in which her greatness was to be shown to the world. By the "small trade" of the wars nearer home, which fall into this first epoch, the Romans made themselves the "capitalists of the peculiar energy with which they were destined subsequently to appear on the stage of the world."

B.—FROM THE SECOND PUNIC WAR TO THE EMPIRE.

In the First Punic War the Romans had shown themselves a match for powerful Carthage, which had in its possession a large portion of the coast of Africa, together with southern Spain, and had also a firm footing in Sicily and Sardinia. The Second Punic War overthrew the power of Carthage, though only after a protracted period of stubborn resistance under the leadership of the great Hannibal. Through this war the Romans came into hostile contact with the King of Macedonia, whom a little later they conquered. Then came the turn of Antiochus, King of Syria, by their victory over whom the Romans became masters of Asia Minor as far as the Taurus. In the Third Punic War Carthage was again subjugated, and the city was reduced to ashes. Next, the liberty of Greece, which along with that of Macedonia the Romans had previously proclaimed, fell a prey to the Roman greed for power. The Romans sought occasion for war, destroyed Corinth in the same year with Carthage, and made of Greece a Roman province.

So Rome became the mistress of the Mediterranean Sea,—that is, of the geographical centre of all culture. In this period of victory it is the ethically great and fortunate individuals — conspicuously the Scipios — who attract our attention. "Ethically fortunate" we term them, notwithstanding the outward misfortune in which the career of the greatest of the Scipios ended, because they were permitted actively to serve their country while it was still ideally sound and whole. But this condition was of short duration. The mind of Rome was the thirst for dominion. In the time of national danger and of those wars in which the fruits of victory were gathered in, Roman *virtus* was at its best; this period over, and the lust for power being satisfied, the Romans suffered, so to express it, a spiritual collapse. The valued fruit of victory to the Romans was booty, riches, renown, and not that noble undisturbed "leisure" so precious to the thought of the Greeks, in which a spirit quick to its own higher interests, to art and science, may ideally recreate, live over again, and enjoy that which it has previously accomplished in the field of action. Accordingly, we now find selfish interests beginning to enter into successful rivalry with the claims of patriotism. Wealth increases, founded on the spoils of war and the spoils of the tax-gatherer, rather than on industry and honest labor. From the Asiatic provinces luxury and license are introduced into Rome; corruption becomes general. Rome as a moral national personality is no more. The sceptre of authority is bandied about among individuals, whose rise and fall are governed by no other law than that of violence. Some of these individualities are "colossal," and animated by loyalty to the old type of Roman patriotism; but none of them are able to keep themselves untouched by the general corruption. The end is — Caesar and the Empire.

This end is not accidental,— it is necessary. The principle of the Roman nationality was dominion, military power. This principle was a sufficient organizing force for the Republic while the dangers imposed by the necessities of self-defence and self-assertion lasted, and in the first exciting hours of victory; but no longer. In Caesar's time the Republic existed only as a shadow. What Pompey, and all those who were on the side of the Senate, called the power of the Republic, and sought to establish, was their own particular dignity, authority, and supremacy. The "power of the Republic" was nothing but a phrase, and its use a piece of empty formalism, to which Caesar put an end. He reconsolidated the Roman nationality by forcibly allaying the internal conflicts of private interests and ambitions, concentrating all power in his own hands, and through his Transalpine expeditions fixing the eye of Rome upon the predestined centre of the next great movement in the history of civilization. That he did not form a false judgment of that for which the times were ripe, is shown by the fact that his work survived his own violent death. Caesar died: the Empire lived.

C.—LATER HISTORY OF THE ROMAN WORLD.

I. *The Empire.*—We have seen, in a measure, how it lay in the character of Rome to stand in the history of civilization for the principle of abstract personality. From this principle,—the principle of the formal, personal, absolutely self-asserting will, —flowed the Roman lust for dominion, as well as the peculiar mechanism of Roman "right," or law. We have now to consider the final developments of this principle in the time of Rome's contact with the new people and the new principle of a stage of civilization destined to take the place of the Roman.

Looking, first, at the character of the imperial rule, we note that its introduction occasioned almost no alteration in the constitution of the social fabric; and this, because the rule of Rome both within and without was so mechanical an affair. The popular assemblies, indeed, came to an end; the various dignities of *princeps senatus*, censor, consul, and tribune continued, at least in name, and were united in the person of the Emperor, in whose hands alone was also lodged the control of the military power. That modicum of organic public spirit which had for a time sufficed to animate this mechanism of different functions, and to maintain the latter in harmonious operation while distributed among different persons, had long since disappeared. The mechanism, none the less, still remained; and the simple and only way to rescue it from destruction and render it longer efficient was to place the whole control of it in the hands of a single person. Who this person should be was determined, not by a fixed law of succession, but in the majority of cases by the choice of the army, on whose support the authority of the Emperor immediately depended.

In the exercise of his authority the Emperor was absolute, irresponsible; in his person an individual, subjective will,— subject, as such, to no law but that of its own arbitrary fancies, — was set upon the throne of the world. "Abstract personality,"— personality in the primary legal acceptation of the term, manifesting itself in ownership as the elementary and original expression of the free and independent human will, — is now rendered supreme; the Roman world is the possession of the Emperor. What differentiates this despotism from Oriental autocracy is the fact that it comes to existence in the midst of a social fabric having a legal mechanism. Imperial ownership, though absolute (like all true ownership), has the formal sanction of law, and is exercised through a mechanism of legal forms which secure for society a certain fixed, even if petrified, character. So it is that the Emperors "rule, but do not govern;" they simply exercise their abstract right of ownership. Those among them who are of noble character and disposition do nothing for the organization of Roman life on a freer basis; while under the abominable tyranny of

Domitian the Roman historians even mention that the Roman world enjoyed a period of repose! In general, however, it is to be said that the "whole empire lay prostrate under a burden of taxation and robbery. Italy was depopulated; the most fruitful lands lay uncultivated. This condition hung like a fate over the Roman world."

Turning next to the condition of individuals as legal persons, we observe that all were on an absolute equality (even the condition of slavery made but slight difference) and without any political rights. The laws relating to persons were the laws relating to the possession of property, in which the equality just mentioned was developed and perfected. In this way the individual, politically a nullity, became in his relation to the social body just an atom, having such right to exist and to possess as a social atom can have, and no other.

Finally, the spiritual condition involved in such a social state is quickly estimated. The elements in this state, once more, are simply these: On the one hand a universal rule, resembling in its relations to individuals an all-inclusive fate; on the other hand individuals, each possessing the enormous spiritual advantage over the subjects of Oriental empires of occupying a recognized legal status as an independent person, but limited in the manifestation and realization of this personality to the exercise of a qualified ownership of external things. Between these two extremes stands a morally empty chasm; they are not joined in the unity of a common, spontaneous, concrete, organic, and organizing public spirit. The inward condition of the individual, conscious of this complete break of continuity between himself and his world, must therefore of necessity be that of one who simply submits to fate and cultivates the spirit of complete indifference to life,—whether thoughtfully, by turning to "philosophy," or by drowning thought in the waves of sensual indulgence. Many of the minds of nobler temper adopted the former course, finding in the systems of the time — in Stoicism, Epicureanism, or Scepticism — the means of rendering the mind indifferent to all the relations of the actual world, or in all things "imperturbable." Scepticism, the last of these philosophies, sought to secure for man the mind undisturbed, by teaching him that in good reason the supreme aim of the human will is or must be aimlessness itself. So this philosophy was a "counsel of despair for a world to which nothing fixed remained. It could not satisfy the living spirit that demanded a higher reconciliation."

II. *Christianity.* — Caesar opened up the locality of the world that was predestined to succeed Rome, — the modern world. Under Augustus its spiritual principle had its birth.

The Roman Emperor was a finite, limited individual, invested with unlimited prerogatives. So the Empire practically asserted for a finite being, considered in his finite quality, a quasi-infinite or absolute character. Near the beginning of the Empire, the supreme organizing force of the modern world was born in the form of a particular person, the Son of Mary, Jesus of Nazareth, — to whom, however, finitude was but the form of his historic appearance, while his true substance, his essential character, was absolute and perfect spirituality, which is the true infinitude.

The whole Roman world under the Empire was, spiritually considered, in pain; and its pain could be compared to the "birth-throes of another and higher spirit, which was revealed with the Christian religion." In this higher spirit the human spirit was brought to be at one with itself; it was elevated into harmony with itself, and was set free through that amplified self-knowledge which came to it through the revelation of the Spirit, which is the Truth. The absolute Reality, the reality of all realities; the absolute Truth, the truth of all truths, — in which human knowledge and human will by their very nature imperatively require to be planted as the only possible condition of final and positive satisfaction, — was at last known as spiritual, as the Triune God. The goal of all previous history, and the starting-point for all history to come, were reached.

But only when the times were "fulfilled" did, or could, God complete the revelation of Himself by "sending his Son." The seed-time goes before the time of harvest. The seed of spiritual self-knowledge, and of the knowledge of God as spirit, was sown in the dark soil of pre-Christian history. The seed sown must first swell in the ground, and then burst, before it can issue forth in a more adequate and glorious form of existence in the upper air. Greece is the swelling seed of the spirit and of spiritual self-knowledge; Rome is its bursting and breaking up; Christianity is the fruit-bearing stock, growing up in the actual sunlight of the spirit, and becoming, in its turn, a distributor of this light for the healing of the nations.

The spiritual law of Grecian civilization had been, "Man, know thyself." Fulfilling this command, the Greek had decidedly the consciousness of himself as a spiritual being, and of the spiritual character of the ruling powers of the universe. But this consciousness was not pure; the spiritual was known only as in immediate unity with the natural and sensible. The Gods accordingly were not one Spirit, but many spiritual individualities clad in various naturalistic forms. The highest spiritual conceptions of the Greeks were therefore only such as art could represent, in which the sensuous is employed as a medium of beautiful expression, but not refined in the crucible of pure thought. While the Greek was conceiving that which is spiritual, we may say that his eye, like that of Xenophanes, was directed outwardly, — "to the visible universe." It was needful that the eye should be turned inwards, upon the things unseen, in the inner sanctuary of conscious personality and will.

What the Greeks thus lacked, the Roman spirit, so inferior to the Grecian in other respects, possessed, though in a manner far too elementary, indefinite, and formal. The Roman certainly had the eye turned within, but what the eye perceived was in the main only a rigid, abstract form, — the form which received its most perfect expression in the theory of legal personality. To have grasped and fixed this form was no small achievement in itself; it was an invaluable contribution to civilization. But this form was capable of being associated with any sort of content; which means that legal personality carried with it no presumption respecting personal character. The legal person might be a good man or a bad one, indifferently. To the development of the spiritual consciousness of man, then, the Romans contributed the notion of formal personality: a spiritual being, whether divine or human, is a person, an individual centre of consciousness and volition, of possible rights and obligations. And this was the whole extent of their contribution. Nothing was included therein respecting the positive and concrete character necessarily involved as a content in all true spiritual reality, nothing regarding God as Spirit Supreme and Absolute, and nothing concerning the essential relations that must connect all the persons of the spiritual world.

To what results the development of the Roman principle led, we have already partially seen. Each person under the Empire was, so to speak, a spiritual atom, having all the characters that belong to an atomic state of existence, and no others; each had the status of an independent being, invested with a recognized abstract right (defined in the law of property); and the right of one was just like the right of another. But all were subject to the inflexible authority of one, the Emperor, who as a sort of *monas monadum* was the incarnate force that no "spiritual atom" could resist. All these legally independent private owners were themselves owned, — to wit, by the imperial head of the State. By the same law, or legalized state of things, the independent personality of the individual was at once formally recognized and denied. This contradiction, Hegel declares, was the misery of the Roman world. But the misery, again, was disciplinary in its character. What the law of Moses was to the Hebrews, that was the law of Imperial Rome to the world included under its sway; namely, a schoolmaster to prepare the spirits of men for the truth as it is in Jesus. It is not, of course, that the Roman world saw in this, its spiritual experience, a disciplinary character, or anything whatsoever but the work of a blind fate; it is only we who standing at a higher and later point of view may see this.

What, now, was the exact situation that had been reached, and what was the next problem to be solved in the onward course of human development? In the Roman world mankind had risen beyond that stage of social development at which the individual — with the *one* exception of the chief or ruler — has no independent moral standing (the Oriental world); and also beyond that other stage (of the Grecian world) at which *some* individuals, — namely, all citizens, — possess in fact such standing, but wear the honors of independent individuality in the main unconsciously, being absorbed and satisfied by the organic public or common life of which each is an unconstrained member. In the Roman world, individuality we may say becomes consciously proud and jealous of its right, which right, however, under the Empire declares itself nothing more than an empty form. The problem now is, wherewith shall this empty form — whose worth and right, as such, are indefeasibly established, and which therefore is not to be cast away — be filled? For what shall the spiritually famished individual hunger and thirst? How while retaining his independent individuality, and without prejudice to that of others, shall he be replenished so as to "possess all things"? How shall he thus be made free indeed, and that with a freedom which can be monopolized neither by one man nor by some, but is the inalienable birthright of all? One thing is certain; the problem in question could not become a practical one, and could therefore not be brought to a practical solution, — in other words, the step forward in the development of the human spirit which is marked by the introduction of Christianity could not be taken, until on the one hand the consciousness of human individuality became as distinctly marked and defined as it was in the Roman world, and on the other the sense of its helplessness and emptiness, or of its inherent want, became equally pronounced. Abstract personality, the individual separate Ego, the self-centred personal will, must become aware of its intrinsic "negativity" in order to be prepared for the influx of positive life and substance. It must be in pain; it must feel the pain of its own nothingness, the misery of its own nature, and the longing for a remedy.

This pain the Romans under the Empire felt, though they understood but little of its meaning; whence also their longing was mainly a hopeless one, a longing of despair, which they sought to drown in a sea of sensuous excitements and pleasures, or else covered up under a mantle of proud resignation to the decrees of inexorable destiny. It is not among the Romans, but among the Jewish people, whom the Romans had brought under the same yoke with themselves, that we find not only the pain, but also a longing that is positive, and full of hope and confidence, because definitely directed toward the quarter whence cometh indeed, and whence alone can come, the help of the human spirit. That which we are speaking of finds purest and most beautiful expression in the Psalms of David and in the Prophets, the burden of which is the thirsting of the soul after God, the bitter pain of spiritual defect and of sin, and the desire for righteousness and holiness.

In harmony herewith is the tale of the fall of man, found at the very beginning of the books devoted to the narration of Jewish history. Man, created in the image of God, forfeited, we are told, his state of absolute satisfaction by eating of the fruit of the tree of the knowledge of good and evil. The deep truth is here expressed, that the condition of sin is conscious knowledge. In knowledge alone did man sin; through it alone did he become separated from his natural happiness. Moral good and evil, spiritual perfection and imperfection, are relative only to a conscious, knowing subject. The brute knows not, and is guiltless; it has in its own eyes neither merit nor demerit. The like is true of the merely natural man. It is only with the awakening of consciousness to the reflective knowledge of good and evil, that conscience itself is awakened; it is only then that the spiritual man is awakened, or that man comes distinctly to exist as a spiritual being, clad with a responsibility that marks in the most intense and decisive manner his independent individuality, and causes him indeed to be "as a god," or "in the image" of the divine independence.

By this story of man's fall the "problem" above mentioned is brought before us in its most elementary and comprehensive form. What the story records is not merely a single event that once occurred in the beginning (as it happened) of human history; it is "the eternal story" of the human spirit. If man is to be a spiritual being at all, he must be a rationally self-conscious, cognitive one. The fulfilment of this condition involves the distinction in thought of the self-conscious Ego, — *of me*, who am conscious of *myself*, — as a free and independent agent of knowledge and volition, from other objects, possible or actual, of its knowledge and will. The very first step in the process whereby I am constituted a spiritual being involves thus among other things, and chiefly, the distinction and hence separation of myself from God. Through this dangerous pass the individual spirit must go, as the very condition of its attaining to real spiritual existence. In this sense, the lapse of man from God, — the breaking up of the original state of unreflecting innocence, of harmony and unity with God, the universal divine Spirit,—is inherently and universally necessary. But to stop at this point is to plant the seed of all evil. It is to succumb to what we may term the first danger of our nature; it is to employ the first-fruits of our knowledge irresponsibly; it is to will and act as though we were "gods," in the sense of beings subject to no law of things, to no universal moral order, to no will of God, to no law even of our own nature, but authorized to do simply "as we like;" it is to incur the pain of spiritual disturbance, of an evil planted in the roots of our active nature, of a bad conscience. It is this feeling of pain and of longing prompted thereby that we detect in David, when he sings, "Create in me a clean heart, O God; and renew a right spirit within me!" This same feeling of self-inflicted spiritual hurt and pain is expressed in the story of the fall, accompanied by the assurance that it is not irremediable. Recovery is predicted and promised, to come in the fulness of time.

Note, further, that the fall is the incident of the first step of self-conscious knowledge and will. It would be only formal and without evil consequence if man, instead of lingering at it and practically conducting himself as though it were the final one, went on without break to the other steps still requisite for perfect intelligence. By this first step he distinguishes and separates himself from all other things and beings, and goes on to ascribe to himself, practically, irresponsible independence. By the steps which must follow, in order that knowledge may be according to its own nature complete, the chasm thus apparently established between him and all objects of his knowledge and will is to be bridged over; he is to know, not only his distinction from all other things and beings, but also his essential connection and union with them. So his self-knowledge is to acquire a positive content, his will a substantial motive, and his conduct a fixed and valid law. And this process, which is at once the perfecting of intelligence and the perfecting of the spiritual man, is, according to the Christian revelation, completed only when the connection mentioned is established in knowledge and will between man and God; between the individual, conscious agent of knowledge and volition and the supreme and final object of knowledge and inspirer of the will ; between the finite, growing spirit, whose nature impels it to seek the truth, and which can truly exist only as it possesses and is possessed by the truth, and the absolute Spirit, who is the Truth. "This is life eternal, that they might know Thee, the only true God, and Jesus Christ, whom Thou hast sent." Salvation is by the truth. Redemption, restoration, spiritual perfection, is by, through, and in the truth. "The truth shall make you free." So the hurt of sin, the lapse from God which came by knowledge, is to be healed, not by ignorance, still less by the suppression of the activity of intelligence, but by and in the sphere of knowledge itself.

But only when the time should come. The need of man could be satisfied only by an infinite object, only by an actual and vital and absolute resting in God. The first satisfactions of man, as traced in the historical books of the Jewish people, were not of this kind; they were finite ones, in the family and in the possession of the land of Canaan. Their satisfaction was not an absolute satisfaction in God. Doubtless many an ardent soul joined in the longing of King David, and prayed, "Uphold me with thy free Spirit!" But the full answer to this prayer was deferred. The service of God was one of visible sacrifices in the Temple, and of penitential regret in the heart; He was not yet fully worshipped, because He was not yet fully known or comprehended, as a Spirit, and as the Truth. God was still afar off. But the Jewish people were robbed of their outward satisfaction, in family and in territorial possession, under the rod of the Roman Empire. The Romans attacked their very individuality; the Temple was destroyed, and the people were trampled in the dust. Thus every satisfaction was taken away, and the Jewish people were thrown back into a condition resembling that depicted in the story of the fall, the leading elements of their consciousness being the sense of a pain lodged in human nature itself and the thought of God, — accompanied, in the present case, by a feeling of intense and despairing longing after a help that could come only from God.

The time was now "fully come." Man in the Roman world at large, man in the more limited sphere of Israel's spiritual development, was now prepared for that fulfilment of knowledge which could only come to him as a new and glorious revelation, and whereby it was to be perceived that the God of whom Adam had been afraid was the spiritual friend whom the individual not only might but must receive within the precincts of his own conscious individual life, in order that he might be truly filled. It was revealed that the truly human " filling" of the empty form of human individuality was at the same time divine. Man's perfection and true strength were in and through union with God; his true increase was to be an "increase of God;" so far as he really followed the command to become perfect even as his Father in heaven is perfect, he was to become a partaker of the divine nature. Thus, though otherwise possessing nothing, he was indeed to possess all things; he was to become in life's battle a conqueror, and more than a conqueror. So Christianity fully revealed man to himself as a *spiritual* being, a *spiritual conscious individual*, the proper fulfilment or perfection of whose own nature as spiritual was to be attained by nothing short of organic union with God, — as the branch is united to the vine. This union was to be reached through the knowledge of the true God, who is a spirit, and by having Him in all one's thoughts; and, on the other hand, by finding in the content of this knowledge the supreme motive of the human will. Thus man, who had for centuries been in quest of his own true and spiritual self, and of his God, was to be brought into the enjoyment of complete self-possession. Instead of being merely a spiritually empty conscious *individual*, alone in the world, he was to be filled and satisfied, and henceforth not alone, but as a son of God dwelling in the protecting companionship of his heavenly Father and of the glorious company of all believers.

We may say that before the coming of the light of Christianity it was just as true as it is now — that is, it was abstractly a universal truth — that the perfection of a spiritual being such as man consists in its organic union, in the spheres of thought and will, with the one absolute Spirit, who is God. It was abstractly true; but the truth, though men felt after it, was not comprehended. In Christianity this truth was, to the infinite comfort and joy of man, and as a source of immeasurable confidence and strength to the human spirit, brought out or revealed.

The union (or "unity," *Einheit*) of man with God, according to this Christian conception, is not, says Hegel, to be superficially conceived, as though man were simply God, — that is, individually identical with him, or God with man. Man "is God" — that is, as a son of God, by a "new" and spiritual "birth," he is a "partaker of the divine nature" and filled with the divine presence — only so far as he puts off the "old man," the "natural man," whose thought and will are engaged and limited by finite things, and puts on the "new" or spiritual man. The individuality of man — of each particular man — is thereby not abrogated, but emphasized. It is simply that from being a spiritually empty and wretched individual he now becomes filled, and is at peace with himself, with God, and with the world. He remains individually distinct from God and dependent on Him, but as an object of the divine love and recipient of God's richest bounty, — namely, of God himself, — he acquires, he is revealed to himself as possessing, infinite worth. So Christianity introduced the thought and the knowledge of the inherent equality, the equal and infinite worth, of all men.

The content of this new, or "Christian," consciousness was subsequently, and correctly, formulated in the doctrine of the Trinity. This doctrine is a formal statement of what God as a spirit is; it is a statement of what Absolute Spirit is, and, since "the Spirit is the Truth," of what the universal and Absolute Reality is that conditions and creates all dependent reality. The *abstract* meaning of the doctrine is to be apprehended and expressed only by considering the nature of the fundamental attributes that constitute a spiritual being, and that are ascribed in the Christian scriptures to God. These attributes are intelligence ("light," "truth") and love; in God, as the perfect being, these attributes are to be conceived and considered as existing in their perfection. Now, the common character of both intelligence (or knowledge) and love[1] is that they imply an object on which they are directed, — an object known and loved. This object is, from the nature of the case, *distinguished* from the intel-

[1] The daily ejaculation of Trithemius, Benedictine Abbot of Sponheim, "To know is to love!" was neither paradox nor fancy.

ligent and loving subject. The completion of the process of intelligence and love implies, nevertheless, that the subject and object mentioned shall not be and remain simply distinct. In spite of their distinction, the object, in order to be known and loved, must come into a vital and organic union with the knowing and loving subject; the object known must enter into the self-consciousness, the self-knowledge, of the knowing agent, and so become one, or at one, with the latter; and the loving agent must, in the spirit of self-forgetfulness and self-abnegation, — that is, treating himself as though he were in himself nothing and of nothing worth, — actively identify with himself the object loved, putting it in his own place and treating it as though it were himself. Both intelligence and love thus alike imply at once the distinction and the identification of terms (things, beings) abstractly opposed to each other as "subject" and "object." Note that the "identification" does not simply follow after and annul the "distinction;" on the contrary, the former is possible only on condition that the latter exists and is maintained. This paradox of sense is solved in the living, active processes of intelligence and love, whereby a spiritual being is constituted, and is the central truth of spiritual being, — the central truth of all truths. This truth is illustrated in a limited way in the experience of a finite spiritual being like man; it is illustrated in exact proportion to the degree in which any individual emerges from merely "natural" into a truly spiritual existence. In God, the Absolute Being, the perfect Spirit, the illustration of it is perfect; and this is just what the doctrine of the Trinity states. The Father, as subject of intelligence and love, is identified with, and identifies with Himself, his co-equal Son, as His absolute or perfect object: in the Son the Father becomes objective to himself. Father and Son are as necessarily distinct as are subject and object in the processes of intelligence and love; they are as necessarily equal as are subject and object in perfect, absolute, or unqualified intelligence and love. Their union in these processes, or their "identification" (in the sense above defined), is the "Spirit." Father, Son, and Holy Spirit, — these three inseparable "persons" are the one God.[1]

Finally, the truth about the world of finite existences, according to Christianity, is that they live and move and have their being in God. The way in which this truth is contained in the doctrine of the Trinity, as a formula logically inclusive of all truth, is as follows: The Son is the creative and sustaining principle of all finite being; he was not simply once in the world, a stranger, incarnate in the Son of Mary, — when in this character he came, he came "unto his own;" the world, Nature, the finite human spirit, had ever existed, and evermore exist, only by the "word of his power;"

---

[1] Pope's line,

"All Nature's difference keeps all Nature's peace,"

has its application in the realm of the divine nature. The "personal" difference in the divine nature "keeps" — is the eternal condition of — the "peace of God."

they are particular works and revelations of him, in whom dwelleth the fulness of the Godhead, — he is the everlasting Word, of which they are the growing historic manifestation. In this sense, Christianity brought to man the consciousness of a vital connection of his nature, or being, with the absolute Power and Reality of the universe, — that is, with God. This connection he was barred from conceiving in any merely carnal, material, or physical way; it was fundamentally spiritual, and by nature rather potential than actual; it could be fully actualized only "through the truth," or through the active spiritual processes of intelligence and love: man must know and love God. Now man could comprehend and become reconciled to the spiritual wretchedness through which he had passed; he could see that it was due to his having distinguished and separated himself in self-conscious, abstract, wilful independence from God, the supreme object of knowledge. He could also see in what sense this was a necessary incident in the actual development in him of true spiritual quality; he could see, too, how the law, whether of the Roman world or of the Jewish church, in emphasizing one-sidedly his individual right and obligation, had really sold him "under sin," at the same time that as a schoolmaster it prepared him for the "grace" revealed in Christ.

The truths we have been considering, which in their interest for man centre in the notion of the both possible and necessary, or required, union of man in the development of his spiritual nature with God, constitute what we may term the speculative, logical, or purely spiritual content of the Christian revelation. But it was not in this abstract form that they were, or could be, first brought to the consciousness and knowledge of man. The truths that man with his mixed intellectual constitution, such that his spiritual intelligence must be a gradual growth out of natural or sensible beginnings, can know, are alone such as are presented to him under forms that correspond to and respect the laws of this growth. The central truths respecting the inner, spiritual nature of man and his relations to God could not possibly enter into his consciousness, except they were first presented to him incarnate in a sensible object;[1] and the only sensible form in which the living Spirit, which is the Truth, could be presented, was that of man. "Christ appeared,— a man, who was God; and God, who was man; in this way peace and reconciliation were brought to the world." God in Christ, the God-man, appeared on earth as a particular, historic individual. Moreover, after passing through many of the ordinary vicissitudes of human life, he died. It was only after his death that the Son of Man became fully declared as the Son of God; it was only then that he could be fully recognized in this character,— that is, in his spiritual character,— or that he could completely manifest himself in it. After he should

---

[1] In this connection the language of Saint John is very significant: "That which . . . we have heard, which we have seen with our eyes, which we have looked upon, and our hands have handled, of the Word of life, . . . declare we unto you." — 1 *John i.* 1. 3.

have gone away he promised to come again, as the "Spirit of truth," to guide his followers into all truth. So it was not while Christ as an historic individual was with them, but only afterward, on the day of Pentecost, that the Apostles were filled with the Holy Ghost; then first the scales fell from their eyes, and they all knew their Master. And so it is that modern criticism, attending exclusively to the details of the historic life of the individual Jesus, may be blind to and deny him in his true spiritual character as the Son of God. The essential question is not, What was Christ, unspiritually considered? but, What was he viewed in the light of the Spirit? What was he in the truth of the Spirit? What was that "truth" and "life" which he declared himself truly to be?

The Christian idea, or principle, was announced with incomparable energy by Jesus. It was announced as an end to be aimed at, as an absolute command; it contemplated the development in man of spiritual purity and perfection, making of man's membership in the spiritual world the supreme reality, upon the demand of which all worldly ties are to be set at nought. "Blessed are the pure in heart, for they shall see God;" "Blessed are the peacemakers, for they shall be called the children of God;" "Blessed are they which are persecuted for righteousness' sake, for theirs is the kingdom of heaven;" "Be ye perfect, even as your Father which is in heaven is perfect," — obedience to these commands of the spirit is represented as the true basis of worldly prosperity: "Seek ye first the kingdom of God and his righteousness, and all these things shall be added unto you." Then the doctrine, because in its first announcement abstract, becomes polemical. "If thy right eye offend thee, pluck it out;" "If thy right hand offend thee, cut it off, and cast it from thee;"—anything that might interfere with the purity of the soul is to be put out of the way. With regard to property and its acquisition, the language used is, "Take no thought for your life, what ye shall eat, or what ye shall drink; nor yet for your body, what ye shall put on. Is not the life more than meat, and the body than raiment?" And again, "If thou wilt be perfect, go and sell that thou hast, and give to the poor, and thou shalt have treasure in heaven: and come and follow me." The doctrine of Christ is even of such exalted character that all ordinary duties and ethico-social ties appear, and are represented as, in comparison with it, inferior and indifferent. "Follow me; and let the dead bury their dead;" "He that loveth father or mother more than me is not worthy of me;" "Who is my mother? and who are my brethren? . . . whosoever shall do the will of my Father which is in heaven, the same is my brother, and sister, and mother." Nay, more, we even read, "Think not that I am come to send peace on earth: I came not to send peace, but a sword. For I am come to set a man at variance against his father, and the daughter against her mother, and the daughter-in-law against her mother-in-law." In these words we find a complete abstraction from all the actually established relations of life, including the social-moral ones. Nowhere, we may say, has such revolutionary language ever been employed, as in the Gospels.

Such was the Christian principle — the seed of Christianity — as historically announced. The next thing was its development. The first step was the forming of a society or church on the part of the friends of Christ. It has already been remarked that it was only after the death of Christ that the Spirit could come upon his friends, so that they could comprehend the true idea of God and the truth that in Christ man is redeemed and reconciled to God; then alone could they see how Christ was himself the revelation of the truth, that the essential nature of man is spiritual, and that man attains the truth only by loosening the bands of his finite relations and cultivating the purely spiritual self-consciousness. And then only could they comprehend that Christ, the "Son of Man," in whom the union of God and man was manifest, had by his life and death pointed out the eternal way of the Spirit, — the way which every man must personally follow in order truly to exist as a spirit, or to become a child of God and citizen of his kingdom. The disciples of Christ, uniting themselves under the inspiration of these truths at last perceived by them, and "living in the spiritual life as their aim," constitute the Church, which is God's kingdom. "Where two or three are gathered together in my name" (that is, in that character, which I am), says Christ, "there am I also in the midst of them." The Church is an actual and present life in the spirit of Christ.

In view of such facts as the foregoing, Hegel adds that the Christian religion is by no means to be judged merely by the express and recorded sayings of Jesus. The Christian truth as developed truth is to be learned from the Apostles. Or, more generally, it was in the Church ("*Gemeinde*") that the content of the Christian principle was positively developed and brought out.

The Church now stood in a double relation,—first to the Roman world; and secondly to the Truth, the development of which was its inherent aim.

Under the first head we have only to remark, briefly, that it was in the Roman world that the Church found itself existing, and that the extension of the Christian religion was to take place. The Church was to constitute a distinct society within the State, holding itself aloof from all political activity; it acknowledged the Emperor, but could not, like the Roman, admit his absolute or unqualified authority. Hence came persecution and hatred of the Christians; and then was revealed the limitless inward freedom of the Christian spirit, through the amazing steadfastness and patience with which sufferings were endured for the sake of the highest truth. It was less the miracles of the Apostles than the truth of their doctrines thus manifested in its power to strengthen and set free the human spirit, which gave to Christianity its outward extension and inward strength.

Regarding the other relation of Christianity,— its relation to the truth implicit in it and awaiting developed expression,— it is particularly important, says Hegel, to note that the theoretical development of the Christian principle, in the form of dogma, occurred before its practical application as an organizing power in the realm of civil and political affairs. The former took place within the limits of the Roman world; the latter, elsewhere and later. It was the Church, through its fathers and councils, that undertook the dogmatic definition of the content of the spiritual revelation made in and through the person of Christ. It was the Church as an " Holy Church," the whole body of the faithful " builded together into an habitation of God through the Spirit," the corporate and living temple of the promised Spirit which was to lead them " into all truth," in whose name the dogmas of the Christian faith were defined. In them the Church declared its mind as the mind and truth of Christ, surviving and growing into clearer consciousness in the Church, which is " his body." In the Nicene Council, 325 A. D., a confession of faith was formulated which is still retained in the Church. "This confession," says Hegel, "had indeed no speculative form; but profound speculative truth is therein most intimately interwoven with the facts of Christ's life and death. In the beginning of Saint John's Gospel we see the beginning of a more thoughtful apprehension of the truth as it is in Jesus; the profoundest thought is connected with the person of Christ in his historic and visible life and work. It is indeed precisely in this that the conspicuous greatness of the Christian religion resides; namely, that with all its speculative profundity it is easily apprehended through its historic facts, which at the same time stimulate to and demand the effort to penetrate to their deeper meaning. Thus it is adapted to every stage of cultivation, and at the same time satisfies the highest demands."

But the dogmatic definition and declaration of Christian truth had a relation, not only to the new and specifically Christian consciousness expressed therein, but also to the spiritual state of the world under imperial Roman dominion, and in particular to philosophy. We have above spoken of the distinct development in the Roman world of the principle or consciousness of personality, or of independent individuality; we have also noticed the painful limit at which this development stopped short. The philosophy of Stoicism and of Scepticism stated this principle in universal form. So the form was prepared for the conception of God as the Absolute Person, having universal relations to all finite persons. After such a conception we may say that the Occidental world was blindly feeling;- and such an one in kind the Jews in Western Asia had already possessed. In the extended Roman world, Orient and Occident were outwardly united. The state of the Occidental mind led it to feel after an inward union. The cultus of Isis and of Mithra was spread over the whole Roman world; the spirit, fed on the husks of purely outward and finite relations, longed for an infinite satisfaction. In Alexandria the principles of East and West were brought together in the crucible of scientific or philosophical inquiry; learned Jews, such as Philo, connected such abstract expressions of ideal values as Plato and Aristotle had discovered with their idea of the infinite, spiritual God. The heathen themselves had found it necessary to criticise and correct their religious notions, in conformity with their philosophical ideas. It became especially common to seek for a spiritual interpretation of the heathen mythology; just as also Philo, in interpreting the Mosaic records, sought for a deeper or "allegorical" meaning. The proceeding of the early Church fathers therefore, in attempting to go beyond the letter of the historical records to the deeper-lying and vivifying spirit, had a superficial analogy with what was a common tendency among the more thoughtful of their Gentile and Jewish neighbors. In their work of defining the Christian faith, they made free use of philosophy, with the result not only of reaching an admirable statement of this faith in itself, but also of meeting palpably those spiritual needs of the age of which, directly or indirectly, the current philosophy was the purest expression.

The next thing of importance is the constitution of the Church as a visible organization. The Christian religion made its appearance in the Roman world, not merely as a new religion on a par with all the others that were recognized, but as a new "kingdom," — a kingdom of mankind and of heaven, at once of this world and not of this world. The Church, the communion of the faithful, is the organ of a new life, whose beginning is here and now, and not simply reserved for the future. Organization is introduced into this body through the selection, as overseers, of men conspicuous through their talents, character, decided piety, godly walk and conversation, learning, and general culture. These men are selected, especially, on account of their knowledge of that universal and substantial life which Christ identified with himself, and which is still incorporated in the body of his followers. They are the teachers of this life, the definers and dispensers of the truth, and in this character receive authority to rule the general body of the believers.

It was involved in the nature of Christian truth, and of the Church as its visible organ, that it should enter as a vitalizing and organizing force into the secular, historic life of man. Christianity is not alone "religion;" it is not alone the revelation and establishment of the connection of the spiritual man in each individual believer with God. It is also the life and truth of the world, and must demonstrate itself as such. That freedom of man as man, which Christianity declared and revealed, — the freedom which is, however, only "through the truth," and is to be won and asserted only through the positive development of the spiritual nature, in thought and will and love, — this freedom, of which the Christian religion was the idea and Christian living the personal illustration, was to be wrought out in the corporate life of mankind, in civil, political, social, and historic relations, for the healing of the nations. This was the problem of Christian history, — a problem to be effectively taken up, not in the Roman but in the Germanic world.

III. *The Byzantine Empire.* — With Constantine

the Great the Christian religion was elevated to the throne of an Empire which embraced the whole civilized world. It was not long before the new religion was spread throughout this immense realm. Under Theodosius the heathen temples were closed, the sacrifices and ceremonies were abolished, and the pagan religion itself was forbidden; by degrees it completely disappeared.

Of the circumstances attending the division of the Empire nothing need be said. It is enough to mention that while the Eastern empire long continued to subsist, in the Western a new people of Christians was formed out of the invading barbarian hordes. "We see now the Christian religion in two forms, — on the one hand, barbaric nations, who in the elements of all civilization, in science, in civil and political constitution, are obliged to begin at the beginning; on the other hand, civilized peoples, in possession of Grecian science and of a finer Oriental culture. The latter had entered on the inheritance of a civil law so completely developed by the great Roman jurisconsults, that in the form in which its elements were brought together by the Emperor Justinian it still excites the admiration of the world. Here the Christian religion is planted in an already developed civilization, not originally inspired by it. In the West, on the contrary, the development of civilization starts wholly *de novo*, and its guiding principle is Christianity. These two Empires offer thus an extremely remarkable contrast, wherein, as in a great object-lesson, there is impressed upon us the truth that the civilization of a Christian people must of necessity be its own work." In the cultured Eastern empire, where we might have expected the spirit of Christianity to be appreciated and illustrated in its truth and purity, the spectacle presented to us is anything but edifying; it is a spectacle of crimes, weaknesses, baseness, and fickleness, at once horrible and uninteresting. The Byzantine empire illustrates conspicuously how possible it is that a great principle of life and human culture like Christianity may remain abstract, — that is, without its appropriate, concrete, and organizing effect. The Christian religion is, on the one hand, an inner life and conviction, claiming the throne of the individual conscience. Opposed to this, on the other hand, and at war among each other, are the passions and lusts, the inward reflex of man's relations to his finite, sensible surroundings; and in order that, in accordance with the Christian conception of freedom, the heart may be kept pure, the will steadfast, and the intelligence clear and just, a process of individual and social self-training is required. So the right is to become the customary, and the whole organization of human relations, social and political, is to become the abiding and consistent expression of an immanent and inspiring reason. Thus the "culture" or civilization of a people free in the Christian sense of this term is, as above intimated, to be its own work, its own self-culture. This condition, in the Byzantine empire, was not fulfilled. The forms and largely the spirit of an old pagan culture here lasted over into Christian times; the whole organization of the State and of the laws was not reconstructed from the bottom in accordance with the central principle of the Christian religion, — the principle of spiritual freedom; the activities of Christians were largely absorbed in passionate and trifling theological or liturgical disputes, in which the great truths of the Spirit were treated most unspiritually.

The Byzantine empire paid the just and humiliating penalty of its own spiritual weakness, when it was destroyed (1453) by the conquering Turks.

CHAPTER VIII.

THE GERMANIC WORLD.

THE Germanic world is the modern world, whose moulding principle is derived from Christianity. This principle is freedom, as the essential attribute of the human spirit and the rightful heritage of all men. The mission which in the interest of universal history fell to the Germanic peoples was, not only to receive the notion of true freedom as a central religious principle, but also to make it the organizing force of secular institutions.

The history of the Christian-Germanic world may be divided into three parts, dealing, respectively, with this world in its initial period, in mediæval times, and in modern times.

A.— THE ELEMENTS OF THE CHRISTIAN-GERMANIC WORLD.

I. *The Barbarian Migrations.*—What must mainly interest us under this head is not so much the statistics of the "migrations," as the character of the "barbarians" who undertook them.[1] We may mention only one of the ultimate results of all this

[1] Hegel, in his work, gives a sufficient review of the statistics.

national movement and fermentation; namely, the constitution of a number of new nations (the Romanic: Italy, Spain, Portugal, France), of mixed composition and speaking composite languages of a common type, — and of three other nations (Germany, Scandinavia, and England), remaining more or less completely Germanic in their speech, and all preserving intact the original tone, as we may call it, of the Germanic character.

We have said that it was the mission of the Germanic nations to receive and to develop in the world the notion of true freedom, which was contained in Christianity as its central principle and ideal. For this mission they were well chosen. They were a wild stock, well suited by native character to receive the engrafted word. The inhabitants of the German forests had always been regarded as a collection of free tribes: not only the tribe, but also in a peculiar sense the individual, was free. Tacitus, in his celebrated picture of Germania, contemplates the character and condition of its inhabitants with an obvious feeling of admiration and longing, contrasting it with the corruption and artificiality of the Roman world to which he belonged. We are of course not to regard this barbarian freedom as of a lofty or developed kind. We must not, for example, fall into an error like that of Rousseau, "who imagined the condition of the savages of America as one in which man was in possession of true freedom. True, there is an immense amount of misery and pain, of which the savage has no knowledge at all; but this is only

THE GERMANIC WORLD. 257

negative, while it is essential to freedom that it should be affirmative. It is only the goods of affirmative freedom that are at the same time the goods of the highest consciousness." The point is simply that in the Germanic tribes a seed of freedom was conspicuously present, ready to be quickened into a larger growth when watered by the principles of Christian liberty.

This point will appear still more obviously, if we consider the native Germanic character from another side. One of the most conspicuous marks of this character is what in the German language is termed *Gemüth*, or *Gemüthlichkeit*, — best described perhaps in English as a general feeling of satisfaction. It is an indefinite feeling, embracing one's whole condition, a sort of "universal enjoyment of one's self." It is very positively self-centred, but no less kindly. "Gemüth" is cumbered about nothing; all things are indifferent to it. On the other hand, we may also say with equal truth that all things are to it equally important, since into anything, no matter what, that engages the attention of its possessor, he throws himself entire. Mere "Gemüth," by itself, implies no mental enlightenment. The Germans in their original condition illustrate this; they were stupid; their ideas were confused and indefinite. Such religious notions as they may have had they appear to have held rather lightly: witness the readiness with which, on the whole, they were led to embrace the Christian religion. And they were equally deficient in political ideas, and ideas of civil law. Murder was not regarded as a crime

17

and punished accordingly; the payment of a fine of money was deemed sufficient. Society exercised no authority in its own right; for the protection of person and property associations were freely formed, and a delegated authority to pass judgment on matters in dispute was exercised, but never in abatement of the absolute right of individual self-assertion. And when it came to the matter of following a leader in war, or of rendering obedience to a prince, it was with the Germans not a question of yielding to compulsion, but of paying the free tribute of personal loyalty; indeed, if the first watchword of the Germans is and has always been Liberty, their second has been Loyalty, personal Fidelity (*Treue*). The relation of such a subjective state to positive, " affirmative " freedom — the freedom of a will enlightened by universal principles and guiding itself by recognized laws — is of course rather negative than positive. It is negative, because undeveloped; but it is also positive, because it is the rich soil in which freedom may grow, and which contains freedom in actual germ.

To all things genuinely and concretely human, and consequently to all historic developments of human civilization, in proportion to their perfection, there belong two sides, — a subjective side of self-conscious feeling, and an objective side of recognized and stable truth; and the former must pre-exist as a preparation for the reception and realization of the latter. The Germanic spirit, with its " Gemüthlichkeit," constituted just such a subjective preparation. The objective element was furnished by Christianity; the historic problem was to bring the two into friendly and vital union. The undeveloped, indefinite, rational subject (individual, race) must take on definite, rational, objective form; it must know, and in its life and institutions realize, the universal truth; it must become inspired with universal interests, act in view of universal and the highest aims, become familiar with law and find its satisfaction therein. In short, it must become concretely spiritual, and bring forth the fruits of the spirit.

With reference to the State, the problem was to combine individual liberty with social solidarity, so that duties and rights should no longer be left at the mercy of private fancy, but become fixed in the form of determinate civil relations. Indeed, one may say that the whole labor of the Germanic spirit, in political regards, has been expended in the effort to breathe into selfish particularism the organizing breath of unity, and to do this, not to the detriment, but in the interest, of real freedom.

Such was the great problem which the Germanic spirit was called, first in its own interest and then in the interest of universal humanity, to solve. It could not be solved suddenly, but only as the slow result of a long process of providential discipline, and of self-discipline. Christianity was received, but the comprehension of it and the actual illustration of its perfect law of liberty in the sphere of life and institutions were the work of time. Accordingly, in the earliest periods of Germanic Christianity we witness the most decided and even shocking moral contradictions. The new and accepted religion comes forward with a requirement of self-restraint, and the passions, which without this interdict upon them had perhaps continued to sleep, are at once aroused to uncontrollable fury. "Clovis, the founder of the Frankish monarchy, commits the worst crimes. Barbarous rudeness and ferocity characterize the whole following line of the Merovingians; and the same spectacle is repeated in the Thuringian and other royal houses. The Christian principle is undoubtedly lodged in the minds (*Gemüther*) of these men, as a problem; but the immediate conditions of these minds is still raw and undeveloped." The will is formally set toward the true goal, but is turned aside from it through its attachment to particular finite aims. So it smites in the face the truth it loves; it finds a law in its members, such that when it would do good, evil is present with it. The good that it really does, it accomplishes, as it were, against its will. Yet even so the truth prevails, the good is achieved. "*La vérité, en la repoussant, on l'embrasse.* Europe comes to the truth only by resisting it, and in proportion to its resistance. Herein we witness, in the exactest sense of this expression, the presence of an overruling Providence, making the misery and suffering, the particular aims and the unconscious will of the nations, the means for the accomplishment of its absolute aim and of its honor."

II. *Mahometanism.* — Among the Germanic nations began, in the manner above described, the slow and long process of giving organized reality to the universal principles of Christian freedom in the world of secular relations. Contemporaneously with or just after this beginning, there sprang up in the Orient a spiritual revolution, the principle of which imposed on those who accepted it a labor capable of being quickly accomplished. For it was an abstract principle, and of an abstract simplicity, — quickly apprehended, therefore, and quickly applied. The principle in question was that of the one God, beside whom there is none other, and whose dominion is absolute. It was the Jewish God, stripped of the limitations included in the Jewish conception of him; it was the Jewish God, conceived in pure and abstract unity, and become the God of all the world. Before Him every knee must bow: this was the simple and universal requirement, which Mahometanism undertook to enforce. Before Him nothing is free, and all differences of high and low, of family, caste, or nation, are of no account: this was the simple consequence which Mahometanism existed to illustrate. In the eyes of its followers the highest merit consisted in dying for the faith; and he who fell for it in battle was certain of entering into paradise.

Animated by such a principle and such a hope, Mahometanism — founded among the Arabians in the seventh century — rapidly made prodigious conquests, extending over portions of Asia Minor, Persia, Egypt and Northern Africa, Spain, and the south of France. An abstract principle flies and consumes like wildfire; and the Mahometans, says

Hegel, were "ruled by abstraction." Their enthusiasm was "fanaticism, which is enthusiasm for anything abstract,— for an abstract idea, whose relation to the existing order of things is negative and destructive." "*La religion et la terreur* was the principle in this case, as in Robespierre's it was *La liberté et la terreur.* . . . Never has enthusiasm as such accomplished greater things. Individuals may be enthusiastic for various specific and lofty objects; a nation's enthusiasm for its independence has also a definite object; but the enthusiasm that is abstract, and hence all-inclusive, restrained by nothing, limited by nothing, and wanting nothing, is that of the Mahometan Orient."

As rapid as the conquests of the Arabians was the rise among them of the arts and sciences to a condition of high development. The great indebtedness of the Western world to the Arabians in the matter of scientific and philosophical knowledge is well known. At the fires of passion which burn in their literature the poetic fancy of the Occident has more than once been kindled; witness, in more recent times, the string of poetic pearls arranged by Goethe in his "Westöstliche Divan." As an aggressive secular force, Mahometanism served to unite the divided interests of the Christian world in opposition to a common foe. And, finally, the form of the principle that animated the Mahometans was complementary to the form of the Germanic consciousness in the period now under consideration. The spirit of the German world was mainly absorbed in the establishment and defence of a multiplicity of separate, particular interests. The universal unifying principles of Christian civilization, of Christian freedom, had scarcely begun to dawn upon the consciousness of the Germanic nations; they were in the Western mind and in Western life only in germ, and their development was destined to take place, as it could only take place, in the form of a slow but solid growth. The universal was here in a sense to grow out of the particular; it was to be, in the strict etymological sense of this term, *concrete;* it was to *grow up with* and through the manifold particular, becoming to it a constructive bond of free and harmonious unity. But for the present, we repeat, it was the particular, — a multiplicity of separate, finite, particular aims, — with which the Western mind was more immediately filled. The Mahometans, on the other hand, set the Christian world the complementary example of complete absorption in the contemplation and service of a formally universal idea. The defect of this idea was, precisely, that it was only a formal universal; that is, that it was abstract, and hence devoid of content and of freely constructive force. Its empire (like that of all abstractions) was tyrannical; no birth of freedom could spring from it.

III. *The Empire of Charlemagne.* — Of the events preceding and attending the establishment of this Empire, of its internal constitution and administration, and of its manifold relations to pre-existing institutions (especially to the Church) and to the development of Western culture, our author gives a brief account, which seems an admirable example of compressed but lucid statement. We can only note that the great realm of Charlemagne was transformed by the latter into the character of a systematically ordered State, — the first grand attempt of Christendom in the direction of civil and political development. The work of Charlemagne was not merely one of mechanical construction and innovation; it was rather — or was intended to be — a work of organization: pre-existing institutions were to be "developed and helped on to a more definite and unhindered efficiency." And yet, excellent as the constitution of the Carlovingian empire appears in the abstract," it proved itself, after the death of Charlemagne, wholly impotent, being incapable of self-defence against the attacks of Normans, Hungarians, and Arabians from without, and ineffective as a barrier against lawlessness, robbery, and oppression of every kind within. We see, thus, along with an excellent constitution the most wretched social condition, and consequently contradiction on every side. Such political constructions, just because they spring up suddenly," are intrinsically weak; they require for their confirmation to be confronted with reactionary forces in all directions, such as manifest themselves in the following period.

B.—THE MIDDLE AGES.

The Western world, at the beginning of the Middle Ages, was an "unbounded lie," a living self-contradiction. This character determines the whole complexion of the following period, of its life and its spirit. It is not a period of stability, but of manifold reactions.

I. *The Feudal System and the Hierarchy.* — The First Reaction is that of the particular nationalities against the universal empire of the Franks. The division of the Empire was not merely the imprudent act of weak princes; it was supported and enforced by the different peoples concerned. The result, speedily attained, was the establishment of numerous minor but independent kingdoms, such as Italy (itself inwardly divided), the two Burgundys, Lorraine, Normandy, Brittany, and, shut in between the foregoing, France proper. Eastern Franconia, Saxony, Thuringia, Bavaria, and Swabia alone remained in the German empire. At the same time occurred the incursions of the Normans into England, France, and Germany, of the Magyars into Eastern Europe, and of the Saracens into Southern Europe.

So, like a dream, disappeared the fair fabric of civil and political organization introduced by Charlemagne. It disappeared, because it was the work of Charlemagne and of his genius alone, for which Christendom was not ripe. Stability in the constitution of a State or Empire is only possible when this constitution is the organic expression of the matured and developed will of a people. This was not the case in the present instance. The Germanic spirit had not yet grown out of its original crude condition of simple "Gemüth" and individual wilfulness into that higher consciousness of common interests and of an organic public life which is the condition of the permanence or effectiveness of any constitution.

The Second Reaction was that of individuals against all established authority. The civic sense, the sense of law and legal order, was conspicuously absent from the minds of men. As soon as the strong hand of Charlemagne was withdrawn, the brilliant civil, military, and judicial administration which he had instituted disappeared, as we have said, and left no trace behind. The result was that private individuals found themselves thrown into a general condition of defencelessness, where defence and protection were imperatively needed. Under the circumstances, no course was left open to the weaker and poorer but to seek the patronage of the strong and rich. This they did. In return for a promise of protection, they made over their possessions to a neighboring lord, cloister, abbot, or bishop, and then received them back burdened with an obligation to render specific services to these masters. So from being freemen they became liegemen, or vassals, and their possessions were held by a feudal tenure. Thus the pledge given by the individual, and the obligation assumed by him in return for the promise of security to life and property, were respectively given to and assumed toward, not the State, but particular individuals; and the bravery which he might show in battle could be credited to no patriotic consciousness of devotion to a public cause, but only to a prudent carefulness for his individual interests, or at best to a feeling of personal loyalty to the feudal lord.

This system of vassalage became well-nigh universal. It was only in a few of the cities, where the united freemen were strong enough to protect themselves alone, that remnants of the former free constitution survived.

As for the imperial authority, it was in words highly exalted. The Emperor was represented as the secular chief of all Christendom; but his real power was in inverse ratio to the magnitude of the common notion concerning it. "France gained extraordinarily by repelling this hollow pretence, while in Germany the progress of civilization was checked by this sham authority. Kings and emperors were kings and emperors, not of States, but of vassal princes, each master in his own territory." The Empire was not held together by that essential bond of unity which consists in the existence of uniform laws and the administration of a uniform justice for all its subjects.

If we have hitherto been considering what a logician would term reactions of the particular and individual against the universal, the Third Reaction, now to be considered, is one counter to the foregoing, proceeding from the universal against the particular and individual. It is the reaction of the Church, as the representative or claimant of a universal authority, against political and moral anarchy. The condition of Christendom was indeed deplorable; in consequence of which Christendom itself would appear to have been tormented by the tremors of an evil conscience. In the eleventh century all Europe was dreading the approach of the judgment-day and of the world's end; at the same time dreadful famines swept away thousands of lives. The immediate results were anything but refining; brutality and lust and violence only increased. The clergy were not unaffected by the universal degeneracy; bishoprics dependent on a feudal sovereign fell into the hands of men of the worst character, and even the right to occupy the papal chair was sold by the Counts of Tusculum for money. At last the condition of things became so intolerable that men of energetic character, in secular as well as ecclesiastical authority, set about checking it. The Emperor Henry III. put an end to the strife of factions by undertaking to appoint the popes himself. Pope Nicholas II. decreed that the popes should be elected by the College of Cardinals; and Pope Gregory VII. sought to secure the independence of the Church especially by two measures, — one rendering obligatory the celibacy of the clergy, and the other directed against simony. Of the secular power, further, Gregory made demands looking to the completer independence of the Church in the ordination of its clergy and to the lodging of the control of the extensive possessions of the Church in the hands of the Pope. The Church, as a divine authority, even claimed the supremacy over the secular powers, proceeding on the abstract principle that the divine is higher than the secular. The Emperor, who might receive his crown only from the Pope, was required to swear constant obedience to the Pope and the Church. "Whole lands and states, such as Naples, Portugal, England, and Ireland, came into a relation of formal vassalage to the papal see."

So the Church acquired an independent position. The bishops assembled their clergy in synods, thus giving them a sense of greater solidarity. Further, the Church undertook to decide in cases of disputed royal succession and to play the part of mediator in war and peace. Such was the general disorder that the intervention of the Church was felt to be a necessity. But through her temporal possessions the Church came into a relation to other temporal powers which was strictly foreign to her own character. She was indeed thereby able the more effectually to make her authority felt in opposition to the wilful violence of the times; but she also confused her temporal interests with those belonging to her in her purely spiritual character. When this began to be perceived, as it quickly was, her spiritual authority began to decline.

Let us now look at the spiritual side of the Church. We have previously seen that Christianity rests on the principle of mediation. This principle supposes a consciousness of the union of the "regenerate," or spiritual, man with God. In Christ this union is completely objectified. The point of main importance then is that each individual be elevated into this consciousness, and that it be kept evermore awake in him. This is the true theory of the Mass; Christ in the consecrated host is God present among men, visible, and the victim of an eternal sacrifice. The perversion of the theory is when the divine guest is present only to the physical eye, and the doors of the spiritual consciousness — of that inner region in which alone God is truly known, and where alone the process of mediation can take place — are closed upon him: then the "present God" remains merely an external sensible object, a thing. This thing is in the hands of the priesthood; the laity have no direct access to it: the former determine upon what conditions the latter may partake of the bread of life. It is the clergy alone whose privilege it is to possess knowledge of divine things, so far as such knowledge is deemed any way possible; the one duty of the laity is obedience. So the priest becomes the mediator on earth between the individual and his God; in heaven it is the saints who perform this office. The veneration of relics becomes very popular. In the confessional the Church takes the place of the individual conscience. The whole work of religion becomes in tendency external rather than internal. The Christian principle of freedom is perverted into one of absolute un-freedom.

Under these circumstances it is not surprising to find the Church turning against the principles of the "ethical world." One of these principles is marriage. Of celibacy we are to say, not that it is unnatural, but rather that it is unethical. While the Church declared marriage a sacrament, it degraded it by pronouncing the single state still holier. Another ethical principle is active, self-supporting labor; in opposition to this, the Church exalted poverty, idleness, and inactivity. A third principle of the ethical world is that of obedience to the claims

of morality and of right reason, as expressed in law
and otherwise, rendered willingly and with full
knowledge; the Church, on the contrary, urged the
superior merit of blind unconditional obedience.
So the three vows of chastity, poverty, and obedience were the exact opposite of what they should
have been, in view of the real character of the
Christian principle of freedom. The Church was no
longer a spiritual but only an ecclesiastical power,
calculated to paralyze in its subjects spirit, will,
and intelligence; the result was shameless vice
and unscrupulousness. The Church of the Middle
Ages was a manifold contradiction; but so also,
as we have seen, was the Empire; and such were
individuals, in many of whom might be witnessed
the most delicate blossoms of piety, accompanied by
a real barbarism of intelligence and will. Really,
such contradiction was, in a vital sense, a sign
and necessary result of the superior character and
comprehensiveness of the truth, on which the human spirit had begun to feed, but which it had
not yet mastered.

The Reaction of the Church against the world was
one that resulted less in the reformation of the
latter, than in its mere reduction under the external
authority of the former.

The period from the eleventh to the thirteenth
century is characterized by the simultaneous development of a number of movements, all bearing
witness to a common impulse. Such were the
erection of immense cathedrals; the prosecution of
a vigorous maritime commerce on the part of the

cities of the Italian, Spanish, and Flemish coasts; the new interest in intellectual pursuits, leading to the highest development reached by the Scholastic philosophy; further, the establishment, at Bologna and elsewhere, of schools of law and medicine. The principal condition of all these movements was the rise and the growing importance of the cities. The rise of the cities was indeed another reaction, like that of the Church, against the violence of feudal rule. The story of their growth, and therewith of legal order, of trade, of the influence of the *bourgeois*, and of the principle of independent ownership of property is a lively one, and has been a favorite theme of investigation in modern times.

Finally, a word about one more Reaction, proceeding from the secular princes, with the Emperor at their head, and directed against the Pope and the cities. The contest thus carried on with the Pope was full of contradictions. Theoretically, the Emperor was the rightful possessor of the " dominion of the world." He could thus claim supremacy over the Pope as a secular ruler; but in attempting to enforce the claim, he was embarrassed by the circumstance that he was contending against one to whose spiritual authority he was subject. Again, the princes, on whose aid the Emperor was compelled to rely in the prosecution of his schemes, were themselves embarrassed by their double allegiance to Emperor and Pope. Further, these princes had special interests of their own; they might be willing to fight in behalf of the empty principle of imperial authority or in opposition to the cities, but could not lose sight of their own desire to secure for themselves, within the Empire, the greatest possible independence of imperial authority and control. The result was, in the main, victory for the cities and the Church.

II. *The Crusades.* — The Church in her contest with the world had triumphed. She had established herself as the mistress of all the relations of life, of science, and of art; she was the recognized storehouse of all spiritual treasures. And yet Christendom was not satisfied; the Christian principle was not fulfilled; freedom through and in the truth was not realized. What was it specifically that was lacking?

It was the sense of the Christian doctrine that man should find his perfect strength in God; that humanity should come to mature perfection, and so to specifically human independence and freedom, through an influx upon it, here and now, of the divine Spirit; through a partaking of the divine nature; through a present recognition and adoption of the will of God as the true will of man. So God was to be known, not as jealously withholding himself from his creation, but as a strictly present God, entering into the secular life and work of man, and elevating the same into harmony with the will and purpose of His own absolute love. The present God, "Immanuel, God with us," — this is the side of Christian truth the full realization and comprehension of which were lacking to Christendom. And yet it was precisely in order to be a living demonstration of this truth that the Church existed.

God, incarnate, had once been sensibly present among men in the form of a visible creature of flesh and blood. But the higher meaning of this presence, as we have previously seen, was spiritual, not sensuous; so that it was only when the visible Christ was withdrawn from before the eyes of his disciples that he became spiritually known to them. Then first was he truly present with them, becoming the informing spirit of his Church, and guiding them to the perception of the essential spiritual truth. So, first of all, in the Church, as the communion of all believers, the true, the spiritual Christ was to be actually present — "God with us" — in the life of the world.

The sensible sign of the present Christ was perpetuated in the Church in the form of the consecrated host; nay, more, the host by transubstantiation became the very body of Christ, and was adored as God sensibly present before the eyes of the faithful. It is not necessary to condemn the doctrine of transubstantiation. The important historic fact to be noted is, that the Christian imagination of the Middle Ages dwelt with exaggerated emphasis on the particular sensible form of the divine presence, while the eyes of its spirit were closed. As a consequence, it sought other signs and wonders, — sensible manifestations of the divine power and presence, — its finding of which is recorded in the multitudinous stories of mediæval miracle. The Christian heart sought to realize the presence of Christ as a sensible fact. It was in pursuance of this impulse that the Crusades were undertaken. The incarnate Son of God was indeed not again to be seen, but the places frequented by him in his life, and above all his sepulchre, were still there, in Palestine. In their presence the wish of the heart could be at least in a measure satisfied; and, besides, it was only fitting that they should be and remain in the possession of Christian hands.

Christendom sought its Christ in his grave. Arrived there it might have heard again the words, "Why seek ye the living among the dead? He is not here, but is risen." Listen not to those who say, Lo here! or, Lo there! Christ is neither here nor there, but within you, in the living heart and conscience, the will and reason. Seek him there, welcome him there, and there shall ye find him! The result of the Crusades was, in its practical tendency, to break up a spiritual illusion; it measurably prepared the way for the practical reception of the Christian truth of the absolute right and worth of spiritual, divinely-sustained individuality. "From this time on," says Hegel, "begins the period of self-reliance and independent activity. At the holy sepulchre the Occident bade the Orient an eternal farewell, and grasped its own principle of subjective freedom. Christendom never appeared again on the historic stage as one whole."

In the Crusades the power of the Church was complete. The Pope stood at the head of the powers of the Christian world. The decline of the Church from this temporal eminence was destined to be the result, not of attack from without, but of the operation of spiritual causes within its fold. The Christian spirit, undeceived and unsatisfied by the turbulent attempt to find its treasure without itself, was to direct its search within, or else to seek satisfaction in the active pursuit of universal human ends,—ends of mercy, of social order, of intellectual culture, and the like. All these movements were to be in the direct line of preparation for the fuller realization of the Christian spirit in the plenitude of its higher freedom.

First to be mentioned in this connection is the founding of monastic and knightly orders, for the practice of those precepts of renunciation which the Church had distinctly enjoined and for the cultivation of purity of heart. Such was the Franciscan order of mendicant friars, and the Dominican order of preaching monks; such also were the orders of knighthood,—the order of Saint John, the Templars, and the Teutonic order. Of the members of these latter orders the same renunciation of worldly advantages was exacted as of the members of the monastic orders. Their chief virtue was to be knightly bravery; they were to protect pilgrims, and to shield and care for the poor and the sick. The principle of these associations presented a radical contrast to the selfish principle of the feudal system. "With almost suicidal bravery the knights sacrificed themselves for the common good. So these orders rose above their environment, and formed a network of fraternal relations extending over the whole of Europe."

We have also to note the development of intellectual interests. The Scholastic philosophy, the chief professed aim of which was the exposition and defence of Christian dogma, reached its brilliant maturity. Much of the intellectual activity of the time was indeed merely formal, and may best be described as a sort of logical fencing or tourneying, quite comparable to the contests of the knightly arena; but even this, as a form of discipline, was far from useless.

Finally, " we notice in this period after the Crusades certain beginnings of art, of painting; and even while the Crusades were in progress, a characteristic form of poetry had sprung up. The spirit, unable to find satisfaction, created for itself fairer images, and in a calmer and freer manner, than the actual world could offer."

III. *The Transition from Feudal Rule to Monarchy.*— The movements last mentioned tended away from selfish particularism and individualism toward the recognition of universal human aims and the pursuit of common interests. A movement of like direction in the political world is what we have now to consider.

The feudal rule was polyarchy,— an improvement no doubt on anarchy, yet removed from it by only a single step. It was a rule by might, of particular individuals, lords, princes, with no fixed standards of right. Over these petty or inferior rulers themselves stands another, a king or emperor, whose authority is formally acknowledged, but is by them freely resisted. Feudal rule is a rule of caprice.

It is not civil rule; it is not the rule of the State; it denotes a social condition founded on the relation of lords and serfs. Monarchy, on the other hand, means the establishment of a single supreme authority, which excludes caprice, and is exercised according to law. It means the establishment of the authority of the State as a political organism, an ethico-social order, all the parts and members of which are harmonized in a common order and subject to one supreme and organic law of the whole. In a monarchy one is master, and no one a serf; serfdom disappears under a rule of civil order and of law. So monarchy, as succeeding feudal polyarchy, became the parent of real freedom. This remains the historic fact, in spite of the circumstance that before the full development of constitutional monarchy it was often necessary to defend the cause of freedom against a residuum of obstructive caprice and tyranny, the door for which was still left open by the lodging of irresponsible power in the hands of one individual.

Of course, the transition from feudalism to monarchism did not take place in a day. It was not the result of chance, nor was it the benevolent work of a few accidental possessors of power; it was the result of the most varied action and reaction, attack and defence, among princes, classes, corporations, cities. The details of all these secondary causes and incidents of the transition are naturally not to be mentioned here. We are concerned only to note that at the period in history at which we have arrived in our review, we "see the beginning of a process of the formation of States, while feudalism knew no States," and to observe the general form of the process in different Christian countries.

In the Roman empire — Germany and Italy — the transition to monarchy took place through a repudiation, on the part of local princes, of their feudal dependence on the Emperor. The vassal princes became independent monarchs. An essential condition of the success of this movement was the existence in both parts of the Empire of a number of distinct tribal or national differences, — such as those by which, in Germany, Swabians, Bavarians, Saxons, etc., were distinguished; and in Italy, Lombards and Normans. In the barbarous period, which in Germany followed the downfall of the Hohenstaufen, it became a maxim of the imperial electors to select weak princes as emperors; and they even went so far as to sell the imperial office to foreigners. Thus the unity of the Empire in substance disappeared, and a number of principalities, or states, in the first instance mainly predatory, were constituted. (When the Hapsburgs succeeded to the imperial throne, they were reduced to the necessity of procuring for themselves, independently, the means and forces with which to maintain the imperial dignity, since the electors refused to grant them.) To the complete anarchy which was the first result of this change a limit was set by the establishment of associations or leagues for public purposes; such was the Hanseatic League in the North, the Rhenish League formed by the cities along the Rhine, and the League of the Swabian cities. In Switzerland the peasants united to repel invasion and defend their independent rights. We must also mention here the invention and use of gunpowder, — one of the principal means of securing freedom from physical tyranny and of reducing the distance between classes.

In Italy the turn of affairs was similar to that witnessed in Germany. In France it was the opposite. The territory belonging to the kings of France was for many centuries smaller than that of many of their vassals; but to the great advantage of the former, the hereditary principle was early established in France. So by inheritance and conquest the territory of the French kings was gradually enlarged, and instead of being, like the German emperors, merely feudal sovereigns, they were territorial rulers. They remained, on the whole, on good terms with the cities. "In this way the kings of France rose very soon to great power, and the successful cultivation of poetry by the Troubadours, as also the development of the Scholastic theology (the chief centre of which was Paris), gave to France a culture superior to that of other European countries, and which caused it to be looked up to with respect in foreign lands."

In England, subdued by William the Conqueror, who introduced there the feudal *régime*, the barons and cities gradually acquired a position of important influence, — so, especially, in the case of disputes and struggles relative to the succession to the throne. Thus the barons forced from King John the *magna charta;* while the cities, favored by the kings against the barons, gained representation as a third estate in the Commons.

The popes meanwhile sought to exercise their authority, but to little avail. Not to speak of other causes operating to weaken their influence, States and communities were at last coming to the consciousness of the inherent right of political independence. In the work of political and civil construction in which they were engaged, they were coming to recognize a universal human aim thoroughly legitimate in itself, and worthy and able to command the will of the individual. Mankind, after passing through a disciplinary servitude both of body and of soul, began to stand upon its feet, and in its secular activity to have a good conscience. This was no insurrection against what is divine; it was simply the manifestation of a better consciousness, recognizing a divine impulse within itself, permeated by genuinely humane motives, and directing the activity of man to universal ends of rationality and beauty. In these latter results, — we refer especially to the so-called revival of learning, the new bloom of art, and the discovery of America and of the way to the East Indies, — we may witness at once the dissolution of the mediæval period and the dawn of a new historic day.

C. — MODERN TIMES.

In this third and last period of the Germanic world the human spirit, set free by Christianity, comes to a new and fuller knowledge of its freedom.

If the ideal of the preceding period had been the establishment of a mechanical universality, — the forcible and universal reign of a single empire, in the secular and spiritual worlds, over dependent and resistant subjects, — the ideal of the modern period is what we will term concrete universality: the individual shall freely know and recognize the true universal (the true, the eternal, law, the will of God) as part and parcel of his own perfected nature, and shall direct his will accordingly. So the universal shall be realized in human affairs, not in the form of an abstract Procrustean rule over spiritual slaves, but as the free and willing work of the individual; and in this work the individual shall find the fulfilment and present fruition of his true freedom. The "spiritual" and the "secular" shall be at one.

I. *The Reformation.* — The Reformation came because the Church was itself in an unsound condition. It is important to understand precisely wherein this unsoundness, perversion, or "corruption" consisted. The root of it lay open before us when we were considering the motive of the Crusades, and consisted in the persistent tendency to seek and worship the divine presence in some external sensible object, rather than in the spirit and in the truth. Art indeed came to the rescue of the Church, furnishing sensible objects (paintings and statues), calculated by their spiritual significance to assist the heart of the appreciative worshipper to rise from the merely sensible and external to the spiritual and internal; but this means of rescue was insufficient. The sensuous, the external, not changed by transfiguration into the spiritual or into a witness of the spiritual, remained as a dominant element within the Church itself; and the Church, in embracing and fostering it, embraced and fostered within itself the very "negative of itself," the necessary principle of its own ruin and corruption. So the Church encouraged a superstitious piety, the "slavery of authority," and an absurd credulity, not to mention other more sensuous vices; or, if it recommended virtue it was a virtue of a negative sort, acquired by fleeing from the world rather than by overcoming it. And in all this the Church was really remaining behind its times. The movements going on in the world of political and civil life, of art and polite learning, of science and discovery, were all in their way exhibitions of the spiritual character of civilized man, and of the spiritual character of the truth that sets man free, which transcended in their scope, not the essential ideas of pure Christianity on these subjects, but the ideas practically adopted by the Church.

While the rest of Christendom was engaged in scouring the world — visiting America, India — in the search for riches and temporal dominion, the simple, fervent German heart rose up, first to correct the corruption of the Church, and then to overthrow the corrupted Church itself. It too — this German heart — wished to "see Jesus," to know the present Christ, to have the comforting witness of the Spirit; and it felt infinitely hurt and scandalized when its spiritual mother, the Church, offered it, instead of the bread of life, a stone. What Christendom had previously sought in an earthly sepulchre of stone, a simple German monk found in that deeper sepulchre of the spirit, where all that is merely sensuous and external either lies dead or is transfigured. The true Christ, the true God, the true man also, is spiritual; Christ is truly and fully present only to the believing spirit,—through this channel God in Christ becomes the bread of the world. This is the simple doctrine of Luther, which may be summed up in the words " faith," and " the witness of the spirit." The Christian consciousness is not the consciousness of a sensuous object as God, nor a mere historic memory; it is the consciousness of something actual and not sensuous. By this removal of the attribute of sensuous externality, all doctrines are reconstructed and all superstition is reformed away. It is especially the doctrine of works that is thus affected, — works being considered as things done outwardly, not in faith, not as the natural expression of the believing spirit, but by command, and the like. As to "belief," or "faith," it is not merely an assured conviction about finite things, such as " that this or that man once existed and said this or that; or, that the children of Israel passed through the Red Sea on dry land." The knowledge of these things does not constitute knowledge of God, nor faith in Him; whether a person possesses this knowledge or belief depends wholly on the accident of his having access to the relevant sources of historic information. Faith is not the function of the individual as individual,—

that is, as distinguished from other individuals by accidents of birth, talent, or historic instruction,— but of the individual considered in that which constitutes the essential nature of all individuals; to wit, his spiritual being. It is the function of that reason in him which, to appropriate the language of Heraclitus, is "common to all." It is the function of that nature in him by virtue of which he is in the image of God, and in this sense one with God. Says Hegel: "Faith is the subjective and certain assurance of the eternal, of the essential truth, of the truth of God. Respecting this assurance the Lutheran church declares that it is effectuated only by the Holy Spirit; in other words, it is an assured certainty, of which the individual is capable, not by virtue of his particular individuality, but by virtue of his [universal] nature. The Lutheran doctrine is therefore wholly the Catholic doctrine, excluding only the afore-mentioned character of externality, so far as this was asserted by the Catholic church, and whatever flows from it. Hence, in the doctrine of the Lord's Supper, in which all Christian doctrine is concentrated, Luther had no option but to remain unyielding. To the Reformed church he could not concede that Christ was [present in the Lord's Supper only as] a mere memory, a reminiscence; the rather, he agreed with the Catholic church that Christ is a real presence, but in faith, in the spirit. The spirit of Christ, he taught, actually fills the human heart. Christ is therefore not to be regarded merely as an historical person; on the contrary, man has an immediate [present] relation to him in the spirit."

Faith, then, with its fruits of the present indwelling divine spirit, is the privilege of no individual or class of individuals. An essential distinction between priest and layman, as though the former were in exclusive possession of the truth and of all spiritual and temporal treasures of the Church, is not to be admitted. Hereby the responsibility of the individual is so much the more increased. Each one, working out his own salvation, is to look out for the accomplishment in himself of the work of spiritual reconciliation; the individual spirit is to receive into itself the Spirit of Truth, and to give him a dwelling-place there. Thus Christian freedom, freedom in the truth, was to become, and did become, actual.

"Hereby," says Hegel, "was the new and final standard raised, about which the nations assemble themselves,— the banner of the free spirit, master of itself *in the truth*, and only so. This is the banner under which we serve and which we carry. The period from then till now has had, and still has, no other work to do than to mould the world according to this principle. . . . This is the essential meaning of the Reformation; namely, that the very nature of man defines him as free."

The Reformation, first directed only against certain sides of the corruption of the Catholic church, ended in complete repudiation of the authority of the Church. In the place of this, Luther put the Bible and the witness of the human spirit. On the importance of this change it is unnecessary to comment.

A word must be added regarding the relation of the Church, as reformed, to the secular life of man. The result of the Reformation in its spiritual character was man finding and welcoming his Lord as a divine guest in his own spirit. God and man were "reconciled." With this was necessarily given the consciousness that the secular is capable of being the dwelling-place of the true; it is not, as previously held, simply and only evil. It is now perceived that the ethical and the just, in the sphere of man's social and political relations, is worthy to be termed divine; that it is the command of God, and that nothing is in kind higher or holier than it. Hence the restitution to honor of marriage and labor, and the principle of free and enlightened, in place of blind, obedience: what is rational in the secular life of man need no longer fear contradiction on the part of the religious conscience. However, it is one thing to see and adopt a principle, and another to develop and apply it. The needful objective realization of the Christian principle of freedom in the form of a system of civil and political laws of freedom could not be the work of an hour. The reformers devoted themselves for the moment to such immediate changes as the abolition of cloisters, bishoprics, and the like; the principle of the reconciliation of God and the world was present as an abstract conviction, but was not at once "developed into a system of the ethical world."

First of all it was, and was felt to be, necessary that the reconciliation in question should be consciously accomplished in the individual. The individual must gain the assurance of the indwelling Spirit within himself, or, in the language of the Church, the assurance that his own heart is broken and contrite, and then filled by the influx of divine grace. Man is not man by simple nature; only through a process of transformation does he become man in full truth. Christian dogmatics called upon each individual to realize for himself this truth in the form of a conviction of his own natural sinfulness, and then of the forgiving and restoring grace of God manifested in his own behalf. The attempt to fulfil this condition led even the most simple and innocent natures into habits of minute introspective self-examination, which gave to Protestant piety for a long time a pitiable and wretched aspect of spiritual self-torment. With this was joined a strange phenomenon, common alike to the Catholic and Protestant worlds, founded in the belief of personified Evil as a tremendous and powerful Prince of the World. With this power it was believed that compacts might be and were made; by pledging one's soul to the Devil *in futurum*, one might purchase unlimited riches and pleasures in the present. Most deplorable of all were the widespread belief in witches, as persons in league with or possessed by the Devil, and the numerous trials of witches; these spread like an epidemic over the principal countries of Europe. Father Spee, a noble-minded Jesuit, and with still more effect the Protestant Professor Thomasius in Halle set themselves in opposition to this pervading superstition, the last vestiges of which were long in disappearing.

II. *Influence of the Reformation on Political Development.* — This topic may be briefly treated. We note first the strengthening of the monarchy by the general adoption of the principle of the hereditary transmission of the royal power following the law of primogeniture. Because in Germany the emperor, and in Poland the king, was elective, Germany failed to become one nation, and Poland disappeared from the list of independent States. At the same time the private possessions or domains of the prince came to be treated as the property of the State, and their administration was made a State function.

Another change, of no less importance, was the transformation of petty princes from the character of independent lords into that of supporters of the monarchy and of the public interest. That such a change should be accomplished was equally in the interest of the monarch and of the people. The change was not effectuated without many contests, the details of which do not concern us here.

Europe came now to be constituted by a system of States. Out of the wars of these States among themselves was developed the sense of a common interest, which was defined as the maintenance of the political equilibrium. To this end diplomacy was necessary, the art of which had been brought in Italy to the highest refinement, and thence transmitted to the rest of Europe. Attempts to disturb the political equilibrium were made by Charles V., Louis XIV., and Charles XII. of Sweden, without permanent result. Mention may be made of the common dread of the Turks, which constituted another temporary bond of union for the European States.

Of particular importance as a consequence of the Reformation was the struggle of the Protestant Church for a political existence. A struggle there had to be, and wars to settle it; for what was at stake was political powers and private possessions, which could be obtained only by wresting them violently from the Church. Such struggles were the Thirty Years' War in Germany, the Wars of the Commonwealth in England, and the resistance of the Netherlanders to Spanish rule.

By the Westphalian Peace the Protestant church obtained recognition of its independence. "This Peace," says Hegel, "has often been praised as the palladium of Germany, because it settled the political constitution of Germany." What this Peace looked to was, in fact, "constituted anarchy, such as the world had never seen before." Germany was (ostensibly) to be one Empire, one political whole, a nation; and yet all the civil and political relations of Germans were to be independent of imperial and determined by local law. In other words, what was inviolably protected and secured was the right of each separate State within the Empire to have in all respects its own laws, and to consult its own interests, even to the detriment of the interest of the Empire. It was complete political particularism. What this "constitution" was good for was directly made evident in the ignominious wars of the German empire against the Turks, and in its still more ignominious impotence to prevent, in very time of peace, the acquisition by the French of flourishing cities and provinces on the western border. "This constitution, which completely made an end of Germany as an empire, was chiefly the work of Richelieu, — through the aid of whom, a Roman Cardinal, religious freedom had been rescued in Germany. At home, Richelieu pursued an opposite policy. While he reduced his enemies to political impotence by securing the autonomy of their empire's different parts, in France he suppressed the independence of the Protestant party, and met in consequence the fate of many great statesmen. His fellow-citizens cursed him, while his enemies looked upon the work by which he ruined them as the most sacred goal of their wishes, their rights, and their liberty."

Later, the political guarantee of the Protestant church was completed by the elevation of a new Protestant State, Prussia, to the rank of one of the leading powers of Europe.

III. "*Illumination*" *and Revolution.*— Protestantism directed supreme attention to the inward man, the interior of the individual soul. But if it taught that here was the true centre of religious emancipation and spiritual peace, it also accustomed its adherents to see in the same place — in the personal, subjective will — the seat of an original power of evil, of "worldliness." To what excesses of subtle, self-examining, analytic introspection this led, we have previously noticed. Something analogous to this was to be observed in the Catholic church, whose casuists (Jesuits) instituted inquiries respecting the inner character of the will and of its motives which were as prolix and hair-splitting as anything in the earlier Scholastic theology. The result of this dialectic, which rendered everything in particular doubtful, was simply to enthrone thought in general; namely, formal thought, the *abstract* function of the spirit. This it was that in the end became the principle of the so-called " Illumination," or "Age of Reason."

Thought is peculiarly a universal activity. Its peculiar products have the form of universality; it considers everything under the form of universality. Moreover, it is the peculiarity of thought that its objects, its subject-matter, are not away from it, but absolutely present to and in it. The presumption of thought is, that all its possible objects lie within and not without its own realm, or within the sphere — to employ a truthful figure — of the rational self of the thinker. Thought may therefore fitly be described as the development or realization of the rational self-consciousness of the thinker. Or, more plainly, thought presupposes that things are thinkable; that it and its objects have a common nature; that a common reason informs and constitutes the thinking subject and the objects of thought; that in truly thinking and knowing things it is just as truly developing and actualizing the potentialities of the subject's own nature, or thinking and knowing itself; and so that wherever it may successfully range, whether in the sensible or in the spiritual world, it is no longer a stranger, but strictly at home, and is free.

Hitherto, both in the Scholastic and in the Protestant theology, the exclusive (ostensible) object of thought had been the doctrines of the Church, — God, the Devil, and so on. Yet this object, according to the hypothesis that had become current, was after all only a quasi-object of thought; in reality, it was held to transcend thought, to be an indigestible morsel for it.

It is, then, the principle of thought as above described that the human spirit acknowledges in the period at which we have now arrived; it is to this stadium in its own development that it has now risen. The historic steps are as follows:—

First, men have the assured persuasion that there must be reason in Nature, in the world, because God, who is reason, has created it. There arises a universal interest in studying and becoming acquainted with the present world. The search for reason in Nature is the search for the universal in Nature; the universal in Nature is genera, species, force, gravity, and the like. These things are not to be discovered by looking away from phenomena, but by observing them. So arises the method of experimental science, consisting on the one hand in direct observation, and on the other in the discovery of laws, forces, and the like, to which, as to their simplest expression, the phenomena observed are reduced. So thought, which in Protestant introspection and Jesuit casuistry had found nothing certain, begins here to have an opposite experience, and thus truly *to come to itself*. True, this exercise of thought remains relatively abstract, and gives abstract results; it does not go so far as to comprehend Nature in the fulness of her (direct or reflected) spiritual life and significance. Perhaps it is for this reason that "in the purely Germanic nations, among whom the principle of the *Spirit* had arisen," this form of science was less cultivated than among the Romanic peoples, whose highest gift was mainly that of abstraction; at all events, experimental science made specially rapid advances among the latter, and among the Protestant English as well. To the men of those times " it was as if God had then first created the sun, the moon, the stars, plants, and animals; as though the laws of Nature had then first been determined, — for now, first, men began to have an interest in these things, when they recognized in the reason that pervades them their own reason. The eye of man became clear, his mind alive, his thought industrious and illuminative. With the recognition of the laws of Nature a barrier was raised against the enormous superstition of the time, as well as against all ideas of alien and mighty powers which could be conquered only by the use of magic." To that extent man was thereby rendered free, — " free through the knowledge of Nature."

In the second place the peculiar activity of thought was directed to the moral side of human experience. For law and morality — previously regarded as only externally imposed by divine command through the Old and New Testaments, or else as having some other equally external origin — a foundation was now sought in the nature of man himself, and of human will. The empirical method was employed in ascertaining the principles of law and justice actually followed by nations in their relations with one another (*Grotius*). Then a source of existing civil and public law was sought, after Cicero's manner, in the natural instincts of man; *e.g.*, the social instinct, or in the principle of security for person and property, the general good, or political necessity, or the inherent right of the State. Frederick the Great is to be regarded as the ruler who, in respect of the last principle mentioned, introduced a new era. Frederick thought out and comprehended the universal aim or "reason" of the State, and was the first ruler who made this his supreme guide, ruthlessly suppressing all particularistic or individualistic pretensions opposed thereto.

To such formal results of the industry of thought as we have now considered — laws of Nature, definitions of the origin and requirements of right and justice — the name of "reason" was given. Insight into the same was " illumination," — illumination by the sole light of "reason." It was in France that the " illumination " so called originated, whence it passed over to Germany, taking with it a new world of ideas. Its professed principle was free thought: every subject of belief or conviction must be clearly present to thought, and stand the test of its formal and analytical examination, before being finally admitted and adopted.

The defect of this principle was its abstract and formal character; it proposed to bring everything to the test of the formal principle of abstract identity and contradiction. But this latter is no principle of comprehension at all, or of penetrating intelligence; at best it is only a principle of formal and superficial identification. It requires him who employs it only to determine that this is A and that is B, and then permits him to judge to the effect that A is A, and B is B, and neither one of them is the other, — A is not B. The immense importance of this principle, and the relative "illumination" which results when by the application of it to the multiform objects and the confused content of thought these are elevated in the mind to the character of clear and separate and distinctly identifiable ideas, are not to be questioned. But this is only the beginning, the scaffolding, for the true work of thought or of thoughtful comprehension, which requires, in addition to the formal principle of dissecting and (to derive an epithet from Wordsworth) "murdering" analysis, a substantial principle of constructive (or reconstructive) synthesis. The abstract principle of the "illumination" was not adequate to the sounding of the concrete depths of the living spirit; the "illumination" was blind to all that is deeply and essentially rational and vital in human and divine things.

The principle of all social relations, as we have

abundantly seen, is the will of man. If it is a question of comprehending or reforming these relations, everything depends on knowing what is the true will of man, — the will essentially conformable to human nature. In Germany it was notably Kant who undertook to throw light on this subject, applying the formal, abstract principle adopted by the "illumination." The result was a thoroughly formal and abstract—that is, empty — conception of will cut off from all intrinsic connection with the actual world of manifold rights, duties, motives; the connection was only extrinsic, formal. The principle was, The will must will itself; or, The will must in all things will to be free. Whatever is assumed to be right, or a duty, must be willed freely for its own sake, and not in obedience to command, or from any other foreign motive. "All this remained among the Germans a matter of peaceful theory, but the French wished to carry it out in practice. The double question arises, Why did this principle of freedom remain merely formal; and why did the French only, and not also the Germans, undertake to realize it?"

The principle in question remained formal because it proceeded from abstract thought, and because in the interpretation and application of it the same abstract thought—the "understanding," as opposed to the "reason"—prevailed. What the French revolutionists, for example, sought to define and secure was the abstract, or "natural," "rights of man." But these were all summed up in the right to liberty, from which by simple analysis they deduced the further right of all men to abstract equality before the law.

To the other question, — to wit, Why did the French, and not also the Germans, undertake to pass immediately from abstract theory to practice? — it will not suffice to say in answer that the French are "hot-headed." The reason lies deeper, and is to be found in the contrasting characters of the German and French spirits, and of Protestantism and Catholicism, and in the fact that in Germany there had been a reformation, while in France there had been none. In Germany the ideas of an abstract philosophy had no power to inflame the minds of men and lead to violent revolution, because the Germans had trodden the path which leads to inward satisfaction of the spirit's needs and to a pacified conscience; they had that moral temper, inseparable from religion, which is itself the basis of all stability and all worth in civil law and political constitution. "Illumination" in Germany was not anti-religious, as it was in France. In regard to temporal and social affairs the Reformation had changed everything for the better; celibacy, poverty, and idleness, previously encouraged by the Church, were by Protestantism held in dishonor. The Church was in Germany no longer invested with an immense amount of unproductive wealth. There was no interference of the spiritual with the secular power; and there was no veneration for the divine right of kings, except so far as the latter ruled with wisdom, justice, and an eye to the good of the whole State. To this extent the requirements of the principle of "thought" were here already satisfied; in addition to which the Protestant world had the consciousness that the principle of spiritual reconciliation, in which it had found peace, contained the germs of further developments of good in the political and social world.

In France all this was different. Here (as, according to Hegel, in all Catholic countries) it was possible for men to have what Protestantism did not admit; namely, a double conscience, — on the one hand a conforming one, and on the other a conscience protesting not only against the superstition of the religion formally accepted, but also against its truth. Besides, the actual condition of social affairs was shockingly bad, and in the perpetuation of it the court, clergy, nobility, and even the parliaments themselves were alike interested. So "illumination" came to the front, declaring that "reason" should reform and rule the world of human affairs. Abstract justice, resting on the unimpeachable authority of abstract thought, should be introduced and made to prevail; unreasoning prescription and brute authority should count for nothing. This declaration was as startling and unheard-of as, to many men of noble temper, the world over, it was exciting and hope-inspiring. With it a new epoch seemed gloriously to dawn, in which it might be expected that things divine and human should reach their final and full reconciliation.

It now remains for us only to consider (1) the course of the Revolution in France; and (2) its *contre-coups* in other lands.

1. The watchword of the Revolution was "liberty." Before considering how the abstract thinkers and the leaders of the Revolution understood this term, and how they undertook actually to realize their conception, a few words of general analysis must be permitted. Liberty, or freedom, involves at least these two sides; namely, the side of objective fact, and the subjective consciousness of that fact. Civil liberty, accordingly, involves, — (*a*) Objective freedom of property, of person, of occupation, and of access to positions in the public service; this freedom can be realized only as it is defined in laws which are executed. (*b*) The execution and maintenance of the laws. Such execution and maintenance constitute the formal office of the Government, whose more substantial offices are to defend the independence of the nation as a separate political individuality against foreign attacks, and, in the form of administration, to look after the welfare of the State internally, and of all its classes. These offices, as also the work of legislation, constitute, as we have previously recognized, the *universal* side of the State. Their exercise constitutes a universal function, affecting all the members of the State, but in which, from the nature of the case, it seems that only a few — and in cases calling for a supreme, immediate, and peremptory decision only one — can participate.

Now, adopting the *abstract* notion of freedom as strictly the attribute of the individual will, and supposing the State to be grounded on this principle, the question arises, How shall laws made to guarantee the objective freedom of the individual not interfere with his subjective freedom, if he have no direct share in the making and execution of them? The difficulty is not removed by the theory of representation, nor by the doctrine of the right of the majority to have their will prevail over the will of the minority; for "representatives," instead of really representing their constituents, often misrepresent and oppress them, and the rule of a majority may be tyrannical. This collision of subjective wills leads us therefore to the recognition and mention of a third essential side of civil liberty (c), to which we may give the name of moral temper (*Gesinnung*). "Moral temper," we say, and not merely "moral custom" (*Sitte*), — an inward willing of the laws, and of obedience to the laws because they are laws; a mind to regard the laws and the constitution as fixed stars in the moral firmament, and to consider it a supreme duty of individual citizens as such to submit thereto their own particular wills. "There may be various views and opinions respecting laws, constitution, and government," but the moral temper of the individual must enable him to pay to the State as such the homage of holding these opinions in due subordination to the actual will of the State, as actually defined in laws and constitution and applied by the governing power. In this way the real subjective freedom of the individual is not only preserved, but elevated into something of the quality of a *universal human* will in distinction from a merely private and individual one. Further, and finally, this temper will have an essentially religious character; it will invest the law and authority of the State, for the State's sake, with something of the sacred and inviolable character that belongs to the religious sphere. " It is, indeed, regarded as a fundamental article of modern wisdom that political laws and constitutions are to be wholly separated from religion; but though State and Religion respect different subject-matters, they are yet one in their root, and laws have their highest authentication in religion."

The " illumination " in France turned against religion, and the political revolutionists took from the former the abstract principle of liberty as exclusively individual in its seat and in its scope. The will was viewed as wholly individual, and each will was immediately regarded as absolute. The State was only the aggregate of the multitude of particular individual wills: it was not, according to the Revolutionary ideal, conceived as a substantial and organic unity, a universal will, to which the will of the individual must be rendered conformable in order that it might itself exist in the character of really true and free will.

The progress of the Revolution in France was as follows. At the outset, the attempt was made to imitate the English method of parliamentary government. But the success of this attempt was hindered by a pervading element of " absolute distrust: the dynasty was distrusted because it had been deprived of its previous power, and the priests refused the oath. Government and constitution could not subsist under these conditions, and they were overthrown." The government was next transferred in theory to the people, in reality to the National Convention and its Committees. It was now the turn for the abstract principles of "liberty" and "virtue" (or "reason") to have the rule. The "virtue" or "reason" in question was that of the "illumination;" and the practical problem given it to solve, when placed in the seat of supreme political power, was the government of the many not yet illuminated, or who through excesses of liberty and passion had become untrue to the illuminated political "virtue" it demanded. But here arose the difficulty of determining who were, and who were not, children of the new light; this being a question of internal condition and disposition, there was no means of settling it, positively and beyond the possibility of unfavorable suspicion, in the case of any individual. And so in fact the ruling power passed at last into the hands of Suspicion; suspicion brought the monarch to the scaffold, and inaugurated a Reign of Terror. This reign was the most fearful tyranny; judicial forms were dispensed with, and the uniform punishment was simply death. It was impossible that this tyranny should last; every human impulse and interest — nay, reason itself — was opposed to the reign of this fearfully and fanatically logical "Liberty." A new, organized government was introduced, having at its head, instead of a monarch, a changeable Directory consisting of five members. These, again, Suspicion overthrew, while the attempts of the legislative assemblies to exercise the powers of government served but to illustrate the absolute need of a governing power. Such a power Napoleon erected in the form of a military government, at the head of which he established himself; that is, his individual will. Napoleon scattered quickly all the lawyers, ideologists, and "men of principle" that remained, and replaced the reign of Suspicion with a rule founded on respect and fear. In all the remainder of French political history, down to the time when he last lectured on the Philosophy of History (Hegel died in 1831), our author saw the outcropping of the same conflicting forces which brought on the first Revolution, and especially of an abstract theory of individual liberty like that above adverted to.

2. Turning, finally, to the *contre-coups* of the Revolution in other lands, we note that all the Romanic nations, notably Spain and Italy, besides France, came under the domination of the so-called principle of political liberalism. And the event proved, according to our author, that it is "a false principle that the fetters of justice and liberty should be removed without emancipation of the conscience, or that there can be a revolution without reformation. . . . External power can effect nothing in the long run: Napoleon could no more force liberty on Spain than Philip II. could force Holland into slavery."

Turning to the other nations of Europe, we remark that Austria and England kept out of the track of the revolutionary tornado, and gave signal proofs of their political stability. England, in particular, is no place for windy abstractions and "principles" to thrive in. England, politically, is constituted of a multiplicity of particular interests having corresponding rights, the administration and defence of which are largely in the hands of those to whom they belong; the bureaucratic centralization of France could not be copied in England. At the same time the English have the sense to see that the ability to govern requires something more than the profession of certain abstract principles. It calls for specific intelligence and training, and the English have not been so silly as to think themselves less free because those who know most about government hold, and succeed in retaining, the highest places in administration.

Germany, traversed by the victorious French armies, was brought to a quickened sense of the defects of her political and civil constitution. In consequence, " the lie of the Empire completely disappeared. The Empire fell apart into sovereign States; feudal obligations were abolished, freedom of person and property being adopted as fundamental principles." In Germany the civil service is open to all qualified citizens; the power of ultimate decision is lodged in the hands of the monarch, but this in great and well-organized States is a point of minor importance. The strength of such a State lies, precisely, in its rational organization; in such a State, far more than in the unstable political constructions of the French revolutionists, the principle of freedom is realized. Not lawlessness, as we have abundantly seen, nor independence of law, nor personal participation in the origination of law, is liberty, but the willing subjection of the capricious individual will to existing laws whose rationality is perceived and recognized.

Thus far have we come in tracing the path of universal history, which "is nothing other than the development of the conception of freedom." We have been obliged to confine our attention exclusively to the progressive development and realization of this conception, "renouncing the attractive labor of portraying in detail the fortunes of nations, their periods of brilliant prosperity, the beauty and greatness of individuals, and the interesting picture of their fate. Philosophy is concerned only with the splendor of the Idea, which is mirrored in universal history." The fact that history is such a development as has been described, — a development of freedom and of the consciousness of freedom, and so an actual and progressive realization of the spiritual nature of man, — "this is the true theodicy, the justification of God in history. The human spirit is capable of being reconciled with the course of past and present history only when it sees that that which has happened and which is daily happening has been and is, not only not without God, but in an essential sense the work of God himself."

THE END.

www.ingramcontent.com/pod-product-compliance
Lightning Source LLC
Chambersburg PA
CBHW030117240426
43673CB00041B/1313